THE EVOLUTION OF THE GOSPEL

THE EVOLUTION OF THE GOSPEL

A New Translation of the First Gospel with Commentary and Introductory Essay

J. ENOCH POWELL

Sometime Fellow
of Trinity College, Cambridge, and
Professor of Greek
in the University of Sydney, NSW

YALE UNIVERSITY PRESS
NEW HAVEN AND LONDON
1994

Set in Linotron Bembo by Best-set Typesetter Ltd, Hong Kong
Printed and bound at the Bath Press, Avon, Great Britain

Library of Congress Cataloging-in-Publication Data

Powell, J. Enoch (John Enoch), 1912–
The evolution of the Gospel : a commentary on the first Gospel, with translation and introductory essay / J. Enoch Powell.
ISBN 0-300-05421-1
1. Bible. N.T. Matthew—Commentaries. I. Bible. N.T. Matthew. English. Powell. 1994. II. Title.
BS2575.3.P684 1994
226.2′077—dc20 93-35985
CIP

A catalogue record for this book is available from
The British Library

CONTENTS

PREFACE

To study documents with a view to discovering how they are related to one another and how their respective contents are to be accounted for is the business of literary and textual criticism rather than of history. But it would be absurd to pretend that the results have no implications for history. In themselves documents belong to history: they were produced at a particular time in a particular place by people who were not insulated from the society and the world around them. In that sense, the mutual relationship and the manner of origin of the gospels belong to history. But their content belongs to history in another sense too. To conclude, as this study does, that the contents, because they are part of a theological debate, are not reportage or narratives is not to conclude that they presuppose no historical events or persons. The *Iliad* is poetry and imaginative creation; but it would not have existed if there had not once been a great war and a long siege. The results of this study therefore raise historical issues, which ought not to be pretended away.

There was a moment when somebody first pointed to a piece of bread and said: 'It is His body.' That action implied on his part and on that of those to whom he spoke that they knew who was the 'He' implied in 'His'. There was also a moment when that knowledge first came to be entertained—a moment before which no such notion existed. The crucial element turns out to be that 'He was the son of God', a statement so startling that it needed to form part of a narrative which explained it and would be capable of being transmitted in writing. The making of that statement and its committal, in whatever form, to writing were also events in history; and the examination of a document purporting to contain that narrative is a study of history, none the less so if the only reliable evidence for it is provided by the document itself.

The attempt to account for the widespread acceptance and prevalence of the ritual meal through time and place belongs to disciplines other than history and criticism, and forms no part of this book. The document, along with others, constitutes, and from an early stage has always constituted, the accompaniment—as the chorus of a Greek tragedy accompanies and interprets the action upon the stage—of the liturgical worship of the Christian Church. That worship does not stand or fall by whatever may have been the textual history of the document, but derives its authority and its persuasiveness from the immemorial practice and the experience of the Church itself.

To ask questions which a document itself poses and to persevere in attempting to answer those questions as rationally as any others offered to human curiosity cannot infringe belief or worship. Indeed, for many of those who find themselves confronting perplexities in their study of the first gospel, it may be a relief to know that those perplexities are not private to themselves but exercised the minds of others from an early stage in the creation and transmission of the book. For me the most surprising experience has been to be led to perceive from how early a period in the evolution of the gospel the forms and ideas of worship were recognizably the same as they have continued down the ages.

The scholarship of centuries has been devoted to the document which forms the subject of this book. It was my method in studying it to clear the mind as far as possible of preconceptions or conclusions arrived at earlier by others; and I have deliberately therefore neither ascertained nor recorded previous agreement or disagreement with the results I propose.

The evolution which I am concerned to explore was complete before the divergences in manuscript transmission which *apparatus critici* record arose. I have used the British and Foreign Bible Society text and apparatus as published in 1958, but those who use a different edition will find no serious inconvenience.

J. ENOCH POWELL

London
Whitsun 1994

ACKNOWLEDGEMENTS

I would like to thank Professor Edward Ullendorff not only for the general encouragement he has given me from the outset of these studies but for undertaking the labour of casting the eye of a Hebraist over the proofs. I am also indebted to the Reverend Professor Henry Chadwick KBE DD and to the Reverend Dr William Horbury of Corpus Christi College, Cambridge, who put both time and patience at my disposal. Needless to say, these gentlemen share no responsibility for my conclusions.

I have benefited immensely from the good offices of that paragon among copy readers, Dr John Waś, and, like so many others, from the help and tolerance of Miss Gillian Malpass of Yale University Press, London.

J.E.P.

INTRODUCTION

The book known as 'The Gospel according to Matthew' has, from an early date, been given pride of place when copied or bound in the same volume as other books of the New Testament. That it was composed, however, as a separate, free-standing work, there is no reason to doubt.

There exist in addition at least three other books of high antiquity which purport to treat what is evidently the same subject. Two of them, the gospels known as 'according to Mark' and 'according to Luke', exhibit striking similarities to Matthew and to one another, including in many places identity of content and even of wording.

The theses which the present work puts forward emerged from a prolonged, repeated, and intensive study of the Greek text of Matthew by the methods of textual and literary criticism. An early outcome of that study was the conclusion that it is possible to demonstrate by rigorous proof that Matthew, in virtually the form in which we possess it, was used by the writers of those two other gospels. With less rigour but with high probability it can also be argued that they had no other source or sources.

The consequences of this demonstration for the study of Matthew are far-reaching. It becomes a unique and primary document, the contents and characteristics of which fall to be studied on their own merits, undistracted by the handling which they received from other authors. Those contents and characteristics alone can afford evidence of the origin and nature of the book: it has to be studied in its own right, in isolation, holding at bay all presuppositions or assumptions derived from elsewhere and insisting that the gospel be made to yield its own explanations.

Thus studied, Matthew discloses that an underlying text was severely re-edited, with theological and polemical intent, and that the resulting edition was afterwards recombined with the underlying text to produce the gospel as it exists. That underlying text was itself the product of earlier processes which involved more than one series of major additions.

In the Translation an attempt has been made to represent typographically, by means of differing founts and by paragraphing, the sort of process by which the book which we possess came into existence. It is an attempt which cannot hope to do more than represent an approximation to what actually occurred; for that process must frequently have involved adaptations which are no longer detectable. Nevertheless, the experiment is invaluable as an instrument of research.

The conclusions stated above are argued at greater length in the remainder of this Introduction.

THE PRIMACY OF MATTHEW

Derivation of one text (Text B) from another (Text A) is demonstrated when Text A can account for the origin of Text B but not vice versa. It is the principle known to textual criticism in the interrogative form *utrum ex utro?*, 'Which (could come) from which?' The following paragraphs adduce passages which demonstrate in this way the derivation of Luke from Matthew and the use by Mark of Luke and Matthew.

At Matt. 6.28 (see Commentary) the undoubted original was 'card not neither do they spin'. This has been corrupted in Matthew into 'how they grow, they toil not neither do they spin'; but the original words 'card not' (οὐ ξαίνουσι) lie concealed under the guise of 'grow' (αὐξάνουσι). Luke (12.27) perceived, as any careful reader would, that 'grow' is not the point of the comparison and that the word 'toil' must be wrong because the general idea of work could not be paired with the specific 'spin' (e.g. 'I have no money and no shillings'). He also realized that, on the analogy of the preceding sentence about the birds who 'sow not neither do they reap' (Matt. 6.26), two successive stages in the manufacture of clothing must have been specified. In Luke accordingly 'how they grow' is omitted and 'spin not neither do they weave' has replaced 'toil not neither do they spin'.

It would have been impossible for the unproblematic text in Luke to give rise to the corrupt text in Matthew, while on the other hand a logical train of reasoning leads from the text in Matthew to that in Luke. That Luke, though he failed to hit upon the original, must have used Matthew and possessed no independent source which could have provided him with 'card', is consequently certain.

A similar case is that of the severed ear at Matt. 26.51, where the severance of the ear is due to textual error and conceals the report of a disciple's abortive attempt to snatch a weapon (see Commentary). Had a deed of actual violence been originally narrated, it could not have been left without sequel. Such a sequel, the miraculous restoration of the ear to its owner, is found in Luke (22.49–51),* but if that had been in the original, it would have been a denouement so striking that no one would have omitted it so as to leave the story incomplete. Mark (14.47) and John (18.10, 11) have no sequel; but they describe the disciple's action as that of drawing his *own* sword, which could not have given rise to the text as it stands in Matthew.

Mark evidently regarded Matthew as his authoritative source which he normally followed. Confronted, however, with too severe a difficulty in Matthew, he held himself entitled to see if Luke could help. He is caught in the act of doing so when faced with Herod's electrifyingly unambiguous assertion (Matt. 14.2) that Jesus is John the Baptist risen from the dead. In transcribing this Mark (6.14) became aware of its appalling implications, noticed that Luke (9.7–9) had toned it down by relating instead that Herod 'heard' various accounts passing current including John's resurrection, and thereupon proceeded inappropriately to insert those alternative accounts before paving his way back to the Herodias story by repeating (6.16): 'Herod said, "John *whom I beheaded* has risen from the dead."' It is possible here to follow the actual thought-processes of an author transcribing Matthew with Luke at his elbow.

In addition to passages where Matthew presents difficulties due to corruption or error, proof of Mark's resort to Luke when flummoxed by Matthew is provided where Matthew's narrative is deliberately symbolical. The woman healed by Jesus without

* This would not be the only case where Luke produced a miracle to solve a difficulty. See on 4.20 (Luke 5.1–11), and 13.58 (Luke 4.30).

his knowing it (Matt. 9.22), inserted into the story of the daughter 'not dead but sleeping' (9.24), was designed to convey important allegorical messages. Failing to interpret these, Luke removed them by means of elaborate and dramatic touches: Jesus healed the woman after she confessed to touching him (8.42–8), and the girl had only *just* expired when Jesus arrived (8.49–52). Mark (5.33–9) copied both touches from Luke, attracted no doubt by their vivid as well as their explanatory character. If original, they could not conceivably have been removed by Matthew in order to produce allegorical instruction, nor could they have been devised by Mark and Luke independently.

The common dependence of Luke and Mark upon Matthew is demonstrable both in miniature and on a large scale. Perhaps the most extensive case is their treatment of the long discourse, the so-called Sermon on the Mount, at Matt. 5.3–7.27. The Commentary analyses how Luke, who retained *in situ* the start and the finish, accommodated numerous items from the rest of the discourse elsewhere in his book, where the subject-matter seemed relevant. Mark, on the other hand, in accordance with his general practice, eschewed the discourse as such but preserved a few striking passages from it in other places in his narrative, *including some passages which Luke had not reproduced.* To deny the dependency of Luke and Mark upon Matthew it would be necessary to resort to the monstrous hypothesis that Matthew (or his source) collected together small items from Luke (in unaltered serial order) and from Mark and built them into a discourse which, as the Commentary shows, has its own internal logic.

Luke was much concerned to render the narrative in Matthew inherently probable. This led him to undertake major changes of order and to make additions, in which Mark often did not follow him. The calling of Peter and Andrew (Matt. 4.19, 20) is not explicitly motivated: no reason is given why at the stranger's command they left all to follow him. Luke (5.1), in the so-called 'miraculous draught', provided—characteristically by a miracle, like the healing of the ear (above, p. xiii)—an irresistible motivation at a somewhat later point to which he removed the calling. It is beyond conception that, if the miracle existed in Matthew's source, it would have been omitted to produce bald, unexplained obedience.

Luke sometimes undertook operations on a still larger scale to remedy deficiencies in Matthew. Perhaps the boldest is that to deal with the 'mission' of the 'twelve' at Matt. 10.5, which causes surprise because the apostles subsequently turn out to have returned without reason and without report. Luke not only provided what seemed to be wanting plus a dramatic success story (Lucifer falling 'like lightning', 10.18) but turned one mission into two (of twelve and seventy-two respectively) in order to meet Jesus' prayer for 'more harvesters' (Matt. 9.38). It defies all probability to suppose that Luke's lively and logical narrative could have been deliberately turned by Matthew into problematic wreckage which happened to offer an invitation to Luke's remedy.

In Matt. 26.17 Jesus responds to the disciples' enquiry, 'where shall we arrange for you to eat the Passover?', with a bald reply, which reflects the incident with the asses at his entry into Jerusalem (21.2): 'Go into the city to so-and-so, and say to him, "Our rabbi says that . . . I want to eat the Passover at your house."' This is replaced in Luke (22.10) by: 'When you go into the city, you will meet a man carrying a jar of water; follow him to the house to which he is going, and say to the owner, "Our rabbi says, 'Where is the lodging where I may eat the Passover with my disciples?'" He will show you a large furnished upper room. Make preparations there.' That narrative is repeated in almost identical terms by Mark (14.12–15). An austere critic, recognizing a fairy-tale, might eliminate it: what is incredible is that the tale should be omitted in order to substitute the brief, lame ('so-and-so'!), and unexplanatory passage in Matthew. Reverse the relationship, and one observes how the creation of minimal data apparently missing can produce elaboration ('large', 'furnished upper room'), including the invention of a link-figure (the water-carrier) to designate the particular house.

At the other end of the scale of size, Mark was not too proud to seek Luke's help over verbal puzzles in Matthew. One such was the Baptist's unworthiness in Matthew (3.11) to 'carry' his successor's shoes. Luke (3.16), who jibbed at this, substituted the pedestrian 'untie the lace', which Mark liked well enough to accept and to adorn with one of his characteristic pathetic touches (1.7 '*stoop down and* untie'). It defies imagination that 'untie' was altered, either by error or by design, into 'carry'; nor could the amendment 'untie' have been made independently twice over, by Luke and by Mark.

Coincidence in omission can be as significant as agreement in alteration. There could be powerful reasons, apart from difficulties of interpretation, for wishing to omit the acclamation of Jesus by Peter in 16.16–19; but the decision to reduce Peter's reply to 'You are the Christ' (Luke 9.20, Mark 8.29) and then cut straight to Matt. 16.20, retaining the tell-tale unexpected verb ἐπιτιμᾶν, could be taken only once by one author.

The striking assertion that 'faith moves mountains' occurs twice over in Matthew (17.21; 21.21). Mark followed Luke's editorial lead and omitted the earlier passage of the two. He replaced it, however, on his own initiative with something quite different ('this sort of devil cannot be exorcised except by prayer'). But prayer is not mentioned in the context: what happened was that Mark had been looking at Matt. 21.22—a tame gloss in the other passage, which Luke (17.6) retained.

That Mark used Matthew directly and did not consider himself subject to Luke's editorial judgement is demonstrated by passages where Mark critically emended words in Matthew which Luke had not found difficult. Luke (6.5) accepted unaltered Matthew's 'the son of man is lord of the Sabbath' (12.8). Mark (2.27) altered it into 'the Sabbath was made for man, not man for the Sabbath', a change betrayed as unauthentic by perversely treating 'son of man' as a periphrasis for 'man' and by presenting the problematical statement as a logical conclusion ('so that', ὥστε). Similarly, when the disciples 'forgot to take loaves with them' (Matt. 16.5), Mark, shrewdly recalling that the miraculous feedings were by multiplication, allowed just a 'single loaf' (8.14). In the incident of the Canaanite woman (Matt. 15.22–8), which Luke did not use, Mark (7.25–30) saw an inconsistency between 'I was not sent except to Israel' and the outcome of the story, and removed it by inserting before 'it is not right to throw the children's bread to the dogs' the words 'Let the children be fed *first*'.

The evidences cited above for the mutual interrelationships of Matthew, Luke, and Mark are not evenly distributed through the book, though cumulatively they are supported by a mass of similar proof-passages, to which attention is drawn in the Commentary. The natural conclusion is that the proposed interrelationships apply to the whole of the three books. To resist that conclusion would involve the difficult hypothesis that Luke and Mark used Matthew in preference to other available sources or 'traditions' where, but *only* where, their dependence upon him would be demonstrable, and that additions and alterations were introduced by them into material from Matthew only when that material gave occasion for them. The hypothesis that Luke and Mark were using independent sources or 'traditions' cannot explain why those sources offered wording designed providentially to solve problems (real or not) posed by the text in Matthew. Divergences from Matthew in Luke and Mark have been shown to represent their critical response to those problems. It is unreasonable to suppose that they resorted to free composition only under the stimulus of difficulties in Matthew. The natural deduction must be that material in Luke and Mark not derived from Matthew was not drawn from any alternative source or 'tradition' but freely composed.

The interrelationships of Matthew, Mark, and Luke may be represented in their simplest form as follows:

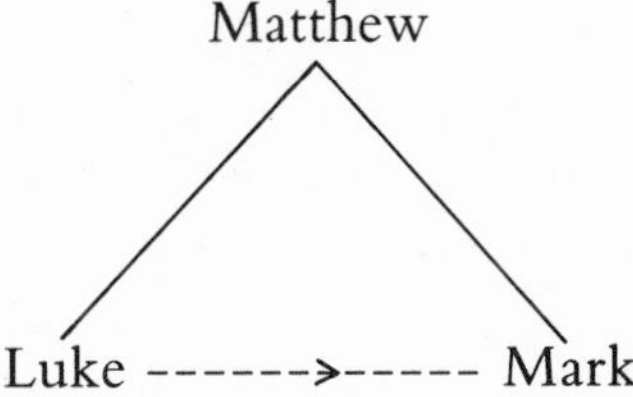

The evidence which proves those interrelationships is valid however many additional links there were between the three books. It would, for instance, be consistent with:

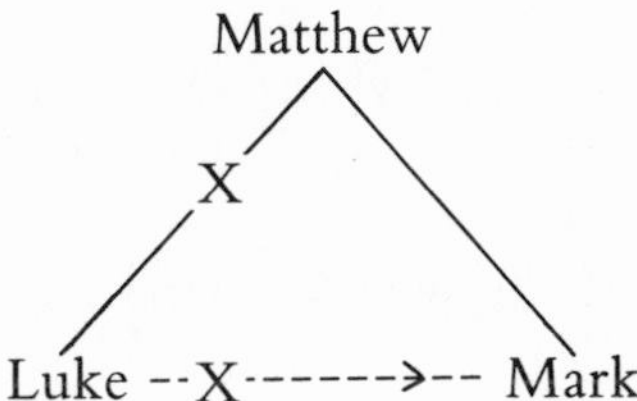

There is nothing, however, which requires the hypothesis of such intervening *entia praeter necessitatem multiplicata.*

THE CHARACTERISTICS OF MATTHEW

The question therefore how, why, and when Matthew, the sole source of Mark and Luke, came into existence can be validly answered on internal evidence by interrogating the text of Matthew in isolation. The results of that study are not susceptible, unlike the interrelationships between Matthew, Mark, and Luke, of completely rigorous demonstration. How difficult is the task may be illustrated by supposing that Matthew had been lost and enquiring how far its text could then have been reconstructed from Mark and Luke. Nevertheless, the text of Matthew presents certain peculiar features, like contradictions, duplications, and abrupt breaks, which suggest that it has not itself been subjected to any smoothing or editorial treatment such as it was later to undergo at the hands of Mark and Luke. Those blemishes would most naturally be explained as traces of the manner in which the book came to be compiled or composed; they would be consistent with its having been produced in haste and under pressure and left without revision or any attempt to remove the blemishes.

The most significant feature of Matthew is the coexistence in it of passages, one of which is an alternative to, or a duplicate of, the other.

Most familiar and best recognized among such alternatives or duplicates are probably the feedings of the five (14.15–21) or four (15.32–9) thousand, where the verbal correspondence is close and the differences, though not necessarily without significance, are limited to variation in numbers and to minor divergences of vocabulary. If two actual events were being recorded, the verbal similarity would be impossible to explain. The only hypothesis to account for it is deliberate duplication.

In most cases it is possible on verbal evidence to detect which of two alternatives was derived from the other. If one alternative uses features or expressions in a less appropriate context than that in which they occur in the other, it is a reasonable deduction that the former was based upon the latter.

Two episodes are narrated as taking place when the disciples are crossing the Sea of Galilee: (A) Matt. 8.23–7, and (B) Matt. 14.24–33. In both the word ὀλιγόπιστος, 'weak in faith', is used by Jesus in a rebuke. In (B) this rebuke is cogently and appropriately addressed to Peter, whose faith is failing to keep him afloat. In (A) it is a harsh and indeed unfair criticism of the alarmed passengers, described as 'cowards' (δειλοί). Again, the exclamation κύριε, σῶσον, 'Lord, save', is dramatically appropriate in Peter's mouth in (B) but less so in that of the crew in (A), who turn out to be unaware of Jesus' identity. In short, (A) is an unsatisfactory substitute for (B), betrayed by its language as derivative.

The same verbal relationship characterizes the most striking and important of the duplicates—the duplicate trials and executions of Jesus: (A) 26.59–66 and (B) 27.11–14. Both contain the same peculiar formula in which Jesus admits the charge: σὺ εἶπας (A), σὺ λέγεις (B), 'thou hast said', 'thou sayest';* but whereas in (A) the admission logically ends the trial, in (B) illogically it precedes instead of following other interrogation. Moreover, 'you say', wounding when addressed to the high priest, is pointless addressed to Pilate. The trial before Pilate is a second-rate duplicate, reusing material from the trial before the high priest, out of which it was manufactured.

A duplicate sometimes betrays itself as derivative by addressing difficulties in the model. For example, in the duplicate healings of the two blind men, (A) 9.27–31 and (B) 20.30–4, the problematic injunction to silence, puzzling in Jesus' mouth after the healing in (A) (9.30), has been attributed in (B) (20.31) to the bystanders *before* the healing.

Duplicate passages are not necessarily lengthy. Despite their brevity, the duplicate 'callings' 4.18–20 (Peter and Andrew) and 4.21, 22 (James and John), are evidently such, despite the intentional variation of the situations—'casting' or 'mending' nets respectively—betrayed by the duplicated εὐθέως ἀφέντες, 'immediately leaving' in the one case their nets, in the other their boat and their father. It is a touch which was as subtly appropriate in the first case as it was otiose in the second: Peter and Andrew had cast a net but abandoned it without retrieving the catch; James and John, if they were to follow at all, could hardly take the boat with them.

The two seed-sowing parables (A) 13.3–8 and (B) 13.24–30 should probably also be classified as alternatives, despite the difference whereby (A) relates to the fortuitous failure of some of the seed, while (B) attributes the presence of weeds to deliberate malevolence.

It is not necessary to suppose that alternatives ever existed for

* It is possible that λέγεις (present) was a deliberate variation on εἶπας (past).

the whole of the underlying text. Substitute passages could equally well have been inserted directly in a copy of it, so as to form, as it were, a 'new edition'. What is certain is that the alternatives cannot have been composed to stand side by side in the same book with the passages to which they were alternative. It follows that they must have been introduced later into the underlying book from the work for which they were composed; and as that process cannot have been accidental or unintentional, it must represent deliberate acceptance or conflation of contradictory material.

We thus have before us the evidence of an alternative gospel being produced and of a subsequent accommodation, however tentative, between the possessors of the respective gospels. It is possible, and unavoidable, to go further. The alternative was hardly created as an exercise in literary or stylistic improvement: its object must have been to alter the content of the underlying book, or at least to eliminate certain elements from it. The alternatives have in common the result of removing references to

(1) the identification of Jesus as son of God;
(2) the pre-eminence of Peter; and
(3) the dissemination of the gospel to the gentiles.

In this, they served to obscure or counteract what must have been the doctrine of the underlying book.

THE UNDERLYING BOOK

The absorption of duplicate passages from an alternative gospel is not the only compositional process in Matthew of which traces can still be found. There were principally two other such processes.

(1) At the cost of sometimes severe disruption wherever they appear, passages about John the Baptist have been inserted. All have the function of displaying him as having recognized in Jesus the fulfilment of his own mission.

(2) A framework which did not fully fit the intended contents was created to accommodate several discourses of Jesus, which appear to have special relevance for Jews who had become Christians without relinquishing their Jewish faith and practice. It is a curious feature of these discourses that they already had a

textual history of their own before they were embodied. At any rate, the incidence in them of corruption and interpolation is exceptionally high.

It is in fact possible that *all* the long discourses put into the mouth of Jesus are artificially introduced. They begin with the 'great sermon' (5.2–7.27), continue with the 'missionary charge' (10.5–42), with the series of parables (13.3–52) and of 'woes' (23.1–36), and end with the advice on behaviour during the siege of Jerusalem (24.5–26) and the warning not to confuse it with the 'end of the world' (24.29–31).

The contexts which the above two processes disturbed were pre-existent. Indeed, unless they had been, the clues to what has happened would not exist. There is an instructive situation at 9.34/12.22, where healings have been carefully repeated so as to create a sort of envelope which encloses one of the discourses (10.5–42) and also a major Baptist insert (11.2–12.21). The implication must be that the Johannine and the Jewish Christian material was absorbed in the course of one and the same operation. It is a process which would be calculated to appeal to members of a sect which held John the Baptist in high esteem as its founder.

We are thus confronted with the fact that the underlying book was itself already composite. In that case, what was the nature of its principal constituent, that is, of what remains when presumable insertions and additions have been removed, the veritable *Urtext* into which all those successive accretions were later to be built, the lowest stratum to which we have the means of penetrating? The question cannot be avoided, and *ex hypothesi* the material partially exists to say something about it.

It was, in form at least, a historical narrative, with each item attached to the foregoing by the terminology of time or movement. Yet it comprised only one event anchored in secular history—the birth of the principal figure, linked to the closing years of King Herod's reign (died 4 BC).

It was a document consisting exclusively of the words and actions of Jesus and preoccupied with establishing and demonstrating his identity as the 'son of God'; he is explicitly so born; and he is put to death by stoning, convicted by the Jewish establishment of the blasphemy of allowing himself to be called 'the son of God'.

The divine sonship of Jesus and the imperative duty of his

followers to convert the gentile world are inseparable; and the scene of the narrative is selected accordingly. Galilee 'of the gentiles' was its starting-point; and the sea around which the narrative is staged was an allegory of the great sea which united the Roman world. The contents were selected with a view to sustaining the three theological propositions on which the gentile mission rested:

(1) Jesus was the son of God, sent as saviour to the gentiles;
(2) believers inherit the kingdom of God or 'everlasting life' by becoming 'sons of God' through faith in Jesus' identity;
(3) they inherit the kingdom without fulfilment of the Mosaic Law, because the death of Jesus procured for them God's 'mercy' or 'forgiveness'.

Of one event only in the secular world did the narrative take note—the Jewish rebellion of AD 66 and its disastrous outcome in the sack of Jerusalem in AD 70. Jesus is represented (23.35, 36) as having interpreted the destruction of Jerusalem as the punishment of the Jews for having denied his identity and thus attempted to prevent the access of the gentiles to the goodness and mercy of their God. The book was given deliberately a bipartite shape, divided at ch. 16 by a scene in which Peter's recognition of Jesus as 'the Messiah, the son of the living God' is acclaimed as 'revelation' and confirmed. Before this point Jerusalem has played no part in the text. Thereafter Jerusalem lies at the centre of attention, incurring Jesus' condemnation and curse, and the narrative is composed with the Jerusalem denouement overtly in prospect.

THE GOSPEL OF PETER

By the side of the principal character, there was one human figure prominent in the underlying book. It was somebody called by the pseudonym—a pre-existent name it is not—of 'Peter' to whom the supreme revelation of Jesus' divine sonship was entrusted. What is more, it was a literal revelation (ἀπεκάλυψεν), directly vouchsafed by God (16.17).

Previous to the acclamation, Peter has appeared in the narrative at the calling (4.18–21), in which he and his brother Andrew were coupled with James and John, 'the sons of Zebedee'.

Henceforth, however, Peter, though prominent, is depicted in an unfavourable light. He endures the ignominy of being addressed as 'Satan' by Jesus himself (16.23) and is used in dialogues to evoke correction (17.24; 18.21; 19.27). He even fulfils the prediction (26.34) that he will 'deny' Jesus, after which he disappears from the scene altogether. 'The sons of Zebedee', on the other hand, are now placed on a level with Peter, sharing his presence at the revelation of the 'transfiguration' (17.1) and in Gethsemane (26.37) and put forward by their mother (20.21) to occupy the dominant position in the 'kingdom' already promised to Peter (19.28). There has, in short, been carried out a thoroughgoing obliteration of Peter inconsistent with his acclamation at 16.17.

The primacy bestowed upon Peter by Jesus at 16.17–19 evidently had to be counteracted, which in itself proves that the original bias of the underlying book was Petrine. It was a book to which it would not be excessive to give the subtitle of 'Gospel according to Peter'—a gospel for the gentiles.

The authors of the underlying book were sensitive, not to say apprehensive, about the relationship between Rome and the mission to the gentile world. The substitution of Jesus' execution by the Romans as a rebel for execution by stoning for blasphemy was made conditional upon Pontius Pilate being exonerated from blame for the verdict. The establishment of the 'kingdom of heaven' on earth—not self-evidently compatible with the *imperium Romanum*—was painstakingly distanced from the Judaean rebellion (24.27) and allowed to remain in an unexplored limbo between individual immortality and a new world order: Caesar's judgement-seat was in no imminent danger of being displaced by God's. Pontius Pilate does not really believe Jesus to be guilty (27.23), and the blame for his execution is laid, like the blame for the destruction of the Temple, upon the Jews themselves.

ALLEGORY

All parts of the underlying book shared with one another and with the inserted discourses a striking characteristic: their meaning depends upon the use of allegory, a use so pervasive that failure to recognize it has been a fruitful source of misunderstanding. It is not too great an exaggeration to claim that allegory was the normal mode in which the characteristic doctrines of the book were promulgated. Allegory, in fact, was its code language. Two specimens may be analysed to illustrate the phenomenon: the healing of the centurion's son (8.5–13) and the parable of the labourers in the vineyard (20.1–16).

The centurion represents the gentile world which it is not necessary for Jesus himself to cross the sea from Palestine in order to convert: like the centurion ordering soldiers, Jesus designates missionaries to do his bidding, and dispatches them to work in the mission field. The healing (which represents conversion, bringing the message of salvation) is performed λόγῳ, 'by the word'. There is, as often, an allegory within the allegory: the belief of the convert—in this case, of the father—is sufficient to procure the salvation of the family. A parallel instance is that of the ruler's daughter, whom the father's belief is sufficient to enable Jesus to raise from the sleep of death into which she has in the meantime fallen (9.18–26). Behind both stories may well lie a defence of the practice of vicarious baptism of relations, including the dead, alluded to at 1 Cor. 15.29.

Allegory becomes manifest when it makes absurdity of the literal meaning of a passage where it is employed. The parable of the labourers in the vineyard (20.1–16) exhibits an apparent absurdity—identical payment for unequal hours—until it is resolved by recognizing that the labourers hired 'at the eleventh hour' represent the gentiles reached by the gospel at a late stage in salvation history. The reward of the gentiles is no less for their being evangelized late. 'Working in the vineyard' is conventional allegory for mission, especially for mission to the gentiles, whose conversion is the 'fruit' (καρπός) which God expects from his vineyard of Israel (21.33–41), on whom he will take his revenge if it is not forth-coming. On this basis, there is behind the obvious allegory a less obvious, more shadowy one: the missionaries sent to convert the gentile world deserve equal reward with those who were sent earlier to Israel.

An allegory regularly used passes over into code, whereby the allegorical meaning which a person or a thing denotes takes their place in a conventional vocabulary. Unless the terms in such a vocabulary are recognized as code, a wrong interpretation will be attached to passages where they occur. A common instance is the code use of 'rich' and 'poor', to denote those who respectively claim, or do not claim, merit accumulated by observance of the Law. Failure to decode has produced paradox at Matt. 19.24, where a preceding allegorical narrative, that of the 'rich' questioner, is summarized in the peremptory proverb of the camel and the needle's eye—a proverb which demands the code meaning of 'rich' and against which the disciples themselves protest. It is the same failure to decode 'poor' which has given rise to the mistaken assumption that Jesus enjoined poverty upon his followers.

The debate between two theological positions—'Son of God' or 'Son of David'—presents itself, as the result of code, as a narrative capable of being read literally. When the theological debate has been settled, the encoded allegory becomes obsolete; but the text survives, with all its difficulties, as narrative. This phase was already past before Luke and Mark used the text of Matthew. In the case of the labourers they left the section 20.1–16 out altogether.

With impressive frequency allegory is used in giving rulings upon the celebration of the sacrament of the bread. This is overt with 'the children's bread' (15.26); but it may be claimed that wherever ἄρτος, 'loaf', occurs it refers to the sacrament. Its all-sufficiency is questioned by the first 'temptation' (4.4). It is asked for in the Lord's Prayer (6.11), where its efficacy is declared conditional upon the prior mutual forgiveness of the participants (the *pax*!). It is the 'good gift' (7.9) which the father will give to his son. King David proves that bread offered to God may be eaten by the needy, to whom it may be distributed on the Sabbath (not yet superseded by Sunday) (12.3–5), to which is possibly attached a ruling in favour of reception in the hand (12.13). Collection of the remnants after the miracle feedings (14.20, 15.37) affirms the validity of the reserved sacrament. The supreme proposition, that the host is the 'body of Christ', is settled (26.26) on no less authority than that of Jesus himself, in a ruling limited allegorically to a unique occasion.

The central issue around which the polemic between the gentile and the Judaizing churches revolved was the availability for the gentiles of the salvation procured by Jesus and the consequent will of God that this salvation should be brought to them. To denote the gentiles there is a whole cluster of code terms. They are 'children', 'infants' (παιδία, νήπιοι), because of their innocence, ignorance, and helplessness. The gentiles' admission to the kingdom is 'mercy' (ἔλεος), which God, in the twice quoted words of Hos. 6.6 (9.13, 12.7), prefers to 'sacrifice' (θυσία), the ritual Law observances of the Temple, no longer possible after the sack in AD 70.

Only when the equation 'children' = 'gentiles' is applied does the narrative at e.g. 18.2, 19.13, or 21.15 cease to be puzzling (see the Commentary). There is a further equivalent, 'little ones' or 'least ones' (μικροί, ἐλάχιστοι), which, like 'poor', expresses the gentiles' dependent status (see on e.g. 18.6, 25.40).

If Jesus provided the means of salvation for the gentiles, his will and that of God must be that the knowledge of that salvation and the sacramental access to it should be taken to them. Salvation is represented by 'healing'—especially, in the case of gentiles, the exorcism of 'evil spirits' (δαιμόνια), i.e. eradication of their belief in the pagan gods.

It was indispensable that the missionaries to the gentiles should be fully penetrated by 'faith' in the sufficiency of the message which they carried across 'the sea', another code term which often, if not always, represents the Mediterranean and signifies the gentile mission field. In the water-walking episode (see above, pp. xviii–xix) Peter's ὀλιγοπιστία ('deficiency of faith') hindered him in crossing the sea like Jesus to heal by exorcism (8.28 ff.); and in the embarrassing incident 17.14–21 Jesus' disciples have been unable because of ὀλιγοπιστία to achieve an exorcism in his absence. The 'mountain' which sufficient faith would have the power to remove and cast into the 'sea' (of the gentile world) at 21.21 was the Law itself, whether represented by Horeb or the Temple mount (see the Commentary).

On the fringes of code are more transparent expressions denoting the gentiles and their conversion. These include ἁμαρτωλοί, 'sinners', since by definition the gentiles do not, and are arguably not required to, fulfil the Law, and the associated term of abuse, τελῶναι, 'tax-gatherers'. In consequence the polemic at e.g. 9.10–11 is more specific than appears on a literal reading of its terms. The gentile mission field was, not unnaturally, a 'harvest' and the work was 'harvesting', which would similarly imply a more specific than general context for 9.37–8, and 12.1 (see the Commentary).

The polemic against the opponents of gentile conversion was carried on with an animosity of peculiar bitterness. Those opponents were, after all, by insisting that fulfilment of the Law remained obligatory, responsible for consigning the gentiles to perdition and frustrating the purpose of God in the incarnation.

The ability of Jesus to bring salvation to the gentile world outide the Law derived from his being 'the son of God': only 'the son of God' could extend God's 'mercy' to it. The question, was he son of God or of David? was therefore burningly important for the gentile churches: a decision taken in the latter sense would not only exclude them from salvation but also be disastrously damaging to their relations with Rome.

DATING

If one enquires where was the natural place for the underlying book to be created, there would be little hesitation about the answer: in Rome, where the pro-Roman bias, not to mention the destination to the gentile world of the salvation brought by Jesus, would be entirely understandable. It would thus be from a 'gospel according to Peter' that the work of the remaining evangelists evolved—presumably in other quarters of the Mediterranean world.

There are not lacking indications which enable the creation of the underlying book to be located in secular history. Up to 16.21 Jerusalem has played no part in the narrative. Thereafter it lies at the centre of attention, attracting Jesus' denunciation and curse, and the narrative is composed with its denouement at Jerusalem constantly visible. This would imply that the composition of the underlying book was commenced before the Judaean revolt and completed after the siege and fall of Jerusalem. In consequence the origin and recombination of the antagonistic editions of the underlying book would fall in the period immediately after AD 70, while rabbinical Judaism was re-establishing itself, at Jamnia and else-where, in the aftermath of the catastrophe.

So late a date may seem to conflict with the conventional dating of the Pauline epistles, based upon the chronology of Acts. On the other hand, the earliest authentic Pauline epistles imply on the part of the writer and his assumed readers a familiarity with the contents of Matthew. The 'faith which moves mountains' of 1 Cor. 13.2 would be meaningless to anyone not already familiar with the striking (and misunderstood)* wording of Matt. 17.21 (=21.21), which is taken literally as intentional hyperbole. The imagery of 1 Thess. 5.7 implies the same scene as is assumed by the parable of the wise and foolish maidens (Matt. 25.11–13). The narrative of the Last Supper is referred to by the phrase 'in the same night in which he was betrayed' at 1 Cor. 11.23. Baptism for the dead (1 Cor. 15.29) implies the same doctrine of posthumous conversion and salvation as the raising of the dead child (9.18–26). In short, the theology of the principal Pauline epistles is quite at home in the environment where Matthew originated.

Missionaries who had converted such gentiles as the addressees of the Pauline epistles could hardly have left them without a narrative into which his theology fitted. Who was Jesus Christ? How did he come into the world? In what circumstances did he leave it again? These are questions to which the most austere theologian could not refuse to reply in some sort of narrative form. A book he would have needed which narrated a birth and a death, but a book which at the same time gave authoritative countenance to the salvation of the gentiles outside the Jewish Law. It would be well if it were a book accepted by every section of Christianity—in Jerusalem as well as in Rome. That would be a book such as might have evolved by AD 100 into the document which we possess under the title of 'the gospel according to Matthew'.

It would have needed a dramatic dating to tie it in with the known course of events in the secular world. The use of allegory, whereby authoritative rulings are attributed to Jesus on questions that could not arise until after his earthly death, necessarily involved anachronism, as well as implying that the intended readership understood and accepted it. But the attribution of such rulings to Jesus would be more acceptable in the last quarter of the first century AD if the sole 'historical' dating in the narrative—birth shortly before King Herod's death in 4 BC—located the implied lifetime of Jesus in the first quarter of that century. The identification of the Roman governor induced to crucify Jesus as Pontius Pilate would then be obtained by adding about thirty years to the date of Herod's death.

* See above, p. xvi.

ABBREVIATIONS

Gesenius–Brown–Driver–Briggs	Francis Brown, with S.R. Driver and Charles A. Briggs, *A Hebrew and English Lexicon of the Old Testament . . . Based on the Lexicon of William Gesenius*, rev. G.R. Driver (Oxford, 1951)
Jos. *Ant.*	Flavius Josephus, *Antiquities of the Jews*
BJ	*Wars of the Jews*
Vit.	*Life*
LSJ	H.G. Liddell and Robert Scott, *A Greek–English Lexicon*, 9th edn., rev. H.S. Jones and R. McKenzie, with supplement (Oxford, 1968)
LXX	Septuagint
M	Masoretic (Hebrew) text of the Old Testament
Strack–Billerbeck	H.L. Strack and P. Billerbeck, *Das Evangelium erläutert aus Talmud und Midrasch*, 8th edn. (Munich, 1982)

TRANSLATION

KEY

1. Text forming part of the underlying book is printed in standard type.
2. Text added to the underlying book by way of amalgamation with the derivative book is printed in small type.
3. Text added by way of introducing references to John the Baptist is printed in sanserif type.
4. Text, other than that to which paragraphs 2 and 3 above apply, which originated later than the surrounding text is inset thus.

   In some places (e.g. 4.5, 8) double inset denotes successive such additions.
5. Interpolations—that is, words added to an already completed text by way of interpretation or correction—*are italicized*. Where they are superfluous to the sense of the surrounding text, they may also be enclosed [*in square brackets*].
6. Omissions supplied conjecturally are enclosed <in angle brackets> (asterisks * * * within these brackets indicate that no restoration of the missing text is attempted).
7. Where a passage forming part of the underlying book and the passage which replaced it in the derivative book both exist (e.g. 14.15–21 = 15.32–8), they may, to facilitate comparison, be printed side by side in parallel columns.
8. Words which translate text conjecturally emended are denoted *thus*.
9. Corrupt words for which no emendation is suggested are surrounded by obelisks †thus†.
10. A row of asterisks

    *　*　*　*　*

    denotes a break in the text, e.g. created to accommodate a major insertion.

11. Line-spaces have been inserted at appropriate points in the narrative, to assist the reader. They have no other significance.

1.1 Table of descent of Jesus Christ, son of David, son of Abraham

Abraham begot
Isaac, and Isaac begot
Jacob, and Jacob begot
Judah and his brothers, and Judah begot
Phares and Zara by Thamar, and Phares begot
Esrom, and Esrom begot
Aram, and Aram begot
Aminadab, and Aminadab begot
Naasson, and Naasson begot
Salmon, and Salmon begot
Boaz by Rachab, and Boaz begot
Jobed by Ruth, and Jobed begot
Jesse, and Jesse begot
David the king, and David begot
1.6 Solomon by Uriah's wife, and Solomon begot
Roboam, and Roboam begot
Abia, and Abia begot
Asaph, and Asaph begot
Josaphat, and Josaphat begot
Joram, and Joram begot
Oziah, and Oziah begot
Joatham, and Joatham begot
Ahaz, and Ahaz begot
Hezekiah, and Hezekiah begot
Manasse, and Manasse begot
Amos, and Amos begot
Josiah, and Josiah begot
Jechoniah and his brothers at the time of the
Babylonian captivity, and after the Babylonian captivity
Jechoniah begot
1.12 Salathiel, and Salathiel begot
Zorobabel, and Zorobabel begot
Abiud, and Abiud begot
Eliakim, and Eliakim begot
Azor, and Azor begot
Sadok, and Sadok begot
Achim, and Achim begot
Eliud, and Eliud begot
Eliazar, and Eliazar begot
Matthan, and Matthan begot
Jacob, and Jacob begot
Joseph, the husband of Mary, of whom was begotten Jesus called Christ.
1.17 *So there were in all fourteen generations from Abraham to David, fourteen from David*
to the Babylonian captivity, and fourteen from the Babylonian captivity to Christ.
And the birth of Jesus Christ was as follows.

In Bethlehem in Judaea in the days of King Herod a woman
1.18 Mary, betrothed to Joseph, a righteous man, became pregnant *by
the holy spirit* before they had had intercourse; and Joseph, not
wishing to expose her, took a private decision to divorce her.
But when he had decided this, an angel of the Lord appeared to
him in a dream, saying, '*Joseph, son of David*, be not afraid. Take
Mary your wife <and do not go in to her until she is delivered>;
for she has conceived by the holy spirit. She will be delivered of
a son, and you shall name him Jesus, because he will save his
1.22 people from their sins.' *All this happened to fulfil what was spoken
by the Lord through the mouth of the prophet: 'Lo, a maiden shall
conceive and bear a son and they shall call his name Emmanuel (which
1.24 translated means "with us is God").'* And Joseph arose *from sleep*
and did as the angel of the Lord had commanded him. He took
his wife, and did not go in to her until she bore a son, and he
called his name Jesus.
2.1 And when Jesus had been born, behold, sorcerers from the east
arrived in Jerusalem, saying, 'Where is the *Messiah* that has
been born? For we have seen his star in the east and have come
to do obeisance to him.' When King Herod heard this, he was
alarmed and all Jerusalem with him; and he summoned all the
high priests and scribes of the people and asked them where the
Messiah was to be born. And they told him, 'In Bethlehem in
Judaea; for so it is written by the prophet: "Thou too, Bethlehem,
land of Judah, art in no wise least among the chiefs of Judaea; for
out of thee shall come a leader who will shepherd my people
2.7 Israel."' Then Herod summoned the sorcerers in private and
ascertained from them the precise time of the portent [*the star*].
And he sent them to Bethlehem, saying: 'Go and find out precisely about the
baby; and when you have found him, report to me, so that I too can go and do
him obeisance.' When they heard the king they went their way, and, behold,
the star which they had seen in the east led them on until it stopped above where
2.10 the baby was. When they saw *the star*, they were overjoyed; and they entered
the house and saw the baby with Mary its mother, and fell down and did
obeisance to it. And they opened their caskets and offered it gifts, of gold and
incense and myrrh. And being admonished in a dream not to return to Herod,
they went back to their own country by another road.
2.13 And when they had departed, behold, an angel of the Lord
appeared in a dream to Joseph, saying, 'Arise, take the child and
its mother and flee to Egypt and be there until I tell you; for
Herod is going to look for the child to destroy it.' And he arose
and took the child and its mother at night and withdrew to
Egypt and was there until Herod's death, *so that what was spoken
by the Lord through the prophet might be fulfilled: 'Out of Egypt I have
called my son.'*

2.16 Then Herod, when he saw that he had been tricked by the sorcerers, was
extremely angry and sent and killed all the children in Bethlehem and
the entire district around it from two years old downwards, *to agree with the time
which he had ascertained from the sorcerers. Then was fulfilled what was spoken
by Jeremiah the prophet, 'A sound was heard in Rama, weeping and
much wailing, Rachel mourning for her children, and she would not be
comforted because they are not.'*
2.19 And after Herod died, behold, an angel of the Lord appeared in a
dream to Joseph in Egypt, saying, 'Arise, take the child and its
mother and go to the land of Israel; for they that sought the life
of the child have died.' And he arose and took the child and its
mother and entered the land of Israel.
2.22 But when he heard that Archelaus was king of Judaea in
succession to his father Herod, he was afraid to go there but,
being admonished in a dream, withdrew into the region of
Galilee.

And he went and settled in a city called Nazareth, that what
was spoken by the prophets might be fulfilled, 'He shall be
called a Nazorite.'

3.1 In those days there arrived John the Baptist, preaching in the desert
of Judaea, saying, 'Repent; for the kingdom of heaven has drawn
near.' For this is he that was spoken of by Isaiah the prophet, 'a
3.4 voice of one crying in the desert, "Prepare the way of the Lord, make
straight his paths."' And he [*John*] had clothing of camel's hair and a
leather girdle round his waist, and his fare was *flat cakes* and
wild honey. Then Jerusalem and all Judaea and all the country round
Jordan went out to him and were baptized in the river [*Jordan*] by
him, confessing their sins.
And seeing many of the Pharisees and Sadducees coming to the
baptism, he said to them, 'Progeny of vipers, who *will show* you
3.10 how to escape the wrath to come? Bring forth then appropriate fruit
of repentance and do not think [*say to yourselves*], "We have Abraham
for father"; for I tell you that God can raise up children for Abraham
3.8 from these stones. Already the axe is laid to the root of the trees.
Every tree therefore that does not produce good fruit will be cut down
3.11 and thrown into the fire. As for me, I baptize you with water [*for
repentance*]; but he that comes after me [*is stronger than I*], whose
shoes I am not capable of carrying, will baptize you with the holy spirit
and fire. His winnowing-fan is in his hand, and he will clean his
threshing-floor and collect his grain into the store but burn the chaff
with unquenchable fire.'
3.13 Then Jesus came from Galilee to the Jordan to John, to be baptized
by him.

But he tried to dissuade him, saying, 'I have need to be baptized
by you. Do you come to me?' But Jesus answered and said to him,

'Let be, now; for so it behoves us [*to fulfil all righteousness*].' Then he allowed him.

3.16 And when Jesus was baptized, as soon as he came up out of the water, behold, the heavens were opened and he saw the spirit of God lighting upon him like a dove; and behold, there was a voice from heaven, saying, 'This is my son, my beloved son, in whom I have taken pleasure.'

4.1 Then Jesus was taken up into the desert [*by the Spirit*] by the Devil to be tempted. And he was without food forty days and forty nights, *and was afterwards hungry*. And the tempter approached and said to him, 'If you are the son of God, command these stones to become loaves.' But he answered and said, 'It is written, "Man shall not live by bread alone but by every word that proceeds from the mouth of God."'

4.5 Then the Devil took him into the holy city and put him on the pinnacle of the temple, and said to him, 'If you are the son of God, throw yourself down; for it is written, "His angels shall be given charge concerning thee, and in their hands they shall bear thee up, lest thou strike thy foot against a stone."' Jesus said to him, 'Again, it is written, "Thou shalt not tempt the Lord thy God."'

4.8 Again the Devil took him to a very high mountain and showed him all the kingdoms of the world and their splendour, and said to him, 'I will give you all these, if you will fall down and do obeisance to me.' Then Jesus said to him, 'Be gone, Satan; for it is written, "Thou shalt bow down before the Lord thy God and serve Him" only.'

Then the Devil left him, and behold, angels came and brought him food.

4.12 <But Herod, being alarmed by John's preaching, sent soldiers and arrested him while he was baptizing and put him in prison. And his disciples came and told Jesus.> And when Jesus heard that John had been arrested, he returned to Galilee.

4.13 And he left Nazareth and went and settled in Capharnaum by the seaside in the bounds of Zabulon and Nephthalim, *so that the saying of Isaiah the prophet should be fulfilled, 'Land of Zabulon and land of Nephthalim, towards the sea, beyond Jordan, Galilee of the gentiles, the people sitting in darkness saw a great light, and as for those sitting in the land and shadow of death, a light arose for them.'*

4.17 From that time Jesus began to preach, saying, 'Repent; for the kingdom of heaven has drawn near.'

4.18 And as he walked beside the sea of Galilee, he saw two brothers, Simon called Peter and Andrew his brother, shooting a seine into the lake; for they were fishermen. And he said to them, 'Come after me, and I will make you fishers of men.' And they immediately left the nets and followed him.

4.21 And going on from there, he saw another two brothers, James son of Zebedee
and John his brother, in the boat with Zebedee their father, preparing their nets;
and he called them, and they immediately left the boat and their father and
followed him.

* * * * *

4.23 And he went about in the whole of Galilee, teaching in their
synagogues and preaching the gospel of the kingdom and
curing every disease and every disability among the people.
And the news of him went out into the whole of Syria; and
they brought to him all that were ill, afflicted with many
kinds of diseases and sufferings, possessed by devils and
lunatic and paralysed, and he healed them. And many crowds
followed him from Galilee and Decapolis and Jerusalem and
Judaea and across the Jordan.
5.1 And when he saw the crowds, he went up into the mountain; and when he had sat down, his disciples came to him
and he opened his mouth and taught them, saying:
5.3 'Blessed are the poor *in spirit*, for theirs is the kingdom of
heaven;
Blessed are the mourners, for they shall be comforted;
Blessed are the gentle, for they shall inherit the earth;
Blessed are the hungry *and thirsty for righteousness*, for they
shall be fed;
5.7 Blessed are the compassionate, for on them there shall be
compassion;
Blessed are the pure *in heart*, for they shall see God;
Blessed are the peacemakers, for they shall be called sons
of God;
5.10 Blessed are those that have been persecuted because of
righteousness, for theirs is the kingdom of heaven;
5.11 Blessed are you when they revile you and persecute you
and speak all evil against you *untruthfully* because of me;
rejoice and triumph, for your reward is great in heaven,
for so they persecuted the prophets that were before
you.
5.13 You are the salt of the earth. If the salt is *not sprinkled*,
with what is it to be salted? It is good for nothing unless it is
thrown out and trampled underfoot by mankind. You are
the light of the world. A †city† cannot be hidden if it is set
upon a mountain, nor do they light a lamp and put it
underneath *the footstool*, but on the lampstand, and it
sheds light upon all in the house. Let your light so shine in
the sight of mankind that they may see your fair works and
glorify your Father in heaven.

5.17 Do not suppose that I came to abolish the Law or the prophets:
I came not to abolish but to fulfil, for verily I say to you, Until
heaven and earth pass away, not one iota or one stroke shall
5.19 pass away from the Law, *until all is over.* Whoever therefore
breaks *the least* of these commandments, and so teaches
mankind, shall be called least in the kingdom of heaven; but
whoever does them and so teaches shall be called great in the
kingdom of heaven.
5.20 For I tell you that, unless your righteousness is in excess
of that of the scribes and Pharisees, you will not enter the
kingdom of heaven.
5.21 You heard that it was said to them of old, "Thou shalt not
murder",

and whoever murders shall be liable to judgement, but whoever says to his brother "Raca" shall be liable to the council, and whoever says "Fool" shall be liable unto hell-fire.

But I say to you, that everyone that is angry with his brother has already murdered him in his heart.

5.23 If therefore you are bringing your offering to the altar and
there remember that your brother has something against
you, leave your offering there before the altar and go first
and be reconciled with your brother and then go and bring
your offering.

5.25 Be of good will towards your adversary *quickly* while you
are with him on the road, lest your adversary deliver you
to the judge, and the judge to the officer, and you be
thrown into prison; verily I tell you, you shall not come
out from there until you have paid the last farthing.

5.27 You heard that it was said, "Thou shalt not commit adultery."
But I say to you that everyone who looks at a woman to desire
her has already committed adultery with her in his heart.
Therefore

if your right eye causes you to fall, take it out and throw it away from you; for it is better for you to lose one of your limbs than for your whole body to be cast into hell; and

if your right hand causes you to fall, cut it off and throw it away; for it is better for you to lose one of your limbs than for your whole body to go to hell.

5.31 And it was said, "Let whoever divorces his wife give her a
bill of separation." But I say to you that anyone who
divorces his wife, fornication apart, causes adultery to
be committed with her, and whoever marries a divorced
woman is an adulterer.

5.33 Again, you heard that it was said to them of old, "Thou shalt
not commit perjury but keep thine oaths to the Lord." But I
say to you not to swear at all

neither by heaven, because it is God's throne, nor by earth, because it is the footstool under his feet, nor by Jerusalem, because it is the city of the great king, neither swear by your head, because you cannot make one hair white or black,

but let your speech be "Yes, yes", "No, no": what is more than that is of the Devil.

5.38 You heard that it was said, "An eye for an eye, a tooth for a
tooth." But I tell you not to resist [*evil*]; but if one strikes you
on the right cheek, turn the other to him; and if a man wants
to go to law and take your coat, let him have your cloak too;
and if a man exacts porterage from you for a mile, go two
miles with him.

Give to him that asks, and do not reject whoever would borrow from you.

5.43 You heard that it was said, "You shall love your neighbour"
and hate your enemy. But I say to you, Love your enemies
and pray for those who persecute you,

that you may be sons of your Father in heaven, because he makes his sun to shine upon bad and good and rains upon righteous and unrighteous.

For if you love those who love you, what reward have you? Do not the tax-gatherers do the same? And if you welcome your brethren only, what do you do that is special? Do not the gentiles too do the same?

Be therefore *perfect* as your Father in heaven *is perfect*.

6.1 Take care not to do your righteous works in front of men, to
be watched by them; otherwise, you have no reward with
your Father in heaven.

6.2 So whenever you do almsgiving, do not cause a trumpet to be
sounded in front of you, as the hypocrites do in the synagogues
and in the alleys, so that they may be glorified by men. Verily
I say to you, They have their reward. But when you do almsgiving, let not *the left hand know whose the right hand is*,
so that your almsgiving may be in secret; and your Father,
who sees in secret, will repay you.

6.5 And whenever you pray, you shall not be as the hypocrites,
because they like to pray standing in the synagogues and at the
street corners, in order that men may see them. Verily I say to
you, They have their reward. But do you, whenever you pray,
enter your closet and having shut your door pray to your
Father in secret; and your Father, who sees in secret, will repay
you.

6.7 When praying do not babble like the gentiles; for they think
that by the multitude of their words they will be listened to.
Do not then be like them; for your Father knows what
things you have need of before you ask him.
6.9 So do you pray thus: "Our Father in heaven, let thy name
be sanctified, let thy kingdom come, let thy will be fulfilled,
as in heaven, so on earth also. Give us our bread *today* and
cancel our debts, as we too have cancelled those of our
debtors.
6.13 And carry us not into temptation but rescue us from the
Devil."
6.14 For if you pardon men their offences, your heavenly Father
will pardon yours; but if you do not pardon men neither
will your Father pardon your offences.
6.16 And whenever you fast, do not be as the hypocrites [*gloomy*];
for they disfigure their faces, so that men may see that they are
fasting. Verily I say to you, They have their reward. But do
you, when fasting, anoint your head and wash your face so
that you may not be seen by men to be fasting, but by your
Father in privacy; and your Father, who sees in privacy, will
repay you.
6.19 Do not accumulate stores for yourselves on earth, where moth
and corruption destroy and where thieves break in and steal;
but accumulate stores for yourselves in heaven, where neither
moth nor corruption destroys and where thieves do not break
in nor steal;
for where your store is, there also will be your heart.
6.22 The eye is the lamp of the body. If therefore your eye is
sincere, the whole of your body will be lighted; but if
your eye is evil, the whole of your body will be in darkness. So if the light within you is darkness, how great the
darkness is!
6.24 No man can be servant to two masters;
for either he will hate one and love the other, or he will
cleave to one and despise the other.
You cannot be servant to God and to Mammon.
6.25 For this reason I say to you, do not worry *for your life* what
you are to eat or drink nor *for your body* what you are to wear.
Is not the life more than food and the body than clothing?
Look at the fowls of the air: they do not sow or reap or gather
into barns, and yet your heavenly Father nourishes them. Are
you not <much> more important than they?
6.27 Who among you by worrying can add a cubit to his life?
6.28 And why do you worry about clothing? Observe the *beasts*

of the field: they do not *card* or spin, <and yet your heavenly
Father clothes them>.

But I tell you that Solomon in all his glory was not dressed
like one of these. And if God so clothes the grass of the
field, which today is and tomorrow is thrown into the oven,
will he not do much more for you, O you of little faith?

6.31 Do not therefore worry, saying, "What shall we eat?" or
"What shall we drink?" or "What shall we wear?"

For the gentiles look for all these things; for your heavenly
Father knows that you need all these things.

Therefore seek his kingdom and his righteousness *first*,
and all these things shall be added to you.

Do not therefore worry about tomorrow; for tomorrow
will worry about itself.

Sufficient for the day is its badness.

7.1 Do not judge, that you may not be judged; for by the judgement by which you judge, you shall be judged; and by the
measure by which you measure, it shall be measured to you.
And why do you notice the splinter in your brother's eye but
not observe the beam in your own eye? Or how will you say
to your brother "Let me take the splinter out of your eye",
when all the time there is the beam in your own eye? Play-
actor, first take the beam out of your eye, and then you will be
able to see to take the splinter out of your brother's eye.

7.6 Give not the holy thing to
the dogs, *lest they turn on you
and tear you.*

Throw not your pearls before
the swine, *lest they trample them
underfoot.*

7.7 Ask and it shall be given to you; seek and you shall find; knock
and it shall be opened to you. For everyone asking receives;
and the seeker finds; and to him that knocks it shall be opened.
Is there any man among you whom his son asks for bread who
will give him a stone? Or if he asks for a fish too, will give
him a snake?

If then you, who are wicked, know how to give good gifts
to your children, how much more will your Father in heaven
give good things to those who ask him?

7.12 All things therefore that you would have men do to you, do
you also do to them; for this is the Law and the prophets.

7.13 Enter (if you will) through the narrow gate;

for broad [*is the gate*] and spacious is that road which
leads to destruction, and many they are who seek to enter
by it; because narrow is the gate and constricted is the

road which leads to life, and few there are who find it.
7.15 Beware of the false prophets, who come to you in the clothes
of sheep but inside are predatory wolves. You will recognize
them by their fruits. Surely men do not gather grapes from
thorn-bushes nor figs from caltrops? Likewise every good tree
makes good fruits, but a rotten tree makes bad fruits. A good
tree cannot bear bad fruits nor a rotten tree bear fair fruits.

Every tree not making fair fruit is cut down and thrown on
the fire. [*You will recognize them by their fruits.*]

7.21 Not everyone who says to me "Lord, lord" will enter the
kingdom of heaven, but he that does the will of my Father in
heaven. Many will say to me on that day, "Lord, lord, did we
not prophesy by your name and cast out devils by your name
and perform many mighty works by your name?" And then I
shall declare to them, "I never knew you: depart from me,
workers of unlawfulness."

7.24 Everyone therefore who hears these words of mine and does
them shall be like a wise person who built his house on the
rock. And the rain descended, and the rivers came, and the
winds blew and fell upon that house, and it did not fall.

And everyone hearing these words of mine and not doing
them shall be like a foolish person who built his house on
the sand. And the rain descended, and the rivers came, and
the winds blew and smote that house, and it fell, and great
was the fall of it.'

7.28 And it was so, that when Jesus had completed these words, the
crowds were astonished at his teaching;

for he was teaching them as one having authority and not as
their scribes.

8.1 And after he had come down from the mountain, many crowds
followed him and lo, a leper came and prostrated himself
before him, saying 'Lord, if you will, you are able to cleanse
me.' And stretching out his hand, he touched him, saying, 'I
do so will: be cleansed.' *And immediately his leprosy was cleansed.
And Jesus said to him, 'Be sure to tell no man* but go and
show yourself to the priest and bring the offering which Moses
prescribed, as evidence for them.'

8.5 And when he had entered Capharnaum, a centurion came to
him, beseeching him and saying, 'Lord, my son is lying in my
house paralysed in dreadful torment.' He said to him, 'I will
go and heal him.' But the centurion answered and said, 'No,
lord; *I am not good enough for you to enter under my roof*; simply

say the word, and my son will be healed. For I too am one
who has men under him [*under command*], and I say to one
"Come" and he comes, and *to another* "Go" and he goes, and
to my servant "Do this" and he does it.'
8.10 And when Jesus heard, he was astonished and said to those
following him, 'Verily I say to you, in no one in Israel have
I found such faith. And I say to you that many from the east
and the west will come and feast with Abraham and Isaac
and Jacob in the kingdom of heaven, but the sons of the
kingdom will be cast out into the darkness outside; there
shall be the wailing and the gnashing of teeth.'
8.13 And Jesus said to the centurion, 'Go; as you have believed, so
be it.'
And his son was cured at that hour.

* * * * *

8.14 And Jesus came into Peter's house and saw his mother-in-law
lying suffering from fever. And he took hold of her hand and the
fever left her; and she got up and served him a meal.
26.6 And as Jesus was in the house of Simon *Peter* [in Bethany],
the woman came to him as he sat at meat with a jar of *costly*
26.8 myrrh and poured it upon his head. And when the disciples saw,
they were indignant
and said, 'Why this waste? This could have been sold for much
and given to the poor.'
But Jesus hearing said to them, 'Why complain of the woman?
For she has done me a good deed; for you have the poor with
you always, but me you do not always have. For in putting
this myrrh on my body, she did it for my embalming.
Verily I tell you, wherever this gospel is preached in the whole
world, what this woman did will also be told in memory of her.'
8.16 And when evening was come, they brought to him many
possessed of devils; and he cast out the evil spirits with a word,
and healed all that were ill, *so that the saying of Isaiah the prophet*
should be fulfilled: 'He took our weaknesses and bore our diseases.'
And when he saw a crowd around him, he gave command to
depart for the other shore.
8.19 And a certain one, a scribe, came and said to him, 'Teacher, I
will follow you wherever you are going.' But Jesus said to
him, 'Foxes have earths, *and the birds of heaven their roosts*, but
the son of man has not *anywhere to lay his head*.' And another
of the disciples said to him, 'Lord, allow me to go back first
and bury my father.' But Jesus said to him, 'Follow me, and
leave burying the dead.'
And when he had gone on board his disciples followed him.

8.24 And behold, there was a great *hurricane* on the sea, so that the boat
was being *swamped* by the waves. But he was asleep. And they went
and woke him, saying, 'Lord, save us, we perish.' And he said to them,
'Why are you cowardly, you of little faith?' Then he rose and rebuked
the winds and the sea, and there was a great calm. And the men
marvelled, saying, 'What sort of person is this, that even the winds and
the sea obey him?' And he came to the opposite shore, to the country of the Gadarenes. And there met him two men possessed,
who came out of the tombs, so very dangerous that nobody was
able to pass by on that road. And behold, they cried out, saying,
'What have we to do with you, O son of God? *Have you come
here before due time to torment us?*' Now not far away from them
was a herd of many swine feeding; and the devils besought him,
saying, 'If you cast us out, send us into the herd of swine.' And
8.32 he said to them, 'Get you gone.' *And they came out and went into
the swine.* And behold, the whole herd rushed down the precipice
into the sea and died in the waters. And the swineherds ran away
and came to the city and reported everything *and what had
happened to those possessed.* And behold, the whole city came out
to meet Jesus, and when they saw him, they besought him to
9.1 depart from their region. And he entered a boat and crossed over
and came to his own country.

9.2 And lo, they brought to him a paralysed man lying on a bed.
And Jesus, seeing their faith, said to the paralysed man, 'Have
courage, child; your sins are forgiven.' And lo, some of the
scribes said to themselves, 'This man blasphemes'; and Jesus,
knowing their thoughts, said, 'Why do you think evil in your
hearts? Which is easier—to say "Your sins are forgiven", or to
say "Get up and walk"? But that you may know that the son of
man has authority on earth to forgive sins', then said he to the
paralysed man, 'Get up, take your bed up and go home.' And he
got up and went home. And the crowds, when they heard, were
astounded and glorified God, who had given such authority to
mankind.
9.9 And proceeding from thence, Jesus saw a man called Matthew
sitting at the customs post, and said to him, 'Follow me.' And he
got up and followed him. And it happened that, when he was
sitting at a meal in the house, lo, many *tax-gatherers and sinners*
9.11 came and joined in the meal *with Jesus and his disciples.* And
when the Pharisees saw, they said to his disciples, 'Why does
your teacher eat with the tax-gatherers and sinners?' And he
heard and said, 'It is not those who are healthy who need a
doctor but those who are ill. Go and learn what "I will have

mercy and not sacrifice" means; *for I came to call not the righteous but the sinners.*'

9.14 Then there came to him the disciples of John, saying, 'Why is it that
we and the Pharisees fast but your disciples do not fast?' And Jesus
said to them, 'Surely those in the bridal chamber cannot *go hungry*
as long as the groom is with them? *But days will come when the
groom is taken away from them and then they will fast.*'

9.16 Nobody puts a brand-new cloak on over an old tunic;

for the patch pulls away from the garment and there is a worse tear;

nor do they put new wine into old skins;

otherwise the skins burst and the wine is spilt and the skins are ruined; but they put new wine into new skins, and both remain intact.

9.18 While he was thus speaking to them, lo, a certain man, *a ruler*,
came and prostrated himself before him, saying, 'My daughter
has just died; but come and lay your hand upon her, and she
will live.' And Jesus arose and went with him, and so did his
9.20 disciples. And lo, a woman who had had a discharge of blood for
twelve years approached him from behind and caught hold of the
fringe of his garment; *for she said to herself, 'If I only catch hold of
his garment, I shall be saved.'* And Jesus turned and seeing her said,
'Have courage, daughter; your faith has saved you.' And the
woman was saved from that moment.

9.23 And when Jesus came to the *ruler's* house and saw the musicians
and the crowd *wailing*, he said, 'Withdraw; for the girl has not
died but is asleep.' And they laughed at him; but when the crowd
had been turned out he went in and took hold of her hand, and
the girl got up. And the report of this went out into all that land.

9.27 And as Jesus proceeded from thence there followed him two
blind men shouting out, 'Have mercy upon us, son of David.'
And Jesus rebuked them; but when he entered the house the
blind men came to him; and Jesus said to them, 'Have you faith
that I can do this thing?' They said to him, 'Yes, Lord.' Then he
touched their eyes, saying, 'Be it to you according to your faith.'
And their eyes were opened. *And Jesus admonished them, saying,
'See to it that no one knows.' But when they came out they noised him
abroad in all that land.*

9.32 And as the men were going out, behold, they brought to him a
mute possessed by a devil. And when the devil had been cast out,
the mute spoke. And the crowds marvelled, saying, 'Such a
thing has never been seen in Israel.' But the Pharisees said, 'It is
by the ruler of the devils that he casts devils out.'

* * * * *

9.35 And Jesus went round all the cities and the villages, teaching in
their synagogues and proclaiming the gospel of the kingdom
and healing every disease and every malady. And seeing
the crowds, he felt compassion for them because they were
bewildered and prostrate, like sheep that have not a shepherd.
Then said he to his disciples, 'The crop is large, but the
workers few. Beseech therefore the owner of the crop that he
10.1 send out workers into his crop.' And he called his twelve
disciples and gave them authority to cast out unclean spirits
and to heal every disease and every malady.

Now the names of the twelve apostles are these: first Simon called Peter and Andrew his brother, and James the son of Zebedee and John his brother, Philip and Bartholomew, Thomas and Matthew the tax-gatherer, James son of Alphaeus and Thaddaeus, Simon the Zealot and Judas Iscariot, the one who betrayed him.

10.5 These twelve Jesus sent out, after giving them charge as
follows: 'Do not go off on the gentile road

and do not enter a city of Samaritans, but go rather to the lost sheep of the house of Israel.

As you go, preach, saying that the kingdom of heaven has drawn near. Heal sick, raise dead, cleanse lepers, cast out devils. You received gratis, give gratis: do not acquire gold or silver,

nor cash for your belts, nor scrip for the road, nor two garments, nor shoes, nor staff; for the labourer is worth his keep.

10.11 And whatever city or village you enter, ascertain who in it is
worthy;

and remain there until you depart. On entering the house, bless it; and if the house be worthy, let your peace come upon it; but if it be not worthy, let your peace return to you.

10.14 And whoever does not receive you and listen to your words,
depart out of that house or city,

and shake the dust off your feet. Verily I say to you, it will be more tolerable for the land of Sodom and Gomorrah in the day of judgement than for that city.

10.16 Behold, I am sending you out like sheep in the midst of
wolves.

Therefore be wise as serpents and undefiled as doves.

Beware of men; for they will hand you over to sanhedrins, and in their synagogues they will whip you; and you will also be brought before governors and kings for my sake,

to be witness to them and to the gentiles.

10.19 And when they hand you over, do not be anxious about how
or what to speak;
for it shall be given to you in that hour what you are to
speak; for it is not you who are speaking but the spirit of
your Father who speaks in you.
10.21 And brother will hand brother over to death, and father will
hand over child, and "children will rise up against parents"
and do them to death. And you will be hated by all because of
my name; but it is he who endures to the end that will be
saved.
But when they persecute you in one city, flee to the other;
for verily I tell you, you will not complete the cities of Israel
before the son of man comes.
10.24 A disciple is not above his teacher, nor a servant above his
master.
Sufficient for the disciple to be as his teacher, and for the
servant to be as his master. If they called the owner of the
house Beezebul, how much more will they his household!
10.26 Do not fear them, then; for nothing is concealed that will not
be revealed, nor hidden that shall not be known.
What I tell you in the dark, say in the light; and what you
hear in your ear, proclaim it on the housetops.
And do not fear those who kill the body but cannot kill the
soul;
but fear rather *to lose* both body and soul in hell.
10.29 Are not two sparrows sold for a farthing, and yet one of
them does not fall to the ground without your Father's
knowledge?
Even the hairs of your head are all numbered. Do not fear
them, therefore; you are worth more than many sparrows.
10.32 Everyone who acknowledges me before men, I too will
acknowledge before my Father in heaven; and whoever denies
me before men, I too will deny before my Father in heaven.
10.34 Do not suppose that I came to bring peace upon the earth. I
came to bring not peace but a sword; for I came to divide "a
man against his father, and a daughter against her mother,
and a daughter-in-law against her mother-in-law; and a
man's enemies will be his own household". He that loves
father or mother above me is not worthy of me; and he that
loves son or daughter above me is not worthy of me; and
whoever does not take his cross and follow after me is not
worthy of me. He that has found his life shall lose it, and he
that has lost his life for my sake shall find it.
10.41 He that receives you receives me,
and he that receives me receives him that sent me. He that

receives a prophet as a prophet shall have a prophet's reward; and he that receives a righteous man as righteous shall have a righteous man's reward; but whoever gives to one of these little ones only a cup of water to drink as a disciple, verily I tell you, will not lose his reward.'

11.1 And it came to pass that, when Jesus had finished instructing his
twelve disciples, he removed thence to teach and preach in their
11.2 cities. And John, having heard in the prison of the doings of Christ,
sent *two of* his disciples, and said to him, 'Are you the one who
is coming, or are we to await another?' And Jesus answering said
to them, 'Go and report to John the things you hear and see. "Blind
men see again and lame men walk, lepers are cleansed and deaf
men hear and dead people are raised" and "Beggars are told the
good news." And blessed is he who is not persuaded to disbelieve
in me.'

11.7 As they went away, Jesus proceeded to say to the crowds about
John: 'Why did you go out into the desert? To watch a reed
swayed by the wind? Well, why did you go out? To see a man
dressed in soft clothing? *Lo, those who wear soft clothing are in
the houses of kings*. Well, why did you go out? To see a prophet?
Yes? I tell you, you saw something much more than a prophet. This
is he about whom it is written, "Behold, I send my messenger in
11.11 front of you, who will prepare your way before you." Verily I tell
you, there has not arisen among those born of women one greater
than John the Baptist; but the least in the kingdom of heaven is
greater than he. [*From the days of John the Baptist until now the
kingdom of heaven suffers violence and men of violence ravish it*];
for all the prophets and the Law were until John. If you will receive
it, he is Elijah [*who was to come*]. Let him that has ears hear.
11.16 To what shall I compare this generation? It is like children sitting in
the squares, who call to the others and say, "We piped to you and
you did not dance; we wailed and you did not beat your breast."
11.19 For John came neither eating nor drinking, and they say, "He has
a devil." The son of man came eating and drinking, and they say,
"Behold, a glutton and a drunkard, a friend of tax-gatherers and
sinners."

And wisdom was condemned by its own works.'

Then he proceeded to rebuke the cities in which most of his mighty works were done, because they did not repent.

'Woe to you, Chorazin, woe to you, Bethsaida, because if the mighty works done in you had been done in Tyre and Sidon, they would long ago have repented in sackcloth and ashes. Verily I tell you that it will be more tolerable for Tyre and Sidon

11.23 in the day of judgement than for you. And as for you, Capharnaum, Say not, "I will be raised to heaven": you shall be cast down to hell. If the mighty works done in you had been done in Sodom, it would have remained standing to this day. Verily I tell you that it will be more tolerable for the land of Sodom in the day of judgement than for you.'

11.25 At that time Jesus lifted up his voice and said, 'I acknowledge my gratitude to you, Father, lord of heaven and earth, because you hid these things from wise and clever men and revealed them to children—yea, Father, because so it was pleasing in your sight. All things have been delivered to me by my Father; and no one recognizes the son except the Father [*nor does anyone recognize the Father except the son*] and to whomever the son wishes to reveal it. Come to me, all you who toil and are burdened, and I will relieve you. Take my yoke upon you and learn from me, *because I am mild and lowly in heart*, "and you shall find surcease for your souls"; for my yoke is kind and my burden is light.'

12.1 At that time Jesus went on the Sabbath through the standing crops, and his disciples, becoming hungry, started to strip ears of corn and eat. And the Pharisees seeing said to him, 'Look, your disciples are doing what it is not permissible to do on the Sabbath.' But he said to them, 'Have you not read what David did when he and those with him were hungry, how he entered the house of God and they ate the shewbread, which it was not permissible for him or those with him to eat but only for the priests? Or have you not read in the Law that the priests in the Temple break the Sabbath and are blameless? I tell you that something greater than the Temple is here. If you had known what "I will have mercy and not sacrifice" means, you would not have condemned the guiltless; for the son of man is lord of the Sabbath.'

12.9 And removing thence, he went into their synagogue. And lo, a man with a withered arm. And they were *watching to see* if he would heal him on the Sabbath in order that they might accuse him. Then said he to them, 'Which man among you shall there be who has one sheep and if it falls on the Sabbath into a pit will not catch hold of it and lift it out? How much more then is a man than a sheep!' [*So that it is permitted to do good on the Sabbath.*] Then said he to the man, 'Stretch out your arm'; and he stretched it out, and it was restored [*whole*] like the other.

12.14 And the Pharisees went out and took counsel together to *denounce* him.

And Jesus, perceiving it, departed thence, and many followed

him; and he healed them all and charged them not to make
12.17 him public, *in order that what was spoken by Isaiah the prophet*
might be fulfilled, namely, 'Behold my son whom I chose, my
beloved whom my soul approved. I will put my spirit upon him,
and he will announce judgement to the gentiles. He will not
contend or shout, nor will anyone hear his voice in the streets. He
will not snap a broken reed, and smoking flax he will not quench,
until he brings judgement to victory. And in his name shall the
gentiles hope.'

* * * * *

12.22 Then was brought to him a man possessed by a devil, blind and
dumb. And he healed him, so that the mute spoke and saw. And
the crowds were amazed and said, 'Surely this is no son of
12.24 David?' But the Pharisees hearing said, 'This man only casts
12.25 out the devils by the ruler of the devils, *Beezebul*.' And knowing
their thoughts, he said to them, 'Every kingdom divided against
itself [*is ruined, and every city or house divided against itself*] will not
stand. And if Satan is casting out Satan, he is divided against
himself. [*How therefore shall his kingdom stand? And if I cast out the*
devils by Beezebul, by whom do your children cast them out? Therefore
they shall be your judges.] And if I cast out devils by the spirit of
God, surely the kingdom of God has come upon you? How can
anyone enter the strong man's house and seize his gear, unless he
12.30 binds the strong man first? *And then he will plunder his house. He*
that is not with me is against me, and he that does not *sow with me
does not reap*.

12.31 Therefore I say to you, any sin [*and blasphemy*] will be forgiven
men except blasphemy against the spirit, and whoever says a
word against the son of man shall be forgiven but whoever says
it against the [*holy*] spirit shall not be forgiven either in this age
or in the age to come. *For the tree is known by its fruit; or will
a good tree bear bad fruit, or a bad tree good fruit?* Progeny of
vipers, how can you speak good, being evil yourselves? For the
mouth speaks out of the superfluity of the heart. The good man
produces good things out of his good store, and the evil man evil
things out of his evil store.

12.36 I tell you that every idle saying that men shall speak, they shall
render account for it in the day of judgement; for by your words
you shall be judged *and by your words you shall be condemned.*

12.38 Then some of the scribes and Pharisees answered him, saying,
'Teacher, we wish to see a sign from you.' And he answered and
said to them, 'An evil and adulterous generation wants a sign,

and a sign shall not be given to it[, *except the sign of Jonah the prophet;*]

for as Jonah was in the belly of the whale three days and three nights, so shall the son of man be in the heart of the earth three days and three nights.

The men of Nineveh will rise up at the judgement with this
generation and will condemn it, because they repented at Jonah's
12.42 announcement, and behold more than Jonah is here. The Queen
of the South will arise at the judgement with this generation and
will condemn it, because she came from the ends of the earth
having heard of the wisdom of Solomon, and behold more
than Solomon is here.
12.43 But when the unclean spirit comes out of a man, it goes through
waterless places, looking for a refuge, but does not find one.
Then it says: "I will return to my house that I came out of" and
it goes and finds it unoccupied and swept and tidied. Then it
goes and takes with it seven other spirits worse than itself, and
they enter and settle there; and the end of that man is worse than
the beginning. *So shall it happen to this evil generation also.*'

12.46 While he was still talking to the crowds, behold, his mother and
brothers were standing outside, wanting to talk to him. And
someone said to him, 'Behold, your mother and your brothers
are standing outside, wanting to talk to you.' But he answered
the person who said this to him: 'Who is my mother, and who
are my brothers?' And stretching out his hand over his disciples,
he said, 'Here are my mother and my brothers; *for whoever does
the will of my Father in heaven, he is my brother and sister and
mother.*'
13.1 On that day Jesus went out of the house and sat down beside the
sea, and many crowds flocked to him,

so that he got into a boat and sat down in it, and all the crowd stood on the beach.

3a, 24b And he spoke much to them in parables, saying: 'The kingdom
of heaven is likened to a man who had sown good seed in his
field. And while the men slept, his enemy came and proceeded
to sow darnel among the wheat, and departed. And when the
shoots of wheat came up *and bore fruit*, the darnel made its
appearance also. And the farmer's servants said to him, "Master,
did you not sow good seed in your field? Whence then does it
have darnel?" And he said to them, "Some enemy did this." And
the servants said to him, "Do you wish us to go and collect the
darnel?" And he said, "No; otherwise in collecting the darnel
you will uproot the wheat with it. Let both grow together until

harvest time, and at the time of the harvest I will say to the
reapers, 'First collect the darnel and bind it in bundles to burn it,
and then gather the wheat into my barn.'"
13.44 The kingdom of heaven is like treasure hidden in a field, which a
man found and concealed; and in his delight he went and sold all
he had and bought that field. Again, the kingdom of heaven is
like a man [*a merchant*] looking for fine pearls who, having found
one magnificent pearl, went and sold all he had and bought it.
Again, the kingdom of heaven is like a net which was let down
into the sea and collected together fish of every sort; and when it
was filled, they pulled it up on to the shore and collected the
good ones in containers but threw the bad ones away; *so shall it
be at the end of the world: the angels will come forth and will separate
the evil from among the righteous and will throw them into the furnace
of fire, where shall be the wailing and the gnashing of teeth.*'
13.36a Then he dismissed the crowds and went into the house; and the
13.10 disciples came and said to him, 'Why do you speak to them in
parables?' And he answered and said, 'To you it has been given
to know the mysteries of the kingdom of heaven, but to them it
has not been given. *For to whoever has shall be given and
shall overflow; but whoever has not, from him even what he has shall be
taken.* For this reason I speak to them in parables, because seeing
they do not see and hearing they do not understand; and there is
fulfilled upon them the prophecy of Isaiah, which says: "You
shall hear with your hearing and not understand; and looking
you shall look and not see; for the heart of this people was
hardened and with their ears they heard dully and they kept their
eyes half-shut, lest they should see with their eyes and hear with
their ears and in their heart understand and take heed, and I
would heal them." But blessed are your eyes because they see
and your ears because they hear. For verily I say to you that
many prophets and righteous men longed to see what you see
and did not and to hear what you hear and did not. Do you
therefore hear and understand the parable of the darnel in the
13.36c field. The man sowing the good seed is the son of man; the field
is the world; the good seed is the sons of the kingdom; the darnel
is the sons of the Devil; the enemy is the Devil; the harvest is the
end of the world; the harvesters are angels. As therefore the
darnel is collected and burnt, so it shall be at the end of the
world: the son of man will send his angels and they will collect
from his kingdom all that lead astray and those that work unrighteousness,
and will throw them into the furnace of fire,
where shall be the wailing and the gnashing of teeth. Then "the
righteous will shine out" like the sun in the kingdom of their
father. Let him that has ears hear.'

13.24 He propounded to them another parable, saying, 'A man went out to sow,
13.3b and *behold*, as he sowed, some seed fell beside the road, and the birds came
and ate it up. And some again fell on the stony ground, where it did not have
much soil, and as soon as it sprang up, [*because of not having depth of soil, when
the sun rose high it was burnt*] it shrivelled because it had no root. And other seed
fell on thorns, and the thorns grew up and choked it. And yet other seed fell on
the good ground and bore fruit, some a hundredfold, some sixtyfold, and some
thirtyfold. Let him that has ears hear.'
13.31 He propounded to them another parable saying, 'The kingdom of heaven is like
a grain of †mustard†, which a man took and sowed in his field, which is the
smallest of all seeds but when it is fully grown is the largest of plants and
becomes a tree, so that the birds of heaven come and pitch their tents in its
branches.'
13.33 Another parable he spoke to them: 'The kingdom of heaven is like <*** of>
yeast, which a woman took and *kneaded* into three seahs of flour, until the
whole of it was leavened.'
13.34 All this Jesus spoke in parables to the crowds. Without parables he said nothing
to them, so that what was spoken by the prophet might be fulfilled, 'I will open
my mouth in parables; I will pour out things hidden from the creation.'
13.36b Then his disciples came to him and said, 'Interpret to us the parable of the
13.18 sower.' And he answered and said, 'When anyone hears the word of the
kingdom and does not understand it, the Devil comes and carries him off [*what
has been sown in his heart*]. That man is the seed sown by the roadside. But
the seed sown on the stony ground is the person who hears the word and
immediately takes it up with joy but has no root in him and is fickle and when
there is oppression or persecution for the sake of the word immediately defects.
The seed sown on the thorns is the person who hears the word but the care of
this world and the snare of wealth choke him [*the word*] and he bears no fruit.
But the seed sown on the good ground is the person who hears the word and
understands it and who does bear fruit, one a hundredfold, another sixtyfold,
another thirtyfold.
13.51 Have you understood all these things?' They said to him, 'Yes.'
And he said to them, 'Because of this, every scribe who becomes
a disciple to the kingdom of heaven is like a householder who
throws out of his store both new things and old.'
13.53 And it was so, that when Jesus finished these parables, he removed from
thence. And he came to his home town and taught them in their synagogue, so
that they were amazed and said, '*Whence has this man this wisdom and these
miracles?* Is this not *Joseph's* son? Is not his mother *called* Mary and his
brothers James and Joseph and Simon and Judah? And are not all his sisters
among us? Whence then has he all this?' And they were turned against him. But
Jesus said to them. 'A prophet is not without honour except in his own town
and house.' And he did not do many miracles there because of their lack of faith.
14.1 At that time Herod the tetrarch heard the report of Jesus and said to
his sons, 'This is John the Baptist; he has risen from the dead, and for
14.3 that reason the mighty powers are at work in him.' For Herod had
seized John and bound him and put him away in prison for the sake of

Herodias, the wife of his brother Philip; for John used to say to him,
'It is not permitted that you should have her'; and though he wanted
to kill him, he was afraid of the crowd because they held him to be a
14.6 prophet. But at Herod's birthday-feast the daughter of Herodias went
on to the floor and danced; and Herod took a fancy to her, so that he
agreed upon oath to give her whatever she might ask. And she,
having been coached by her mother, said, 'Give me the head of John
the Baptist here *on a dish.*' And though mortified, the king, *because
of the oaths and the other guests*, commanded that she be given it.
And he sent and decapitated John in prison. And the head was
brought on a plate and given to the girl; and she took it to her mother.
And his disciples came and took up the corpse and buried it, and went
and informed Jesus.

14.13 And when Jesus heard, he withdrew from thence in a boat
to a desert place by himself; and when the crowds heard, they
followed him on foot out of the cities.
And coming ashore, he saw a large crowd. And he had compassion on them and healed those of them who were sick.

15.32 And Jesus called his disciples to
him and said, 'I have compassion
on the crowds, because they
have been attending on me for
three days now and have nothing
to eat; and I do not want to dismiss them hungry, in case they
faint on the way.' And his disciples said to him, 'From where
can we get enough loaves in the
wilderness to feed so large a
crowd?' And Jesus said to them,
'How many loaves have you?'
And they said, 'Seven, and a
few little fishes.' And he instructed the crowd to recline on
the ground, and took the seven
loaves and the fishes and after
giving thanks broke them and
gave them to the disciples and
the disciples in turn to the
people. And all ate and were
fed; and they took away the
surplus of the broken bread,
seven hamperfuls. And those
eating were four thousand men,
besides women and children.

And it grew late, and the disciples came 14.15
to him, saying, 'The place is desert and
the hour has already passed. Dismiss
the crowds therefore, so that they may
go away into the villages and buy
eatables for themselves.' And Jesus
said to them, 'They have no need to
go away: do you give them food to
eat.' And they said to him, 'We have
nothing here but five loaves and two
fishes.' And he said, 'Bring them here
to me.' And having told the crowd
to sit down on the grass and taken
the five loaves and the two fishes, he
looked up to heaven and blessed them,
and broke the loaves and gave them to
the disciples, who in turn gave them to
the crowds. And all ate and were fed.
And they took away the surplus of
broken bread, twelve basketfuls. And
those eating were about five thousand
men, besides women and children.

14.22 And immediately he compelled the disciples to embark in the
boat and precede him to the further shore, until he could send the
crowds away.

And when he had sent the crowds away, he went up into the
mountain by himself to pray. And when evening had come, he
was alone there; and the boat was already many furlongs away
from the land, buffeted by the waves, because the wind was
contrary. And in the fourth watch of the night he came to
them walking over the sea. But the disciples, when they saw
him walking on the sea, were alarmed and said, 'It is a ghost',
14.27 and they cried out in fear. And immediately Jesus spoke to
them, saying, 'Be of good cheer, it is I: fear not.' And Peter
answered him and said, 'Lord, if it is you, tell me to come to
you across the water.' And he said, 'Come.' And Peter got out
of the boat and walked over the water and came to Jesus; but
when he saw the †wind† he was afraid and began to sink and
called out saying, 'Lord, save me.' And immediately Jesus
stretched out his hand and caught hold of him and said to him,
'O you of little faith, why did you doubt?' And when they got
into the boat the wind fell; and the men in the boat prostrated
themselves before him saying, 'Truly you are the son of God.'
14.34 And when they had crossed over they came to land at Gennesaret. And the people of the place, when they recognized
him, sent into all that neighbourhood and brought to him all
that were ill and begged him to let them simply touch the
fringe of his garment. And all who touched it were cured.
15.1 Then there came to Jesus from Jerusalem Pharisees and scribes,
saying, 'Why do your disciples break the tradition of our elders?
They do not wash their hands when they eat bread.'

And he answered and said to them, 'Why do you break God's commandment because of your tradition? For God said, "Honour thy father and thy mother", and "He that curses father or mother, let him die the death." But you say, "Whoever says to his father or mother, Whatever you are due from me is offered to God, need not honour his father or his mother"; and so you have annulled the word of God because of your tradition. Hypocrites, well did Isaiah prophesy concerning you, saying, "This people honours me with their lips, but their heart is far off from me; and in vain do they worship me, teaching as doctrines the commandments of men."'

15.10 And he called the crowd and said to them, 'Hear and understand:
not what goes into the mouth defiles a man; but what comes out
of the mouth, that is what defiles a man.' Then the disciples
came to him and said, 'Do you know that the Pharisees, when

they heard what you said, were turned away from you?' And he
answered and said, 'Every plant which my heavenly Father did
not plant will be rooted up. Let them go; they are blind leading
the blind, but if one blind man leads another blind man, both
15.15 will fall into a hole.' And Peter answered and said to him, 'Show
us the parable.' And he said, 'Are even you still uncomprehend-
ing? Do you not see that everything which goes into the mouth
passes into the belly and is expelled in the privy? But the things
that come out of the mouth come out of the heart, and these are
what defiles a person. For out of the heart come evil thoughts,
murders, adulteries, fornications, thefts, perjuries, and blas-
phemies. *These are what defile a person; but to eat with unwashed
hands does not defile a person.*'

15.21 And Jesus went out from thence and withdrew to the region of
Tyre and Sidon. And behold a Canaanite woman from those
parts came out and shouted, saying, 'Have mercy on me, lord,
son of David; my daughter is sorely afflicted with a devil.' But
he answered her not a word. And the disciples came to him
and requested him, saying, 'Get rid of her, because she is
shouting after us.' But he answered and said, 'I was not sent
except to the lost sheep of the house of Israel.' But she came
and prostrated herself before him and said, 'Lord, help me.'
But he answered and said, 'It is not fit to take the children's
bread and throw it to the curs.' But she said, 'Yes it is, lord;
for the curs eat of the scraps that fall from the table of their
masters.' Then Jesus answered and said to her, 'Woman, great
is your faith; let it be for you as you wish.' And her daughter
was healed from that hour.

15.29 And Jesus passed on from thence and came by the sea of Galilee;
and he went up into the mountain and sat there. And there
came to him many crowds having with them persons crippled,
maimed, blind, dumb, and many besides; and they threw themselves at his feet, and he healed them, so that the crowd marvelled
to see the dumb speaking, the maimed whole, and the crippled
walking and the blind seeing, and they glorified the God of
15.32 Israel. And Jesus called his disciples to him . . .

See above, at 14.15

. . . besides women and children. And when he had dismissed the
crowds, he entered the boat and came to Magadan.

16.1 And the Pharisees and the Sadducees came and *to try him* asked him to show
them a sign from the sky. But he answered and said to them,

'When it is evening, you say, "Good weather; the sky is fiery"; and in the morning, "Storm today, for the sky is fiery *with wrath*." So you know how to interpret the face of the sky but cannot interpret the signs of the times?

An evil and adulterous generation wants a sign, and a sign shall not be given to it *except the sign of Jonah*.' And he left them and went away.

16.5 And when the disciples came to the opposite shore, they forgot to take loaves;

And Jesus said to them, 'Be sure to beware of the leaven of the Pharisees and Sadducees.'

And they were saying to one another, 'We have brought no loaves.' And Jesus, knowing this, said, 'Why do you of little faith say to one another that you have no loaves?' Do you not yet understand or remember the seven loaves of the four thousand and how many hamperfuls you picked up, or the five loaves of the five thousand and how many basketfuls you picked up? How do you fail to understand?

that it was not about loaves that I said, "Beware of the leaven of the Pharisees and Sadducees"? Then they perceived that he had told them to beware not of leaven in loaves but of the doctrine of the Pharisees and Sadducees.

16.13 And Jesus came to the region of Caesarea Philippi. And he asked his disciples, 'Who do men say the son of man is?' And they said, 'Some say John the Baptist, and others Elijah, and yet others Jeremiah or one of the prophets.' He said to them, 'But who do you say that I am?' And *Simon* Peter answered and said, 'You are the Christ, the son of the living God.' And Jesus answered and said to him, 'Blessed are you, Simon-bar-Jonah, because flesh and blood did not reveal it to you but my Father in heaven.

16.18 And now I say to you that you are Peter, and on this rock (*petra*) I will build my church. And the gates of hell shall not prevail against it. And I will give you the keys of the kingdom of heaven, and whatever you bind on earth shall be bound in heaven, and whatever you loose on earth shall be loosed in heaven.'

Then he charged the disciples strictly to tell no one that he was the Christ.

16.21 From that time he [*Jesus Christ*] began to show his disciples that he needs must go *up* to Jerusalem and suffer much at the hands of the elders and high priests and scribes, and be killed, and rise on the third day.

And Peter laid hands on him and began to upbraid him, saying, 'God forbid, lord; this thing shall not happen to you.' But he turned and said to Peter, 'Get you gone [*behind me*], Satan; you

are a stumbling-block to me, for you think not as God but as
men.'

16.24 Then Jesus said to his disciples, 'If anyone will come after me, let
him deny himself and take up his cross and follow me. For
whoever will save his life will lose it; and whoever loses his life
for me will find it. For what shall a man be profited if he gains
the whole world but his life is forfeit? *Or what will a man give in
exchange for his life?* For the son of man is going to come in the
glory of his father with his angels, and then "he will repay
everyone according to his deeds". Truly I say to you that there
are some of those standing here who will not taste death before
they see the son of man coming in his kingdom.'

17.1 And after six days Jesus took along Peter and James and his
brother John and carried them up on to a high mountain by
themselves. And he was transformed in front of them, and his
face shone like the sun and his clothes became white as the
snow.

And behold there were seen by them, talking with him,
Moses and Elijah. And Peter answered and said to him,
'Lord, it is good for us, if you wish, to *set up* here three
pillars, one for you and one for Moses and one for Elijah.'

17.5 While he was still speaking, behold, a shining cloud over-
shadowed them, And behold, there was a voice out of the
cloud, saying, 'This is my beloved son, in whom I have taken
pleasure: hear him.' And when the disciples heard, they fell on
their face and were exceedingly afraid. And Jesus came and
took hold of them and said, 'Get up, and do not be afraid.'
And when they lifted up their eyes they saw nobody, except
17.9 only Jesus himself. And while they were coming down from
the mountain, Jesus commanded them, saying, 'Tell nobody
the thing you have seen, until the son of man has risen from the
dead.'

17.10 And the disciples asked him, saying, 'Why then do the scribes say
that Elijah must come first?' And he answered and said, *'"Elijah
comes and will restore everything": but I say to you that* Elijah
came already, and they did not recognize him *but worked their
pleasure upon him. So is the son of man also about to suffer at their
hands.'* Then the disciples understood that he spoke to them of John
the Baptist.

17.14 And when they had come to the crowd, a man approached him
and fell upon his knees before him and said, 'Lord, have mercy
upon my son, because he has fits and is in a bad state; for he
frequently falls into fire and frequently into water. And I brought
him to your disciples, and they were not able to heal him.' And

Jesus answered and said, 'O unbelieving and perverse generation,
how long shall I be with you? *How long shall I bear with you?*
Bring him here to me.' And Jesus rebuked him and the evil spirit
17.19 came out of him, and the boy was healed from that hour. Then
the disciples went to Jesus privately and said, 'Why were we
unable to cast it out?' And he said to them, 'Because of your little
faith; for truly I say to you that if you have faith like a mustard-
seed, you shall say to this mountain, "Move from here thither",
and it will move, *and nothing shall be impossible for you.*'
17.22 And while they were gathered together in Galilee, Jesus said to
them, 'The son of man is going to be handed over into the hands
of men, and they will kill him, and on the third day he will
arise.' *And they were exceedingly grieved.*
17.24 And after they came to Capharnaum, the collectors of the two-
drachma tax came to Peter and said, 'Does your teacher not pay
the two-drachma?' 'Oh yes, he does,' said he. And when he
entered the house Jesus anticipated him, saying, 'What do you
think, Simon? From whom do earthly kings collect taxes or
tribute—from their own sons or from those of others?' And
when he said, 'From those of others', Jesus said to him, 'So then
their sons are exempt. But in order that we may not lead them
astray, go and cast a hook into the sea and take the first fish that
comes up and open its mouth and you will find a four-drachma
piece. Take that and give it to them on my behalf and yours.'
18.1 In that hour the disciples came to Jesus, saying, 'Who is greatest
in the kingdom of heaven?' And he called a child to him and put
him in the middle of them, and then said, 'Verily I tell you,
unless you turn and become as children, you will not enter the
kingdom of heaven. So whoever abases himself *as this child* is the
greatest in the kingdom of heaven.
18.6 And whoever receives one such child in my name, receives me,
but whoever causes one of these little ones who believe on me to
fall away, it would be to his advantage that an upper millstone
were hung round his neck and he were drowned in the depth of
the sea. For defections must needs come; howbeit, woe to the
man through whom they come. *Woe to the world from defections!*
18.8 If your hand or your foot leads you astray, cut it off and throw it
away from you; it is good for you to enter into life mutilated or
crippled sooner than having two hands or two feet to be thrown
into the eternal fire. And if your eye leads you astray, take it out
and throw it away from you; it is good for you to enter into life
one-eyed sooner than with two eyes to be thrown into the fire of
Gehenna.
18.10 See that you do not despise one of these little ones; for I tell you

that in heaven their angels continually look upon the face of my Father in heaven. What do you think? If any man has a hundred sheep and one of them goes astray, *does* he not leave the ninety-nine and go **to the mountains** and look for the lost one? And if he happens to find it, truly I tell you he is more glad of it than of the ninety-nine that have not gone astray. *Even so it is not the will of your father in heaven that one of these little ones be lost.*
18.15 If your brother errs, go and confute him, with him and yourself
alone present. If he listens to you, you have gained your brother.
But if he will not listen, take with you one or two others, so that
"everything may be established by the mouth of two witnesses
or of three"; and if he disregards them, tell the congregation; and
if he disregards the congregation, let him be for you as the
18.18 gentile and the tax-gatherer. Truly I tell you that all that you
bind on earth shall be bound in heaven, and all that you loose on
earth shall be loosed in heaven. Again, I tell you that if two
among you agree on earth about anything *that they ask*, they
shall have it from my Father in heaven. For where two or three
are gathered together in my name, I am there in the midst of
them.'
18.21 Then Peter came to him and said, 'Lord, how often shall my
brother transgress against me and I forgive him? *Seven times?*
Jesus said to him, 'I say to you not seven times but seventy times
seven. For this reason the kingdom of heaven is like a man
[*a king*] who decided to settle accounts with his servants. When
he started this, one was brought to him who owed ten thousand
talents; and as he was not able to repay, the master ordered him
to be sold with his wife and children and all that he had, and
repayment made. Then the servant fell at his feet, saying to him,
"Be patient with me, and I will repay you all." And the master
had compassion on that servant and let him go free and cancelled
18.28 his debt. But that servant went out, and finding one of his fellow
servants who owed him a hundred denarii, he laid hands on him
and pressed him, saying, "Pay what you owe." Then the servant
fell and besought him, saying, "Be patient with me and I will
repay you." But he would not, but went and threw him into
18.31 prison till he paid what was owing. Now, when his fellow
servants saw what had happened, they were exceedingly sorry,
and they went and reported to their master all that had happened.
Then his master summoned him and said, "Wicked servant, all
that debt I cancelled when you besought me. Ought you not also
to have had mercy on your fellow servant as I had on you?" And
his master was angry and handed him over to the torturers till he
paid back all that was owing to him. *So too will my heavenly Father*

do to you if you do not each pardon his brother from the bottom of your
heart.'
19.1 And it was so, that when Jesus had finished these words he
removed from Galilee and came into the confines of Judaea *the*
other side of Jordan. And many crowds followed him, and he
healed them *there.*
19.3 And Pharisees came to him to try him and asked him if it is
permitted *for a man* to divorce a wife for any cause. And he
answered and said, 'Have you not read that he who created male
and female at the beginning [*made them and*] said, "Because of this
a man shall leave his father and his mother and shall cleave to his
wife and the two shall be one flesh", so that they are no longer
two but one flesh? Therefore what God joined together let man
19.7 not separate.' Then they said to him, 'Why then did Moses
command "to give a bill of divorce and put her away"?' He said,
'Moses permitted you to divorce your wives because of the
hardness of your hearts; but in the beginning it was not so.
But I say to you that whoever divorces his wife, except for
fornication, and marries another woman commits adultery.'
19.10 The disciples said to him, 'If it [*the matter of the man and the wife*]
be thus, is it better not to marry?' And he said to them, 'Not all
can *be continent*, but only those to whom it is given. *For there*
are eunuchs who were born so from their mother's womb, and there are
eunuchs who were made eunuchs by men, and there are eunuchs who
made themselves eunuchs for the sake of the kingdom of heaven. Let
him that can be continent.'
19.13 Then children were brought to him for him to lay hands on them
and pray. And the disciples rebuked them. But Jesus said, 'Allow
the children to come to me *and do not prevent them; for to such as*
these belongs the kingdom of heaven.' And he laid hands on them,
and departed from thence.
19.16 And behold, a man came to him and said, 'Teacher, what *good*
thing shall I do to get life eternal?' And he said to him, 'Why ask
me *about good*? *One only is good.* If you want to enter into life,
keep the commandments.' Then he said to him, 'Which?' And
Jesus said, '"Thou shalt not murder, Thou shalt not commit
adultery, Thou shalt not steal, Thou shalt not commit perjury,
Honour thy father and thy mother", and "Thou shalt love thy
neighbour as thyself."' Then he [*the young man*] said to him,
'*From my youth up* I have observed all these. What do I still
lack?' Jesus said, '*If you want to be perfect,* Go, sell your possessions
and give to the poor, and you shall have treasure in heaven, and come
hither and follow me.' And when he [*the young man*] heard the
answer, he went away grieving, *for he had many possessions.*

19.23 And Jesus said to his disciples, 'Truly I tell you, *that a rich man will with difficulty enter into the kingdom of heaven; and again I tell you that* it is easier for a camel to enter through the eye of a needle than for a rich man to enter into the kingdom of God.' And when the disciples heard, they were exceedingly amazed, saying, 'Who then shall be saved?' But Jesus looked upon them and said, 'With men this is impossible, but "with God everything is possible".'

19.27 Then Peter answering said to him, 'Behold, we have left everything and followed you. What then shall we have?' And Jesus said to them,

'Truly I tell you that *at the rebirth* when the son of man sits on the throne of his glory, you who have followed me shall also sit on twelve thrones, judging the twelve tribes of Israel. And everyone who has left houses or brothers or sisters or father or mother or fields for the sake of my name shall receive many times as much *and inherit eternal life.* [*And many that are first shall be last and last who shall be first.*]'

20.1 'The kingdom of heaven is like a man [*an owner*] who went out at dawn to hire workers for his vineyard. And having agreed with the workers at a denarius for the day, he sent them into his vineyard. And going out about the third hour, he saw others standing *in the market-place idle*; and to them he said, "Get you also gone into the vineyard, and whatever is just I will pay you." And they departed. Again, going out about the sixth and the ninth hour, he did likewise; and about the eleventh hour going out, he found others standing around and said to them, "Why have you stood here all day long *idle*?" They said to him, "Because nobody hired us." He said to them, "Get you also gone into the vineyard." And when evening came, he [*the owner of the vineyard*] said to his steward, "Call the workers and pay the wages, starting with the last ones, *through to the first.*" And they [*those of the eleventh hour*] came and received a denarius each. And when the first came, they thought that they would receive more; but they also received the denarius. And when they had received it, they murmured against the owner, saying, "These last *laboured* one hour, and you have made them equal to us who have borne the burden of the day *and the heat.*" But he answered and said to one of them, "Fellow, I do you no wrong. Did you not agree with me at a denarius? Take what is yours and be gone; and if I wish to give to this last one as to you, is it not permitted me to do as I wish with my own? Or is your eye evil because I am good?" So the last shall be *as the* first, and the first *as the* last.'

20.17 And being about to go up to Jerusalem, Jesus took the twelve aside by
themselves, and on the road he said to them. 'Lo, we are going up to Jerusalem, and the son of man will be handed over to the high priests and scribes, and they will condemn him to death, and hand him over to the gentiles to mock and scourge and crucify; and on the third day he will be raised.'

20.20 Then there came to him the mother of the sons of Zebedee with her sons,
prostrating herself, to ask him for something. And he said to her, 'What do you want?' And she said to him, '*Command* that these my two sons may sit one on your right and the other on your left in your kingdom.' But Jesus answered and said, 'You do not know what you are asking. Can you drink the cup which I am about to drink?' And they said to him, 'We can.' He said to them, 'My cup you shall drink, but as for sitting on my right and left, that is not mine to give *but belongs to those for whom it has been prepared by my Father*.'

20.24 And when the ten heard, they were indignant about the two brothers. And
Jesus called them to him and said, 'You know that the rulers of the gentiles lord it over them, and their great ones use authority over them. Not so shall it be among you; but whoever wishes to be greatest among you shall be your servant, and whoever wishes to be first among you shall be your slave,

> as the son of man came not to be served but to serve and to give his life as a ransom for many.'

And as they were departing from Jericho there followed him a large crowd. And behold, two blind men sitting by the road, when they heard that Jesus was going by, called out, saying, 'Lord, have mercy upon us, son of David.' And the crowd reprimanded them to be silent; but they called out all the louder, saying, 'Lord, have mercy upon us, son of David.' And Jesus stopped and called them and said, 'What would you have me do for you?' They said to him, 'Lord, let our eyes be opened.' And Jesus took compassion and touched their eyes; and immediately they saw again and followed him.

21.1 And when they approached Jerusalem and came to Bethphage *to the Mountain of*
Olives, then Jesus sent two disciples, saying to them, 'Go into the village which is opposite to you, and immediately you will find a she-ass tethered and a colt with it. Untie them and bring them to me; and if anyone says anything to you, you shall say that "The lord has need of them but will send them back directly."' *This happened so that what was spoken through the prophet should be fulfilled: 'Say to the daughter of Zion, "Lo, your king comes to you meek and mounted upon an ass, nay, upon a fool, the son of a beast of burden."'*

21.6 And the disciples went, and having done as Jesus instructed them, brought the
she-ass and the colt, *and put the clothes on them*, and he sat upon them. And most of the crowd spread their clothes on the road, and others cut branches from the trees and strewed them on the road. And the crowds which preceded and followed him shouted, 'Hosanna to the son of David. Blessed is he that comes
21.10 in the name of the Lord. Hosanna in the highest.' And when he entered
Jerusalem, the whole city was shaken, saying, 'Who is this?' And the crowds said, 'This is Jesus, the prophet from Nazareth in Galilee.'

21.12 And Jesus went into the Temple and threw out all who sold and bought in the

Temple, and overturned the tables of those who changed money and the *cages* of those who sold doves. And he said to them, 'It is written, "My house shall be called a house of prayer" *but you make it a "bandits' cave".*' And there came to him blind people and cripples in the Temple, and he healed them. And when the high priests and the scribes saw the *things* which he did and [*the children*] the *people* shouting [*in the Temple*] 'Hosanna to the son of David', they were offended and said to him, 'Do you hear what these are saying?' And Jesus said to them, 'Yes, have you never heard, "Out of the mouths of children, yes, of sucklings, thou hast ordained praise"?' And he left them, and went outside the city to Bethany, and he lodged there.

21.18 And in the morning when he *made his way* into the city, he was hungry. And seeing one fig-tree by the road, he went to it and found nothing on it except leaves only. And he said to it, 'Nevermore shall there come fruit from you for eternity.' And instantly the fig-tree shrivelled up. And the disciples were astonished to see this and said, 'How did the fig-tree instantly shrivel up?' And Jesus answered and said to them, 'Truly I tell you, if you have faith and do not doubt, you shall not only do what I did to the fig-tree but also, if you say to this mountain, "Rise up and be cast into the sea", it will happen. *And all that you ask in prayer, believing, you shall receive.*'

21.23 And he came into the Temple.
And the high priests and the elders of the people came to him *as he taught*, saying, 'By what authority do you do these things? Who gave you this authority?' And Jesus answering said to them, 'I too will ask you a thing, which if you tell me, I will tell you by what authority I do this: the baptism of John, from whence was it, from heaven or from men?' *Then they consulted among themselves, saying, 'If we say, "From heaven", he will say, "Why then did you not believe him?" But if we say, "From men", we are afraid of the crowds; for all hold John to be a prophet.'* And they answered Jesus and said, 'We do not know.' Then he said to them, 'Then I too will not tell you either by what authority I do these things.

21.28 What think you? A man had two children; and he went to the first and said, "Child, go and work in the vineyard today." And he answered and said, "Yes, sir", but he did not go. And he went to the second and spoke to him likewise. And he answered and said, "I will not"; but afterwards he changed his mind and went. Which of the two did the father's will?' And they said, 'The second.' Then Jesus said to them, 'Truly I tell you that the tax-gatherers and the whores will be before you in the kingdom of God. For John came to you in the way of righteousness and you did not believe him; but the tax-gatherers and whores believed him; and you, when you saw it, did not even change your mind afterwards and believe him.

21.33 Hear another parable. There was a man [*an owner*] who "planted
a vineyard and set a fence round about it and dug a vat in it and
built a tower", and he leased it to tenant farmers and went
abroad. And when the time of the fruits drew near he sent his
servants to the tenants to receive his fruits. And the tenants
took his servants, and one they flogged *and another they killed*
and another they stoned. Again he sent other servants, more
numerous than the first, and they treated them the same. And
afterwards he sent to them his son, saying, "They will respect
my son." But the tenants, when they saw the son, said among
themselves: "This is the heir. Come, let us kill him and get his
inheritance"; and they took him, and threw him out of the
vineyard, and killed him.

21.40 So when the owner of the vineyard comes, what will he do to
those tenants?' They said to him: 'He will destroy them as they
deserve and will let the vineyard to other tenants, who will
render to him the fruits in their seasons.'

Jesus said to them, 'Did you never read in the scriptures,
"The stone which the builders rejected, the same became the
head of the corner; this was from the Lord, and it is wonder-
21.44 ful in our eyes"? And he that falls on the stone shall be
21.43 smashed, and whomever it falls upon it will crush. *Therefore
I say to you that the kingdom of God shall be taken from you and
given to a nation which produces the fruits of it.*'

21.45 And when the high priests and Pharisees heard his parables, they perceived that
he was talking about them; and desirous though they were of arresting him,
they were afraid of the crowds because these held him for a prophet.

22.1 And Jesus answering spoke again in parables to them, saying,
'The kingdom of heaven is likened to a man [*a king*] who made
a wedding for his son, and he sent out his servants to call those
who had been invited to the wedding; but they would not come.
And again he sent out other servants, saying, "Tell those who
were called, See, *I have my breakfast ready*, *my bulls and* my
fatlings have been butchered, and everything is ready: come to
the wedding." And they paid no attention but went their ways,
one to his field, another to his shop,

22.6 and the rest seized his servants and maltreated and killed them.
And the king was angry, and he sent his army and destroyed
those murderers and burnt their city.

22.8 Then said he to his servants, "The wedding is ready; but those
invited were not worthy. Go therefore into the highways [*of the
roads*] and call to the wedding however many you find." And
those servants went out *into the roads* and collected together all

whom they found, bad and good; and the marriage-room was filled *with guests sitting at table.*

22.11 And the king, coming in to look at those at table, saw there a man not wearing wedding-garb; and he said to him, "Friend, how came you in here not having on wedding-garb?" And he was speechless. Then the king said to the waiters, "Bind his feet and hands and throw him out into the outer darkness: there shall be the wailing and the gnashing of teeth." For many are called but few chosen.'

22.15 Then the Pharisees went and made a plot to trap him in his speech. And they sent to him their disciples with the Herodians, saying, 'Teacher, we know that you are truthful and teach the way of God in truthfulness, *and that you care for no one; for you are no respecter of persons.* Tell us, therefore, how think you? Is it permitted to pay tax to Caesar?' But Jesus, perceiving their badness, said, 'Why do you try to trick me, you hypocrites? Show me the coinage of the tax.' They brought him a denarius, and he said to them, 'Whose is this likeness and inscription?' They said, 'Caesar's.' Then said he to them, 'So give Caesar what is Caesar's *and God what is God's.*' And when they heard, they were astonished and left him and went away.

22.23 On that day there came to him Sadducees, *saying that there is no resurrection.* And they asked him, saying, 'Teacher, Moses said that if one dies childless, his brother shall thereupon espouse his wife and raise issue for his brother. Now, there were among us seven brothers; and the first married and died, and not having issue left his wife to his brother; and likewise the second and the third, up to seven, and last of all, the woman died. At the resurrection, to which of the seven will she be wife? For they all had her.' And Jesus answering said to them, 'You err, not knowing the scriptures *nor the power of God.* At the resurrection they shall neither marry nor be given in marriage but be like angels in the sky. As for the resurrection, have you not read what was said to you by God, "I am the god of Abraham and the god of Isaac and the god of Jacob"? He is not god of the dead but of the living.' And when the crowds heard, they were astonished at his teaching.

22.34 But the Pharisees, when they heard that he had silenced the Sadducees, gathered together, and one of them [*a lawyer*] asked him a question, to tempt him: 'Teacher, which commandment is the greatest in the Law?' And he said to him, '"Thou shalt love the lord thy God with all thy heart and with all thy soul and with all thy thought." This is the greatest and first commandment. A second is like it, "Thou shalt love thy neighbour as thyself."

In these two commandments [*hang*] are contained the whole Law and the prophets.'

22.41 And the Pharisees being gathered together, Jesus asked them, 'What think you concerning Christ? Whose son is he?' And they said to him, 'David's.' Then he said to them, 'How then does David under inspiration call him lord, saying, "The Lord said to my lord, Sit on my right hand until I put your enemies under your feet"? If David then calls him lord, how is he his son?' And no one could answer him a word, nor did anyone from that day dare to ask him anything more.

23.1 Then Jesus talked to the crowds and to his disciples, saying: 'The scribes and the Pharisees have seated themselves in Moses' chair, [*so do and observe all that they tell you,*] but do not act as they behave; for they talk and do not do: they bind heavy burdens *and put them* on to men's shoulders *but do not themselves lift their finger to move them.* And all their actions are to be observed by men; for they broaden their phylacteries and widen their fringes, and they love the top places at dinners and the front seats in the synagogues and salutations in the squares and being called by men "rabbi".

23.8 But as for you, do not you be called "rabbi"; *for you have one teacher.* And do not call anyone *on earth* your father; *for you have one father, the heavenly one, and you are all brethren.* And do not be called "instructor"; *for you have one instructor, Christ.* But the greatest of you shall be your servant. He that shall exalt himself shall be abased, and he that shall abase himself shall be exalted.

23.13 Woe to you, sanctimonious scribes and Pharisees, because you shut the kingdom of heaven in men's faces; for you will not enter, neither do you let those who will enter do so.

23.15 Woe to you, sanctimonious scribes and Pharisees, because you traverse sea and land to make one convert, and when you get him, you make him twice as much a son of Gehenna as yourselves.

23.16 Woe to you, blind guides, who say, "If a man swears by the Temple, that is nothing; but if he swears by the gold of the Temple, he is bound." Fools *and blind men*! Which is greater, the gold or the Temple which has sanctified the gold? And you say, "If a man swears by the altar, that is nothing; but if he swears by the offering upon it, he is bound." Blind men! Which is greater, the offering or the altar which sanctifies the offering? So he that has sworn by the altar swears by it and by all that is upon it; and he that has sworn by the Temple swears by it and by him that inhabits it; and he that has sworn by heaven swears by the throne of God and by him that sits upon it.

23.23 Woe to you, sanctimonious scribes and Pharisees, because you tithe mint, anise, and cumin, and have omitted the heavier demands of the Law, *judgement and mercy and faith, whereas you ought to have done these things and not omitted those.*

Blind guides, who sieve out the gnat and swallow the camel!

23.25 Woe to you, sanctimonious scribes and Pharisees, because you cleanse the outside *of the cup and the bowl*, but *the inside* is full of robbery and incontinence. *Blind Pharisee, cleanse first the inside of the cup, so that the outside of it may be clean too!*

23.27 Woe to you, sanctimonious scribes and Pharisees, because you resemble plastered tombs, which outwardly appear fair but inside are full of dead men's bones and all uncleanliness. Likewise you outwardly appear righteous to men but inwardly are filled with pretence and unlawfulness.

23.29 Woe to you, sanctimonious scribes and Pharisees, because you build the tombs of the prophets and adorn the graves of the righteous and say, "If we had been in the days of our fathers, we would not have been partners with them in the blood of the prophets."

So you bear witness against yourselves that you are the sons of those who murdered the prophets. *Serpents*, progeny of vipers, how shall you escape the judgement *of Gehenna*? And you shall fill up the measure of your fathers. For this reason, behold, I will send to you prophets and wise men and scribes. Some of them you will kill and crucify; and some of them you will whip in your synagogues and drive from city to city, in order that upon you may be visited all the righteous blood spilt on the earth from Abel the righteous to the blood of Zacharias the son of Barachiah, whom you murdered between the holy of holies and the altar. Truly I tell you, all these things will be visited upon this generation.

23.37 Jerusalem, Jerusalem, that kills the prophets and stones those who are sent to it, how many times have I wanted to bring your children together in the way that a hen gathers together its chicks *under its wings*, but you did not want it. And now, behold, your house is left deserted; for I tell you that henceforth you shall not see me until you say, "Blessed is he that comes in the name of the Lord."'

24.1 And Jesus went out *from the Temple*, and was going his way; and his disciples came to him, to show him the buildings of the Temple. And he answered and said to them, 'Do you *not* see all these things? Truly I tell you, there will not be one stone left here *upon another stone that shall not be brought down*.'

24.3 And when he had seated himself on the mountain *of Olives*, his
disciples came to him privately, saying, 'Tell us, when shall these
things be,

and what will be the signal for your visitation and the end of the world?'

And Jesus answered and said to them: 'See that no one leads you astray; for many will come under my name, saying, "I am the Messiah" and will lead many astray. You will be going to hear *wars and* reports of wars. See you do not get excited;

for so it must happen, but the end is not yet;

for "nation will rise against nation and kingdom against kingdom" and there will be famines and earthquakes in places.

And all these things are only the beginning of the pangs.

24.8 Then they will hand you over to oppression and kill you, and
you will be hated by all *the gentiles* for my name's sake. And many will defect and hand one another over; and because unlawfulness has been multiplied, the love of the many will grow cold. But it is he who endures to the end that will be saved.

And this gospel of the kingdom will be promulgated in the whole world as a witness to all the gentiles. And then shall come the end.

24.15 So when you see the "abomination of desolation set up in the
holy place" as said by the prophet Daniel—let the reader note—let those in Judaea flee to the mountains, a person on the rooftop not going downstairs to get his belongings nor a person in the field going home to get his coat.

Bad luck for those who are pregnant or suckling babies at the time! Just pray that the flight be not in winter—nor on a Sabbath!

24.21 Then there will be "great tribulation such as there has not been
since the beginning of the world" until now, nor ever shall be.

And if those days had not been shortened, all flesh would not have been saved;

But for the sake of the elect those days will be shortened. Then if someone says to you, "Lo, the Messiah is here" or "Here", do not believe it; for false Messiahs and false prophets will arise and
perform great signs and miracles, so as to lead astray, *if it were*
24.25 *possible*, even the elect. Lo, I have told you in advance.

So if they say to you, "Lo, he is in the desert", do not go out, or "Lo, he is in the closet", do not believe it.

24.27 For the coming of the son of man will be like the flash of
lightning *from the east to the west of the sky. "Where the carcass is, there the eagles gather."* And immediately *after the tribulation of*

those days "the sun will be darkened and the moon will not give
its ray, and the stars will fall from the sky and the powers of
24.30 heaven will be shaken". And then shall appear the sign of the son
of man in the sky. And then shall "all the tribes of the earth see
[*mourn*] the son of man coming on the clouds of the sky with
power and great glory"; and he will send out his angels with a
great trumpet, and they will collect his elect "from the four
winds, from one end of heaven to the other end of it".

24.32 Learn from the fig-tree the parable: when its *fruit* is already
soft, and it produces its leaves also, you know that summer is
near. Likewise you too, when you see all these things, must
24.34 know that it is [*nigh*] at the door. Truly I tell you that this
generation will not pass away before all these things happen.
Heaven and earth will pass away; but my words will not pass
away.

But as regards that day and hour nobody knows, not even the
24.37 angels in heaven, nor even the son, but only the Father. For like
the days of Noah, even so shall be the visitation of the son of
man.

For as in those days *before the flood* they ate and drank, married
and gave in marriage, until the day when Noah entered the ark,
and they did not know until the flood came and carried them all
away, so will it be when the son of man comes.

24.40 Then there will be two men afield, one taken and one left, two
women grinding at the mill, one taken and one left. Keep awake,
therefore, because you do not know on what day your lord will
come.

But of this you can be sure, that if the householder had known
at what hour of the night the burglar was coming, he would
have stayed awake and not allowed his house to be broken
into. Therefore do you also be ready, because the son of man
will come at a time you do not expect.

24.45 *It is like* a servant, whom his master <on going away> put in
charge of the household to give them their food at the right time.
Blessed is that servant, *the faithful and wise servant*, if his master
comes and finds him doing so. Truly I tell you, he will put
him in charge of all his possessions. But if that servant, *the bad
servant*, says in his heart, "My master is long away" and starts to
beat his fellow servants and eats and drinks with the drunkards,
the master of that servant will come *in a day he does not expect and*
at an hour he does not know and will cut him in two and give
him his portion with the hypocrites: there shall be the wailing
and the gnashing of teeth.

25.1 Then the kingdom of heaven will be like ten maidens who took

their lamps and went to greet the bridegroom. And five of them
were foolish and five were wise. For the foolish ones took the
lamps but did not take oil with them, but the wise ones took oil
in jars as well as their lamps. And when the bridegroom was
long in coming, they all dozed off and slept. And at midnight
there was a shout, "Here is the bridegroom, go to meet him."
25.8 Then those maidens all woke up and trimmed their lamps. And
the foolish ones said to the wise, "Give us some of your oil,
because our lamps are going out." But the wise ones answered
and said, "No, there may not be enough for us and for you. Go
to the shops instead and buy some for yourselves." And when
they had gone off to buy oil, the bridegroom came; and the
maidens who were in readiness went in with him to the wedding-
feast, and the door was shut. And afterwards came the rest of the
25.13 maidens, saying, "Sir, sir, open to us." But he answered and
said, "Truly I tell you, I do not know you." *Therefore keep
awake, because you do not know the day or the hour.*
25.14 [*For just as*] *A certain man*, on going away, called his servants
and handed his property over to them. And to one he gave five
talents, and to another two, and to another one, to each according as he willed. And [*he departed and*] immediately the one who
received the five talents went and invested them and gained
another five, and likewise the one who received the two talents
made another two. But the one who received the one talent went
25.19 away and dug in the earth and hid his master's money. After a
long time the master of the servants came and called them to
account. And the one that received the five talents came and
brought five more talents, saying, "Master, you handed five
talents over to me: see, I have gained another five talents." His
master said to him, "Well done, good and faithful servant; you
were faithful in little, I will put you in charge of much. Enter
into your master's joy." Also the one who received the two
talents came and said, "Master, you handed two talents over
to me: see, I gained another two talents." His master said to
him, "Well done, good and faithful servant; you were faithful in
25.24 little, I will put you in charge of much. Enter into your master's
joy." And the one who had received the one talent also came and
said, "Master, I knew that you are a *strict* man, who *reaps where
he has not sown and* gathers from where he has not scattered; and I
was afraid and went away and hid your talent in the ground. See,
you have your own back." But his master said to him, "Bad *and
timid* servant, you knew that I *reap where I have not sown and*
gather from where I have not scattered. You should therefore
have put my money with the bankers, and when I came I should

have got back my own with interest. Take the talent away from him therefore and give it to the one who has the ten talents; for to everyone that has shall be given to overflowing, but from the one that has not, even what he has shall be taken away.

And throw the unprofitable servant out into the outer darkness: there shall be the wailing and gnashing of teeth."

25.31 But when the son of man comes in his glory and all his
angels with him, then he will sit down on the throne of his
glory and there shall be brought together in front of him all
the nations; and he will divide them from one another, as
the shepherd divides the sheep from the goats, and will put
some [*the sheep*] on his right and the others [*the goats*] on his
25.34 left. Then will the king say to those on his right, "Come,
blessed of my Father, inherit the kingdom prepared for you
from the foundation of the world; for I hungered and you
gave me to eat, I thirsted and you gave me to drink, I was a
stranger and you received me, naked and you clothed me, I
was sick and you cared for me, I was in prison and you
came to me." Then will they [*the righteous*] answer him,
saying, "Lord, when did we see you hungry and feed you,
or thirsty and give you drink? And when did we see you a
stranger and receive you, or naked and clothe you? And
when did we see you sick or in prison and come to you?"
And answering the king will say to them, "Truly I tell you,
inasmuch as you did it to one of these my brethren, the least
ones, you did it to me." Then will he say also to those on
the left, "Go from me, accursed, into the everlasting fire
prepared for the Devil and his angels. For I hungered and
you did not give me to eat, I thirsted and you did not give
me to drink, I was a stranger and you did not receive me,
naked and you did not clothe me, in prison and you did not
care for me." Then will they also answer, saying, "Lord,
when did we see you hungry or thirsty or a stranger or
naked and not attend to you? And when did we see you sick
or in prison, and not come to you?" Then he will answer
them, saying, "Truly I tell you, inasmuch as you did not do
it to one of these, the least ones, you did not do it to me
either." And these will depart to everlasting destruction and
the others [*the righteous*] to everlasting life.'

26.1 And it was so that when Jesus had finished all these sayings, he
said to his disciples, 'Know that on the next day it is Passover,
and the son of man will be handed over to be crucified.'

26.3 Then the high priests and the elders of the people assembled
in the palace of the high priest called Caiaphas, and resolved

to arrest and kill Jesus *by a trick*; but they said, 'Not at the
feast, lest a disturbance arise among the people.'
26.14 Then Judas *called Iscariot*, one of the twelve, went to the
high priests and said, 'What will you give me, and I will
hand him over to you?' And they weighed him out thirty
pieces of silver. And from that time he sought an opportunity
to hand him over.
26.17 And on the first of the days of unleavened bread the disciples came to Jesus saying, 'Where do you want us to
prepare for you to eat the Passover?' And he said, 'Go into
the city to the first person you meet, and say to him, "Our
teacher says, My time is near: I will keep the Passover at
your house with my disciples."' And they did as Jesus
instructed them, and prepared the Passover.
26.20 And when evening came, he sat at table with the twelve. And
as they ate, he said, 'Truly I tell you that one of you will
betray me.' And they were exceedingly grieved and began
each to say to him, 'Surely it is not I, lord?' But he answered
and said, 'He that has dipped *his hand* with me in the dish, he it
is that will betray me. The son of man goes his way as it is
written concerning him; but woe to that man through whom
the son of man is betrayed. It would be well for him if he [*that
man*] had not been born.' And answering, Judas, who betrayed
him, said, 'Surely it is not I, rabbi?' And he said to him, 'You
have said it.'
26.26 And as they ate, Jesus took bread and having given the blessing
broke it and gave it to his disciples and said, 'Take, eat, this is
my body.'

And he took the cup and having said grace, gave it to them, saying, 'Drink from it, all of you; for this is my blood of the covenant, poured out for many, for remission of sins.

And I tell you: from now I shall not drink from it [*from the product of the vine*] until that day when I drink [*it*] new wine with you in the kingdom of my Father.'

26.30 *And having sung a hymn, they went out to the Mountain of
Olives.*

Then said Jesus to them, 'All of you will fall away from me this night; for it is written, "I will strike the shepherd, and the sheep of the flock will be scattered." But after my resurrection I will go before you to Galilee.' And Peter answered him, 'If all fall away from you, I will never fall away.' Jesus said to him, 'Truly I tell you that this night before cock crow you will deny me thrice.' Said Peter to him, 'Even if I must die with you, I will not deny you.' So likewise said all the disciples.

26.36 Then Jesus went with them to a spot called Gethsemane and he
said to the disciples, 'Sit here while I go away yonder and pray.'

And he took with him Peter and the two sons of Zebedee; and he began to be grieved and dejected. Then said he to them, 'My soul is exceedingly grieved, *even to death.* Remain here and stay awake with me.'

And he went some little way off and fell upon his face, praying and saying, 'O my Father, if it is possible, let this cup pass from me. Howbeit, not as I will be it, but as you will.' And he came back to the disciples and found them asleep, and said *to Peter*, 'So you were not able to keep awake with me a single hour! Watch and pray, so that you may not fall into temptation. The spirit is ready, but the flesh is weak.' And again a second time he went away and prayed, saying, 'O my Father, if this cup may not pass by, unless I drink it, let your will be done.' And when he came back he found them asleep; for their eyes were weighed down. And he left them, and went away again and prayed a third time, saying the same thing again.

26.45 And he came to the disciples and said to them, 'Is now the time
for you to sleep and take your rest? Lo, the hour has arrived
when the son of man is delivered into the hands of sinners.

Awake, let us be going. Lo, my betrayer has arrived.'

And while he was still speaking, lo, Judas, *one of the twelve*, came, and with him a big crowd, with swords and staves, from the high priests and elders of the people.

And the betrayer gave them a signal, saying, 'Whomever I kiss is the man: seize him.'

And he went straight up to Jesus, and said, 'Greetings, rabbi' and kissed him. And Jesus said to him, 'Friend, have your way.'

26.50 Then they came and laid hands on Jesus *and arrested him.* And lo,
one of those with Jesus put out his hand and struck the high
priest's servant *and took his sword away*, and snatched his sidearm.
Then said Jesus to him, 'Give it back. *Put your sword back where it*
came from; for all who take the sword shall perish by the sword.
Or do you think I can not call upon my Father and he will at once
provide me with more than twelve legions of angels? How then
are the scriptures to be fulfilled, that thus it must needs happen?'
In that hour Jesus said to the crowds, 'Have you come out with
swords and staves to capture me as if I were a robber? *Daily* I sat
in the Temple teaching, and you did not seize me. *All this has*
happened in order that the scriptures [*of the prophets*] *might be fulfilled.*'
Then all the disciples left him and fled.

26.57 And those that had arrested Jesus led him away to Caiaphas the
high priest, where the scribes and the elders were assembled.

And Peter followed him at a distance to the courtyard of the high priest, and went in and sat down with the servants *to see the end*.

And the high priests and the whole council sought false witness against Jesus in order to put him to death and they did not find it, though many false witnesses came forward.

And afterwards, two men appeared and said, 'This man said, "I can pull down the Temple of God and build it in three days."'

And the high priest rose and said, 'Do you hear what these men are witnessing against you? Have you no answer?' And Jesus was silent. And the high priest said to him, 'I conjure you by the living God to tell us if you are the Messiah, the son of God.' And Jesus said to him, 'You have said it.

Howbeit, I say to you, from henceforth you shall see "the son of man seated at the right hand of Power" and "coming upon the clouds of heaven".'

Then the high priest tore his clothes, saying, 'He has blasphemed. What more need have we for witnesses? Lo, now you have heard the blasphemy. What is your verdict?' And they answered and said, 'He is guilty; let him die.' Then they spat upon his face and slapped him, and some struck him saying, 'Prophesy to us, Messiah: *who was it that hit you?*'

26.69 And as Peter was sitting outside in the courtyard, a servant girl went up to him saying, 'You too were with Jesus the Galilean.' But he denied it in front of them all, saying, 'I do not know what you are talking about.' And he went out into the porch, and another maid saw him and said to the men there, 'This man was with Jesus of Nazareth.' And again he denied it with an oath, 'I do not know the man.' And after a little while those standing there came up to Peter and said, 'Surely you too are one of them; for your speech betrays you.' Then he began to curse and swear, 'I do not know the man.' And immediately a cock crew. And Peter remembered the words of Jesus when he said that 'Before cock crow you will deny me thrice'; and he went out and wept bitterly.

* * * * *

27.1 And when morning came all the high priests and elders of the people took counsel against Jesus to put him to death. And they bound him and took him away and handed him over to Pilate the governor.

27.3 Then Judas, who betrayed him, when he saw that he was condemned, repented and took the thirty pieces of silver back to the high priests, saying, 'I have sinned, betraying an innocent man.' But they said, 'What do we care? That is your affair.' And he threw down the pieces *in the Temple*, and went away and hanged himself. And the high priests picked up the pieces and said, 'It is not permissible to pay these into the chest, because they are the price of blood.' And after taking counsel they bought with them the potter's field to bury *him* [*strangers*], for which reason that field was called Field of Blood and is so to this day. *Then was fulfilled what was spoken by Jeremiah the prophet, who said, 'And I took the thirty pieces of silver, the price of him that was valued out of the children of Israel, and put them into the potter's field, as the Lord instructed me.'*

27.11 And Jesus was brought before the governor. And the governor questioned him,
saying, 'Are you the king of the Jews?' And Jesus said, 'You say it.' And while
he was being accused by the high priests and elders, he made no answer. Then
Pilate said to him, 'Do you not hear all that they are accusing you of?' And he
answered him not a word to anything, so that the governor marvelled greatly.
27.19 *And as he sat on the judgement-seat, his wife sent a message to him, saying,
'Have nothing to do with that righteous man; for I saw much to alarm me
27.15 about him in a dream today.'* Now it was the governor's custom at the time of
a feast to release to the populace one prisoner whom they wanted, and at that
time *he* had a notorious prisoner called Barabbas. Therefore Pilate, when
they were gathered together, said to them, 'Whom is it your pleasure that I
release to you, Barabbas or Jesus called the Messiah?'
27.20 And the high priests and the elders persuaded the populace to ask for Barabbas
and destroy Jesus. And the governor answered and said to them, 'Which one *of*
the two shall I release to you?' And they said, 'Barabbas.' Then Pilate said to
them, 'What then shall I do with Jesus called the Messiah?' And they all said,
'Let him be crucified.' But he said, 'Why? What has he done wrong?' But they
27.24 shouted all the more, saying, 'Let him be crucified.' And Pilate, seeing that it
availed nothing but that instead a riot was arising, took water and washed his
hands in the sight of the populace, saying, 'I am clear of this deed of blood; see
you to it.' And all the people answered and said, 'His blood be upon us and
upon our children.' Then Pilate released Barabbas to them and sentenced Jesus
to be scourged and crucified.
27.27 Then the governor's soldiers, taking charge of Jesus, collected the cohort
around him in the praetorium. And having stripped him, they put on him a
scarlet cloak, and plaited a wreath of acanthus and put it on him [*his head*] and a
reed in his right hand; and they genuflected before him and mocked him,
saying, 'Hail, king of the Jews.'

And having spat upon him, they took the reed and hit him on the head.
27.31 And when they had mocked him, they took the cloak off him and put on him
his own clothes and took him away to crucify him.

And as they were going out, they found a man of Cyrene, Simon by name. Him they pressed into service to raise his cross.

And having come to a place called Golgotha—that is, 'place *called* of the skull'—they gave him wine mixed with bile to drink; and when he had tasted it, he would not drink.

27.35 And when they had crucified him, they 'divided his clothes among them,
casting lots', and sat down and watched him there. And they attached above
his head his offence in writing: 'This is Jesus, the king of the Jews.'

Then were crucified with him two robbers, one on the right and one on the left.

27.39 And the passers-by reviled him, 'wagging their heads' and saying, 'You that
pull down the Temple and build it in three days, save yourself, if you are the son of God,

and come down from the cross.

"He trusted in God; let him rescue him now, if he will"; for he said, "I am the son of God."' Likewise the high priests with the scribes and elders mocked him, saying, 'Others he saved; can he not save himself?

If he is the king of Israel, let him come down from the cross, and we will believe in him.' And the robbers that were crucified with him also cast the same reproach at him.

27.45 And from the sixth hour there was darkness over all the earth until the ninth
hour. And at the ninth hour Jesus cried out with a loud voice, saying, 'Eli, Eli, lema sabachthani', that is, 'My God, my God, why hast thou deserted me?' And some of those that stood there, when they heard, said, 'This fellow is calling for Elijah.'

And immediately one of them ran and got a sponge and filled it with vinegar and stuck it on a stick and gave him to drink; but the rest said

'Let us see if Elijah will come to save him.' And Jesus cried again with a loud voice and gave up the ghost.

27.51 And lo, the veil of the holy of holies was split in two from the top to the
bottom, and there was an earthquake and the rocks were split and the tombs were opened; and many bodies of the saints that were asleep arose and went out of the tombs *after his resurrection* and went into the holy city and were seen by many.

And the centurion and those with him watching Jesus, when they saw the earthquake and the happenings, were exceedingly frightened, saying, 'Truly, this was the son of God.'

And there were many women there watching from a distance, who had accompanied Jesus from Galilee to serve him,

among whom were Mary of Magdala and Mary the mother of James and Joseph,

and the mother of the sons of Zebedee.

27.57 And when it was evening there came a rich man from Arimathaea, whose name
was Joseph, who had also become a disciple of Jesus. He approached Pilate and asked for the body of Jesus. Then Pilate ordered it to be handed over. And Joseph took the body and wrapped it in a clean linen cloth and put it in his new tomb which he had hewn in the rock and rolled a great stone against the doorway of the tomb, and went away. And Mary of Magdala was there and the other Mary, sitting opposite to the tomb.

27.62 And on the morrow, *which is the day after the Friday*, the chief priests and the
Pharisees went to Pilate, saying, 'Sir, we have remembered that that impostor said when he was still alive, "After three days I shall arise." Give orders, therefore, that the grave be made secure until the third day, lest the disciples

come and steal him away and tell the people, "He has risen from the dead", and the last imposture will be worse than the first.' Pilate said to them, 'You have custody; go your ways and take precautions as you think best.' And they went, and made the grave secure by sealing the stone, with the guard.

28.1 And late on the Sabbath, as it was dawning on the first day of the week, there came Mary of Magdala and the other Mary, to watch the tomb.

And lo, there was a big earthquake; for an angel of the Lord descended from heaven and came and rolled away the stone and sat upon it. His face was like lightning and his garments white as snow. And for fear of him those keeping guard were shaken and became like dead men. But the angel answered and said to the women: 'As for you, do not be afraid; for I know you are looking for Jesus who was crucified. He is not here; for he has risen, as he said. Come hither and see the place where he lay, and go at once and tell his disciples, "He is risen from the dead and behold he goes before you to Galilee: you will see him there." Lo, I have told you.'

And they went away from the tomb at once with fear and great joy, and ran to give the news to his disciples.

28.9 And lo, Jesus met them, saying, 'Greetings.' And they approached and clasped his feet *and prostrated themselves before him.* Then said Jesus to them, 'Fear not: get you gone, and give the news to my brethren. Let them go back to Galilee, and they will see me there.'

28.11 And while the women were on their way, lo, some of the soldiers of the guard went into the city and reported to the high priests all the happenings. And having assembled with the elders and taken counsel, the high priests gave considerable money to the soldiers, telling them, 'Say, "His disciples came at night and stole him while we were asleep." And if this is heard in front of the governor, we will intercede with him and see that you have no cause for anxiety.' And they took the money and did as they were instructed; and this report was noised abroad among the people of Judaea down to the present day.

28.16 And the eleven disciples went to Galilee *to the mountain*, where Jesus appointed them; and when they saw him they prostrated themselves, but some of them had doubts.

* * * * *

And Jesus approached and spoke to them, saying, 'There is given to me all power in heaven and upon earth. Go therefore and make disciples of all the gentiles, baptizing them in the name of the Father and the son and the holy spirit, teaching them to keep all that I have enjoined upon you. And lo, I am with you, all the days until the ending of the world.'

COMMENTARY

1.1 The book cannot originally have commenced with the genealogy of somebody whose name and existence were as yet unknown to the reader. That genealogy has displaced the original commencement, of which elements survive (see 2.1) and which corresponded with the identification of Jesus as 'the Messiah, the son of God'. The genealogy implies an alternative identification as 'son of David, king of the Jews'.

Being put first, the genealogy created the misleading appearance of a title to the book; but the insertion in the heading of the epithet Χριστοῦ, 'the Messiah', was procured at the price of accepting 'called'—'*called* Christ' (cf. 27.22)—in the concluding transitional sentence, 1.16. These are the only places in the book, apart from a variant reading at 16.21, where the expression 'Jesus Christ' occurs.

As it happens, only one of the other gospels has a title sentence. In 'Luke' that sentence states the subject and contains a dedication but no indication of the author's name; the sentence, however, is under suspicion of being an addition designed, when taken together with the similar prefatory sentence to Acts, to link the two books together. The original beginning of 'Mark', like the end of it, has been lost, presumably a victim to the common fate which overtakes the first and last pages of books, more easily if in the form of a codex rather than a roll.

'John' has no title sentence but contains internal claims of authorship. Though 'Luke' and 'Mark' as author names lack internal authority, it is not only convenient to use them, as well as 'John', to designate the respective books, but also appropriate, because each of those three books is substantially the product of an individual mind and pen. As that is not the case with this book, use of the traditional author name 'Matthew' is inherently misleading, however unavoidable.

The expression 'table of descent', βίβλος γενέσεως, is the equivalent of ספר תולדת, 'book of progeny' as in Gen. 5.1 ('this is the book of the progeny of Adam: Adam begot Seth, Seth begot Enos, Enos begot Cainan', etc.). That sort of list reads downwards and takes its name from the first ancestor, who stands at the head of it. As there Adam, so here it would be Abraham. When, however, the table was inserted at the beginning of the book, 'Jesus Christ' was substituted for 'Abraham' and the words 'son of David, son of Abraham' were added. The description of Jesus as 'son of David' was of course significant; but the description of him as 'son of Abraham' was not, since all Jews were 'sons of Abraham' (cf. 3.9). Thus arises that feeling of bewilderment which has been shared by readers ever since at finding a table of descent from Abraham prefixed to a book about Jesus.

The section of the genealogy from Abraham to David corresponds to 1 Chr. 1.34–2.15 and that from David to Jechoniah to 1 Chr. 3.5–16, omitting, however, three names after Oziah and a fourth, Jehoiakim, after Josiah. The nine names between Zorobabel and Joseph are otherwise unknown. They are quite inadequate, even at three per century, to fill the gap of five hundred years between Zorobabel (*c*.536 BC) and Herod.

Luke saw the difficulties, and two in particular—that of starting his book with a table of the descendants of Abraham, and that of a table which landed Jesus in the third or second century BC. He dealt with the first difficulty by waiting until his narrative was well under way (3.23) and then introducing a genealogy which started with Jesus and ascended to 'Adam, son of God'. His David-to-Abraham section is identical, apart from having two names, Arni and Admin, instead of the one name Aram; but the line up to David is taken not through Solomon but through another of David's sons, Nathan, possibly in order to avoid the 'curse' of Jer. 22.30 on the seed of Jechoniah. In this section Luke has only one point of contact with the table here—the names Salathiel and Zorobabel, which marked the return from exile. Into the section from Salathiel to Jesus Luke put nine more names, thus bringing Jesus, on the basis of four generations to a century, down to 'the days of King Herod'. The threefold division he entirely dropped. Instead, with wholly different theological consequences, he carried the line back to the fall of man, thus creating one continuous 'age' from the fall to salvation.

Those who wish to believe that Luke's genealogy between Zorobabel and Joseph is other than fictitious must face the fact that he had different names, with nine more added to correct the chronology, amongst which 'Matthias' or variants of it occur five times—twice as 'son of Levi', the latter the grandfather of Jesus' putative father, Joseph.

A genealogy purporting to establish the identity of Jesus as 'son of David' did not need to include David's descent from Abraham. A document of which the original purpose was dif-
1.17 ferent has been used and the embarrassing fact disguised by
inserting the claim that the genealogy discloses a significant tripartite pattern, produced apparently by counting 'the Babylonian

captivity' twice over, once at the end of the second of the three sections and again at the beginning of the third.

1.18 A transition to the original commencement has been contrived by reintroducing the putative parents, already designated at 1.16, and using the word γένεσις in a different sense from 1.1. This led by way of correction to the variant reading γέννησις 'procreation'.

For the designation of place (Bethlehem) the reason is that given below at 2.5. The designation of time—'in Herod's reign'—is more remarkable than familiarity has rendered it. It is emphatically not a date. A date must specify a much shorter period, if not a particular year; and Luke, although he adopted the Herod phrase for his opening (1.5), was careful to introduce a date when he came to the birth of Jesus (2.2) and, even more so, to the appearance of John the Baptist (3.1). 'In the days of King Herod' reads like the introduction not to history but to a tale: the chronology is vague and the period remote from the narrator and his hearers. Herod was king for nearly forty years—from 40 BC to 4 BC—and a reference to his reign rings like a reference to 'the Victorian era'.

'Betrothed' (μνηστευθεῖσα) is used in the New Testament in this context only (= Luke 1.27, 2.5). Though in the sequel Mary is called 'wife' (γυνή) by the angel and by the narrator, betrothal was indispensable to set the scene for Joseph to become aware of Mary's condition without having caused it. The words 'by the holy spirit' officiously anticipate and ruin the angelic announcement to Joseph in his dream. They are manifest interpolation: while Mary could be 'found' to be pregnant, only supernatural revelation, which yet has to be related, could disclose the identity of the father to anyone except her.

1.19 On finding his bride pregnant, Joseph had decided (naturally) to reject her; but he was prevented by the dream before he had told anybody or taken any overt step: in the event, so far as the rest of the world was concerned, the child was his, and the supernatural nature of the birth was known only to the parents. If Joseph had communicated to anyone the fact that he had not had intercourse with Mary, events would have taken a different—and public—course. In fact, in the original form of the narrative of the star, which is to follow, the identity of the child remains unknown except to the parents: at every stage the supernatural communications are made by dream, so that, in the nature of things, only Joseph could know that they had occurred.

To emphasize the crucial point that when the dream happened the decision to divorce Mary was only in Joseph's own mind, the word λάθρα 'secretly' was employed, a word used again in this book only just below (2.7). Construed with 'divorce', it creates nonsense, because secret divorce is a contradiction in terms, and raises the problem: why had Joseph wished to behave so curiously? If Joseph was indeed δίκαιος—a description by which, as in Luke (1.6), he may have been introduced in the first place—that would make him 'righteous' and 'orthodox', but there was nothing in that which obliged a wronged husband to conceal the cause of offence. What it could not mean is that he was compassionately disposed to draw a veil over another's embarrassment. 'Wanted', ἐβουλήθη, is not natural with λάθρα—all volition is private—and may be a corruption of ἐβουλεύθη 'took a decision': Joseph consulted nobody; his decision was a matter of his (and the narrator's) private knowledge, but necessitated the supernatural intervention.

1.20 The patronymic υἱὸς Δαυειδ, which has the effect of lending divine sanction to the genealogy, is suspicious, not so much because the nominative form υἱός is used for the vocative υἱέ—both apparently occur (8.29, 9.27, 15.22, 20.30, 31)—as because of its superfluity, there being no need for the person addressed by an apparition, especially in a dream, to be named. The expression Ἰωσηφ υἱὸς Δαυειδ is moreover curious in itself. It seems always to have been assumed that υἱός thus in the singular could mean what Luke (1.27) called ἐξ οἴκου 'of the house of David'; but though בני (plural construct) often means 'descendants of', it is doubtful if the singular in Greek or in Hebrew ever meant anything but literally 'son of'.

The angel—called 'of the Lord',* because without that addition ἄγγελος could mean just any messenger—begins with the normal preface which apparitions use to prevent their auditors being too frightened to hear the message properly or to remember it (e.g. 28.5; Luke 1.13, 2.10). It is less appropriate in a dream. Here it has attracted the following word from the original imperative (παράλαβε 'take', 2.13, 20) into the infinitive (παραλαβεῖν 'to take'), thus producing the absurdity 'don't be

* Luke (1.26) knew his name: it was Gabriel. It is only in the phrase 'angel of the Lord' and in the citation formula 1.22 and 2.15 that 'the Lord' is ever used in this book to mean God. Apart from the resurrection angel at 28.2 all the occurrences of the phrase are in the nativity narrative 1.20–2.19.

afraid to take Mary'. Joseph was not *afraid* to take her, just unwilling to do so because of her pregnancy by someone else.

When below Joseph proceeds to 'do as the angel of the Lord instructed him', he does three things: (1) 'takes' Mary; (2) refrains from intercourse with her before delivery; and (3) names the child Jesus. The instructions given by the angel therefore included (2), a prohibition which makes the reason adduced ('for she is with child by God') the more pertinent: the human may not go where God has been. Adopted by Joseph of his own volition, there would be less point in noting the abstinence.

Mary had been made pregnant by a breath (πνεῦμα, רוח), but whose breath? Only one answer would make sense to Joseph or the first readers: God's. The breath by which Mary had conceived was holy, the breath of the Holy One, the Holy One of Israel קדוש ישראל. Luke (1.35), though his use of the term in the nominative ('the holy breath will come upon you') was unambiguous, nevertheless interpreted it with a poetical paraphrase which caught the essential meaning: 'the power of the Highest will come over you like a shadow.'

1.21 The name 'Jesus' is, as the reason given for it shows, not יהושע, the equivalent of Joshua, but ישוע (*yēshuʿa*), a common Levitical family name, interpreted as a play upon יושיע (*yōshiʿa*), 'he will save'. The sentence 'for he will save . . .' tacitly assumes that readers will know the Hebrew word (it is not Aramaic) for 'will save' and understand the explanation without assistance. It is the only place in the book where such knowledge is assumed. The piece of information is one which Joseph did not need and could not grasp: 'from their sins' implies an already accepted theology of propitiation.

Luke reflected that, if the angelic message in Joseph's dream were true, there would be a second person who must know the true identity of the father—namely, the mother. He therefore provided (1.26ff.) for Mary to be informed of it—logically—before the act of conception and not, like Joseph here, afterwards. Equally logically, her angelic intimation was received waking, unlike Joseph's here. The method of communication to Joseph he used (1.11ff.) for the father of John.

.22, 23 Between the supernatural command to Joseph and his execution of it stands a sentence which cites Isa. 7.14 as prophetic confirmation of the divine parentage and of the virgin conception, the latter taking 'maiden' to mean 'virgin', which the Greek παρθένος does but Isaiah's Hebrew עלמה does not necessarily. This is the first of ten such passages, introduced by identical or almost identical formulae, six of which occur before 4.14, the remainder being at 8.17, 12.17, 13.35, and 21.4. Seven are citations from Isaiah and one each from Jeremiah (2.17), Hosea (2.15), Zechariah (21.4), and Psalms (13.35). Most fit their context imperfectly, and some cause serious difficulty. This one is no exception: that it was added to an already existing context is shown by the fact that it contradicts the command to call the child Jesus and provides a translation from Hebrew which readers of the immediately preceding sentence had been assumed not to need, the name 'God with us' (i.e. incarnate) being evidently the crucial point of the citation.

1.24 'From sleep' is an officious interpolation: 'he arose' is the conventional response to a command, e.g. 2.13, 20.

2.1 The narrative must, as Luke (1.5) realized, have begun with the date, which cannot be thrown in as an afterthought. The original commencement of the book has been cannibalized.

2.2 The child declared by revelation to be 'son of God' is hailed as such at birth by the gentile world in the person of 'sorcerers from the east'. Herod's enquiry as to where 'the Messiah' would be born (2.4) proves that nothing less unambiguous was the object of the sorcerers' enquiry, which has been altered by substituting 'the King of the Jews' (who would hardly interest orientals, nor have his own star, nor claim worship from strangers). Logic is suspended for the sake of the allegory: we are not to ask how 'sorcerers from the east' came by knowledge of the Messiah.

The word for 'sorcerers', μάγοι, is an uncomplimentary one—cf. Acts 13.6, the only other occurrence in the New Testament—and seems chosen to imply heathen strangers in preference to a neutral word such as ἀστρολόγοι. Though the 'star of David' is of modern origin, a prophesied conqueror had indeed been likened to a star ('There shall come a star out of Jacob, and a sceptre shall arise out of Israel' Num. 24.17) and Balaam, whose prophecy this was, was 'brought out of the mountains of the east' (Num. 23.7). Curiously, the east where the sorcerers saw the star is ἀνατολή, singular, whereas the east whence they came is ἀνατολαί, plural: they may have seen the star 'at its rising (ἀνατολή)'.

2.3 The words 'and all Jerusalem with him' serve no purpose, and the alarm of 'all Jerusalem' is barely compatible with the following narrative. There is a perhaps intentional echo at Jesus' entry (21.10). This is the only place in the book where 'Ιεροσολυμα—

the alternative feminine singular Ἱερουσαλημ occurs only at 23.37—is demonstrably feminine singular, not neuter plural.

2.4 The expression 'all the high priests and scribes of the people' is the first appearance of numerous similar but not identical phrases. The word 'priests', ἱερεῖς, is found no more than twice in the book (8.4, 12.5), and in the other gospels only in the corresponding passages and one or two others—Luke 10.31 (the parable of the Good Samaritan), also 1.5 and John 1.19. Its place has been taken by 'high priests', ἀρχιερεῖς, which would have been an impossibility unless, at the time when the vocabulary was settled, the office of high priest was filled, by lot or otherwise, from a group of eligibles. 'Scribes', γραμματεῖς, is coupled with 'high priests' again at 16.21, 20.18, and 21.15, but nowhere else is 'of the people' attached to it, as it frequently is to 'the elders' (οἱ πρεσβύτεροι). The word 'all', if strictly construed, implies that the persons described here were a limited number forming a recognized body.

2.6 The citation (from Mic. 5.2, not expressly named) is superfluous: the sense is complete with 'it is written'. Elsewhere in Matthew the expression is 'spoken' (ῥηθέν), not 'written', διὰ προφήτου (-τῶν). The series of Old Testament prophecies discussed above (p. 58) is different in form. The words γῆ Ἰούδα, unintelligible in apposition to Bethlehem, could have originated from γῆ being appended as a note to Ἰούδα in the next line.

2.7 The officious interpolation of 'the star' turned the expression τὸ φαινόμενον into an ungrammatical φαινόμενος ἀστήρ; a similarly officious interpolation of 'the star' occurs below (2.10).

Two plots have been combined. In the first Herod ascertains the place of the birth from the high priests and the date of it from the sorcerers, so that he can put to death any child born at the specified place at the specified time. This plot is foiled by the escape to Egypt. With this plot a second has been combined in which Herod requests the sorcerers, with the help of the star, to pinpoint the child for him. The second plot, in which the child features as 'king that shall be', converted a simple and consistent narrative into a series of events which could not have escaped notoriety and whose central figure could not have been overlooked. It differs in vocabulary and style from the context in which it has been inserted. Note, in contrast with the almost jejune basic narrative, the excitably emotional language (the sorcerers 'overjoyed', Herod 'extremely angry') and touches of colour, such as the unnecessary but graphic 'opened their caskets'.

The supernatural warning to the sorcerers, though conveyed in a dream, is expressed by a special word,* and there is silence as to the nature of the warner, because the writer, though he needed a *deus ex machina*, shrank from sending 'the angel of the Lord' to the sorcerers. This second plot creates insoluble problems. If the sorcerers could see and follow the star, so could Herod's police, and Tom, Dick, and Harry; or was the star mysteriously invisible to everybody except the sorcerers? Can one be sure over which precise house a star has 'stopped', or did it acquire vertical as well as horizontal motion?

It is the second plot which is the secondary one: it separates 'after Herod died' (2.19) from 'until Herod's death' (2.15). The quotation from Jeremiah at 2.18 is far-fetched, and that from Hosea at 2.15 would fit better with the order to return from Egypt than with that to go there.

Behind so destructive an alternative narrative there must have lain a powerful motive, which it is not difficult to identify. It was to transform a Messianic birth into a royal (Davidic) birth avoiding the 'gentiles' of Isa. 60.3 and concentrating on 'kings shall come to the brightness of thy rising'. If the birth was royal, it must be acknowledged by homage and the royal gifts from the same prophetic context: 'they shall bring gold and incense'. Though later elaboration along the same train of thought was to turn the sorcerers into kings and make their number three to correspond with the gifts, the incense and the myrrh may, in the light of Isaiah, have originally been alternatives (on myrrh for anointing see below, p. 98). Publicity, not secrecy, had to be the keynote of this secondary narrative, whence both the contradictions and the improbabilities.

Luke had no patience with the resultant muddle but substituted a completely new angelic identification of the newborn saviour to persons sufficiently obscure to render the avoidance of publicity credible: only Mary (Luke 2.19) noted the portents 'in her heart'.

2.19 The narration need not, and presumably at one stage did not, continue beyond 'go to the land of Israel'. It turns out, however, that the 'angel of the Lord' was less alive than Joseph to apprehend the danger if he simply returned to Bethlehem. Joseph's apprehension results in another supernatural warning, described by the same abnormal term χρηματίζειν as the warning

* χρηματισθείς, 'warned', is a debased usage, not found elsewhere before the 2nd cent. AD. Luke, influenced by this passage, used it in his birth narrative (2.26).

to the sorcerers at 2.12. It motivates Joseph to take his family to Galilee—quite illogically, since Galilee too was ruled by one of Herod's sons.

There are signs in the diction of 2.19–21 of conscious embarrassment with two conflicting supernatural instructions: Herod is paraphrased as 'they that sought the life of the child, and the expression 'land of Israel', which occurs nowhere else in Matthew, avoids 'Bethlehem' and is wide enough to embrace Galilee. The implication is that a complete nativity account has been prefixed to a narrative of which Galilee was the starting-point. Luke (1.26) solved the same problem conversely, placing the begetting by the holy spirit in Galilee (Nazareth) and devising a non-existent census to account for the actual birth taking place at Bethlehem.

2.23 The concluding sentence is dispensable: fear of Archelaus could motivate withdrawal to Galilee (another tetrarchy) but not settlement at 'Nazareth', for which an untraceable prophecy is cited. N. is not material to the narrative—Jesus merely quits it (4.13)—and only recurs, problematically, at 21.11 (q.v.).

3.1 'In those days' can mean nothing other than the time when Joseph left Egypt and settled in Galilee, which is incompatible with the appearance of Jesus as an adult at Jordan. The problem was acknowledged by Mark (1.9), who transferred the phrase to the arrival of Jesus at Jordan. The void was also felt by Luke, who filled it with a 'childhood of Jesus' (2.21–52) and proceeded then to provide an elaborate new dating for the arrival of John (3.1) and to attribute to Jesus at his encounter with John the specific age of thirty (3.23). But it is inconceivable that 'in those days' could be intended to span the gap of a quarter of a century.

The block of text thus introduced is not one which could have been excerpted from a book about John the Baptist. Despite treating John the Baptist as sufficiently known to the reader—like 'Herod the king'—to be mentioned without further ado, it begins with a compendious description, specially composed. The word for 'arrive' (παραγίνεσθαι) is used above (2.1) of the sorcerers and below (3.13) of Jesus, but nowhere else in the book.

'Preaching' is a translation which masks the peculiarity of the word κηρύσσων, which ought to mean 'announcing' something and is used as here without an object only at 4.17 (repeating this passage) and in the close parallel at 10.7. The sense is probably 'with the announcement "Repent etc."', the word 'saying' being merely a Hebraism (לאמר) to denote direct speech.

The antithesis in the Hebrew of Isa. 40.3 ('*in the desert* prepare the way . . . and smoothen *in the wilderness* the highway') shows that 'in the desert' originally belonged with 'prepare' and not with 'crying'. The form quoted here agrees with LXX in suggesting (though not absolutely requiring) that 'in the desert' be read with 'crying'; and that is no doubt how the writer here construed it. Indeed it may have given rise to the location of John's appearance 'in the desert'.

'The desert of Judaea' could no doubt mean the desert country west of the Jordan; but there is no point in preaching in uninhabited country. Anyhow, it presently appears that John was *at* the Jordan and baptized people there, presumably at one of the crossing-places east or north-east of Jerusalem. Luke (3.2) deftly removed the difficulty: it was the word of the Lord that came to John in the desert, and he then went 'into all the places round the Jordan' to preach.

3.2 'Repentance' (μετάνοια) is absent from the rest of the book—as markedly (with the significant exception of 28.19) as baptism—and the corresponding verb μετανοεῖν recurs only at 11.20, 21 and 12.41.

John's brief announcement takes for granted that 'the kingdom of heaven' will 'come', and states only that its coming is imminent.

The expression 'kingdom of heaven' (literally, 'of the heavens', βασιλεία τῶν οὐρανῶν)—the plural is a Hebraism, the Hebrew word for heaven having a plural form (שמים)—occurs 34 times in the book. Whether 'kingdom' is understood as active (kingship) or passive (realm), 'heaven' is meant as a periphrasis for God. 'Kingdom of God', which occurs in this book only four times (12.28; 19.24; 21.31, 43), though implied by other expressions elsewhere (e.g. 'thy kingdom', 6.10), was the term invariably used by Luke and Mark.

3.4 'And he', αὐτὸς δέ, recalls the use of αὐτός in 1.21 and below at 3.11; the gloss 'John' is superfluous.

The items of clothing are a deliberate allusion to the description of Elijah (cf. 11.14; 17.12, 13) at 2 Kgs. 1.8 as a man בעל שער and 'girt round the waist with a leathern belt', where the expression בעל שער 'hirsute', though translated δασύς 'shaggy' in LXX, appears to have meant 'wearing as garment a hairy skin'.

The dietary items convey no such specific allusion. Wild honey was kosher but 'locusts' (ἀκρίδες) scarcely would be. In Exod. 16.31 manna was described as tasting like ἐγκρίδες ἐν μέλιτι, 'wheatcakes in honey'. So there may have been intended an allusion to the Israelites being fed on manna in the wilderness. Luke (3.6) omitted the description.

3.5 'Jerusalem' is personified (cf. 2.3), as are the other localities, though 'went out' is strictly appropriate only to the inhabitants of a walled city. The expression 'all the country round the Jordan', πᾶσα ἡ περίχωρος τοῦ Ἰορδάνου, occurred at Gen. 13.10, 11. Otherwise, since Judaea came down to the river on the west side, 'the other bank' might have been expected, producing the sense that people converged on John at the Jordan from both sides. As when Naaman was physically cleansed of leprosy by the water of the Jordan at Elisha's command (2 Kgs. 5.10), the people are here symbolically cleansed by John of whatever were the 'sins' which would endanger them at the coming of the kingdom.

3.6 The innocent simplicity of 'confessing their sins' conceals a problem. Specification of the 'sins' is imperatively required. Of what kind were they? Did John exact a confession from each individual before baptizing him? Or was there a 'general confession', implicit or explicit? The difficulty was felt by Luke, who posed the question (3.10 'the multitude asked him, "What are we to do then?"') and provided some pretty hackneyed answers (3.11–14), which, if they had always been there, would not have been dropped.

The lacuna was also faced and filled in different style by the writer of Jos. *Ant.* 18.117, by describing John as: 'a good man, who called the Jews to come to baptism practising virtue and behaving righteously towards one another and piously towards God, since only so would the baptism appear acceptable to him if they used it not for the remission of particular offences but for the purity of the body when the soul had already been purified by righteousness'.

3.7 John preaches μετάνοια, 'repentance' (3.2); but the meaning of that term is nowhere defined or even implied. On the contrary, when John sees 'many of the Pharisees and Sadducees', he accuses them, not of failure to 'repent', but specifically of not producing 'fruit' and of an exclusivity based upon their vaunted descent from Abraham. Their 'unfruitful tree' is about to be consumed by fire. John's more potent successor, to whom he points forward, will shortly separate the wheat from the chaff. His baptism (ironic) will be 'with the holy spirit and fire'.

There is a verbal echo (complete with rhetorical question) of

23.33 ('progeny of vipers, how shall you escape the judgement of *Gehenna*?'). John is denouncing that same second generation* who were to perish in the sack of Jerusalem. He anticipates the activity of Jesus, who 'raised up children of God' and predicted the destruction of the Temple as punishment for the failure of the Pharisees and Sadducees to 'bear fruit'.

John is announcing in summary the whole doctrine of Jesus—his divine parentage by the holy spirit (1.20), his demand for the extension of salvation to the gentiles—the 'fruitfulness' expected from Israel—and his prediction of imminent destruction of the Temple by fire as punishment for failure to obey. The attribution of Jesus' doctrines to John the Baptist is a breathtakingly bold bid for the allegiance of John's followers. It implies prior knowledge of the Jerusalem narrative (including the Woes of ch. 23) and incidentally of οἱ λίθοι οὗτοι (4.3). The 'repentance' which John preached is turned into acceptance of the demands which will be made by Jesus. This is why καρπὸς καλός (3.10) can be described as καρπὸς ἄξιος τῆς μετανοίας (3.8). The anachronism is as blatant as it was deliberate.

John's discourse, introduced by the conventional formula 'when he saw . . .' (cf. 5.1, 9.36), is addressed not equally to all who came to be baptized but only to 'many Pharisees and Sadducees'.† Luke (3.7) scotched the problem by omitting the 'Pharisees and Sadducees' altogether.

The vituperative preface 'progeny of vipers', γεννήματα ἐχιδνῶν, occurs again, also prefacing rhetorical questions, at 12.34 (in the context, as here, of trees being cut down) and at 23.33 (addressed to the 'scribes and Pharisees'). The latter passage is similar for two reasons: (1) it is followed by the question 'How are you to escape the judgement?' (κρίσις, for which ὀργή 'wrath' is substituted here, a word used nowhere else in Matthew); and (2) γεννήματα ἐχιδνῶν, unless treated as a mere periphrasis of ἔχιδναι, appears to be deliberately chosen at 23.33 in order to attribute to the 'offspring' the iniquity of 'your fathers', a context quite lacking here.

The question 'Who told *you* how to escape the wrath to come?' is reduced by the past tense ὑπέδειξεν, 'told', to a fatuously

* The allusion to 23.33 shows that 'progeny of vipers' is not mere abuse but literal reference to a second generation (cf. 23.30).

† Only in one other passage (16.1–12) are the 'Pharisees' coupled as here with the 'Sadducees', who themselves make only a single other appearance (22.23).

facetious sneer. Asked in the future, ὑποδείξει, 'will tell', the implication becomes 'You must wait for someone mightier than me, namely, the son of God.'

3.11 'Is stronger than I' is a faint attempt to paraphrase the uncomprehended description 'whose shoes I am not strong enough (or worthy) to carry', for which Luke (3.16) did his conjectural best by substituting 'untying the shoelaces' as a mark of humility, which Mark (1.7) then characteristically underlined with 'bending down'. On a slate palette of the fourth millennium from Hierakonpolis in Egypt, King Narmer is shown, barefoot and followed by a tiny sandal-bearer, in the act of clubbing a defeated enemy. If this was a normal presentation, the text could mean: I am not even sandal-bearer to the Great Conqueror.

Unfruitful like a tree that does not bear good fruit or like chaff among the grain, the P. and S. are doomed to be destroyed by fire, an operation described ironically as 'baptism' not with water but 'with the holy spirit and fire'. The 'holy spirit' refers to Jesus' parentage (1.20), the 'fire' to the fall of Jerusalem, an allusion confirmed by the metaphor of the threshing-floor connected (2 Sam. 6.6) with the Temple. John is represented as anticipating Jesus' predictions of that event.

13–16 The purpose of Jesus' baptism by John is to express the acceptance of John (and of his followers) by the gentile church. As, however, John had so strikingly asserted Jesus to be his superior, it was necessary for him to demur and be overruled. That in turn involved John's ability to recognize Jesus, an unexplained feature which prompted Luke (see especially 1.44) to compose a companion nativity for John. (John 1.33ff. resorted to even more extensive elaboration.) The reasons, moreover, which Jesus gave for insisting upon being baptized had to be sufficiently vague and general to repress further enquiry: 'for so it behoves us' (οὕτως γὰρ πρέπον—here only in the New Testament—ἐστὶν ἡμῖν) discourages anything further by way of explanation. The officious efforts of an interpolator only cause problems: there was nothing in 'righteousness', δικαιοσύνη, fulfilment of the Law, which demanded baptism; and what is 'all righteousness', πᾶσα δικαιοσύνη? The dialogue between Jesus and John was composed with wording roughly plundered from the following passage about Jesus and the Devil (cf. 3.9 above).

3.13 If Jesus was going to come 'from Galilee' to be baptized at Jordan, it is strange that the fact of John's public being drawn from Judaea is gratuitously emphasized (3.5). Luke removed the difficulty: with him (3.21) it is simply 'all the people' who are baptized (though the verb '*came out* to be baptized' (3.7) betrays consciousness of 3.4 above) and 'Jesus too' was amongst them.

3.15 'Leave (me) now' is the meaning, and the only possible meaning, of ἄφες ἄρτι. It cannot mean 'let me (be baptized by you) for now' or the like, nor can 'he left him' (ἀφίησιν αὐτόν) mean 'he (reluctantly) consented (to baptize him)'. The word for 'leave' and the exact phrase 'then he left him' (τότε ἀφίησιν αὐτόν) occur in their correct and normal meanings below at 4.10: 'Then Jesus said to him, "*Be gone*, Satan; for it is written . . .". *Then* the Devil *left him, and behold* . . .'

3.16, 17 The counterpart to Jesus accepting baptism by John is to make the latter witness supernatural confirmation of Jesus' divine sonship. The subject of 'saw' (εἶδεν)* is therefore John, however awkward grammatically; and the problems raised by the presence of other spectators are ignored. The confirmation comprises two elements: the verbal declaration is accompanied or preceded by the visible descent of the holy spirit out of an open heaven 'like a dove'. Taken together, the two manifestations amount to the assertion that Jesus was 'begotten by the holy spirit' (1.20). Isa. 42.1 (quoted in full at 12.18ff.), which is here being fulfilled literally, couples with the declaration 'my beloved son, in whom I have taken pleasure' the promise 'I will put my spirit upon him'.

4.1 The theophany is followed immediately by three 'temptations'. The transition to them has been ruined by the impertinent interpolator of 'by the spirit', who failed to perceive that ἀνήχθη is to be construed with ὑπὸ τοῦ διαβόλου. The spirit, after informing Jesus directly of his divine sonship, can hardly proceed: 'And now we will subject you to some tests' and deliberately organize the Satanic temptations.

The absurd 'and was afterwards hungry' was generated by ἐνήστευσε above, replaced by νηστεύσας.

It was hardly unreasonable to invite Jesus, who could supernaturally multiply sacramental bread, to 'command these stones to become loaves' (for 'these stones', cf. 3.9). He chooses, however, not to do so, citing Deut. 8.3, where the word 'alone' (μόνῳ) is utterly destructive: man is saved ('will live', ζήσεται) not solely by the sacrament but by obeying every single divine command (πᾶν ῥῆμα), i.e. by entire fulfilment of the Law.

* Luke (3.22) appears to have read or amended εἴδει ('in shape').

The scene shifts to Jesus' self-immolation, significantly located at the Temple, and the problem is posed, as at the crucifixion mockery (27.41–3), why there was no angelic rescue (cf. 26.53). Jesus offers tamely only the general objection (Deut. 6.16) against 'tempting God'.

The third test, framed upon the second but unconnected with the alleged divine sonship, challenges the universal mission to convert the whole world. The third test, designed perhaps to supplant the others, was combined with them by πάλιν.

Only the first temptation takes place 'in the desert' and is original: the remaining two are artificial and unsatisfactory, the responses being, unlike 4.5, vague and less than logical. In the first temptation, on the other hand, Jesus is represented as repudiating the sacrament in favour of complete obedience to the Law. To this temptation the petition included in the sacramental prayer (6.13), which asks not to be 'led into temptation but rescued from the Devil', evidently relates.

With the possible exception of Gethsemane (26.36ff.), the 'temptations' are unique in that there could be no possible witnesses to the dialogue. The insertion of the first (and original) temptation, designedly destructive of acceptance of Jesus as 'son of God' and presumably intended to counteract the theophany, has caused serious disruption.

4.12 John's arrest must have been mentioned as taking place after Jesus arrived from Galilee (3.13)—to which ἀνεχώρησεν here refers back—and, by implication because of ἀκούσας ('heard'), during his absence. The event itself, knowledge of which is presupposed by the reference at 11.2 to John being 'in *the* prison', has been deleted—possibly because of inconsistency with 14.3, 4—without the text being adjusted. The word παρεδόθη need mean no more than 'taken into custody', but is curious in view of its later use for Jesus' 'betrayal'.

Mark (1.14) was not bothered, but wrote up a conflation of this sentence with 4.17. Luke (3.19, 20), on the other hand, took an explanation to be indispensable, and supplied, as best he could, what was obviously wanting. In order to relieve another difficulty, namely, so that Jesus does not expressly come back from the desert to learn of John's fate and turn tail for Galilee, Luke (4.1) made him set off home from Jordan before the temptations in the desert, which thus became, as it were, incidents *en route*. Luke then, using material from 14.4, inserted *before* Jesus' baptism, as a round-off to the potted biography of John (3.1–17), the passage: 'But Herod the tetrarch, whom John had shown up in the affair of Herodias, his brother's wife, and all the wicked things he did, crowned them all by shutting John up in prison' (3.19).

Luke had no other source: he knew, because of 11.2, that he must get John into prison, and he obtained Herodias from 14.3, 4. But his vague and overstrained expression, treating John's arrest as the climax of Herod's (unspecified) iniquities, betrayed his consciousness of really having nothing to work on. He is producing a stopgap; but he acknowledged there *was* a gap to be stopped, the gap which confronted him and which confronts us.

4.13 That Jesus 'left Nazareth' had to be stated here, because the place was introduced in 2.23. The introduction of Nazareth is the more notable because it does not appear subsequently until Jesus is hailed in Jerusalem (21.11) as 'the prophet from Nazareth' (see there).

The mystery is deepened by the fact that Nazareth is not found at all outside Christian sources until the fourth century, raising the possibility that some town was then renamed Nazareth by Christian pilgrims (Helena?). But if Nazareth was not a real 'city', why invent it, and is there any connection with Gennesar(et)(eth) in 14.34? It is treated as not known to the reader, but introduced, as are only Gethsemane (26.36) and Golgotha (27.33), as a city 'called' Nazareth.

The answer may lie in the citation at 2.23. Nazareth does not occur in the Old Testament, where the quoted saying of 'the prophets' (plural!) is not to be found. Significantly, this particular citation is not formulated in the same way as the other annotations discussed already (p. 58). The nearest Old Testament passage would be Judg. 13.5: 'Thou shalt conceive and bear a child; and no razor shall come on his head; for the child *shall be a devotee* to God from the womb, and he shall begin to deliver Israel out of the hand of the Philistines'; but there the word meaning 'devotee' is nāzīr (נזיר), not Ναζωραῖος as here. If there had to be somewhere specific for Jesus to go and live, 'Capharnaum' was available in the subsequent narrative (8.5, 17.24).

Jesus has to return to Galilee because it is from Galilee that his
own mission will commence; but the indispensability of the
Galilean starting-point, which the end of the nativity account
4.14–16 prepared (see p. 61), calls for explanation. The explanation is
immediately forthcoming: Galilee is 'of the gentiles' and lies

'along the sea', which will allegorically represent the gentile mission field across the Mediterranean. Jesus' salvation was, and was from the beginning intended to be, for the gentiles. If the Isaiah quote is interpolated (see pp. 57–8 on 1.22), the allusion to Zabulon and Nephthalim in 4.13 must have been considered sufficient to trigger the crucial words 'gentiles' and 'sea' in a reader's mind.

Never mentioned in the sequel, Z. and N. were two of the 'lost tribes' whose former territory comprised Galilee: they had no existence on the map of post-exilic Israel. For Capharnaum see below on 8.5. Quitting one named place (Nazareth) involved going to live in another. The name Καφαρναουμ did not need to be qualified by τὴν παραθαλασσίαν, as though there were two C.s of which one was, and the other was not, 'on-Sea'. It was 'beside the seaside' that Jesus went to live.

4.17 The sentence 4.17—see on 16.21—interrupts the intended sequence between 4.13 'dwelt beside the sea' and 4.18 'walked beside the sea'. In turn, the calling of Peter, 4.20, was designed to be followed directly by 8.14 'came into Peter's house'. The long discourse inserted between required the previous acquisition of celebrity and of a large audience, which are provided by the verbose fustian of 4.23–5.2. For this preliminary the way had been paved by the insertion of 4.17, attributing to Jesus a preachment of which the content was handily available at 3.1, 2.

The identical framework into which to insert a discourse was reused, word for word, at 9.35, which raises the presumption that the two discourses were inserted by the same hand.

.18–22 However the name Πέτρος may have originated—16.18 (q.v.) is *not* a name-giving—it is the invariable style of this disciple, 'Simon' not being used again for him except (of necessity) in the allocution 'Simon bar Jona' at 16.17, where a different name was indispensable.

The two callings, despite details, such as the different words for 'net', designed to differentiate them, are duplicates. The second, lacking the vigorous point of the first ('fishers of men' . . . 'left the nets' as against 'called them' . . . 'left the boat'), is recognizable as derivative, composed to accord equal status with Peter to the 'sons of Zebedee', James and John, who are to be associated with him in the sequel at important moments (17.1, 26.37) and to claim a pre-eminent role (20.20ff.) in the kingdom. It is, however, to Peter that is assigned the missionary function of 'catching mankind'* and a 'brother', who does not reappear but whose name is of Greek origin (connected with ἀνδρεῖος 'brave')—a point noted by John 12.22, who used him to usher 'Greeks' into Jesus' presence.

The absence of any explanation why the summons of Jesus was unquestioningly obeyed was found unacceptable by Luke, who provided—not here only (see on 26.51)—a miracle, the 'miraculous draught' (Luke 5.1–11), which, if it had been original, would surely not have been deleted. It was an audacious and imaginative essay.

4.23 After recruiting Peter and Andrew, Jesus went to Peter's house (cf. 9.10 after the recruitment of Matthew), where he met and healed the mother-in-law—8.14 is designed to follow 4.20 immediately—but there intervenes a huge interruption (4.23–8.13) consisting principally of a long discourse, the so-called Sermon on the Mount (5.3–7.27), which it must have been desired to present at as early a stage as practicable.

The discourse is framed by an introduction (4.23–5.2), the first part of which is reused later (9.35) to introduce another discourse. The message of Jesus 'in the whole of Galilee' was delivered, like Paul's (e.g. Rom. 1.16), in the first place to the Jews ('in their synagogues'). Its content is described, with conscious repetition of the foregoing (4.17) claim that Jesus continued John's preachment, as 'the gospel of the kingdom'. The word 'gospel', εὐαγγέλιον, is not used in this book except with κηρύσσειν, 'preach'. Its original meaning, whether in the singular or the plural, was the reward given to a bearer of good news; the singular in the sense of the good news itself is apparently not found before the first century AD.

The requirement for the introduction was to provide an explanation of the size of audience and acclaim appropriate to so long and important a delivery. What resulted is a verbose exercise in rhetorical bombast, characterized by lavish use of pleonasm, two expressions with the same meaning where one would have sufficed—'disease and sickness' (νόσον καὶ μαλακίαν), 'suffering and complaining' (κακῶς ἔχοντας, νόσοις συνεχομένους†)—and enriched with grandiose terms like 'among the people' (ἐν

* 'Men', ἀνθρώπων, is not just an antithesis to 'fish', but intentionally wide enough to embrace 'mankind'.

† Luke was uneasy with the word, unique in Matthew and not in Mark, and substituted ἐνοχλούμενοι (6.18) for it here; but it haunted him, and he used it himself of Peter's mother-in-law (4.38 πυρετῷ) and the Gadarenes (8.37 φόβῳ).

τῷ λαῷ) or 'variegated' (ποικίλαις) diseases. There is no need, therefore, to seek specific reasons why 'Syria', the Roman province, or 'Decapolis' make their sole appearance here or to enquire why δαιμονιζόμενοι ('possessed by devils') is duplicated by the rare σεληνιαζόμενοι ('moon-struck') or why Jesus 'opened his mouth' (ἀνοίξας τὸ στόμα) before speaking.

5.1 'The mountain' is quite undefined (cf. 14.23, 15.29, 28.16). This is not geography: a mountain is the place for authoritative promulgation. Instead of addressing 'the crowds', Jesus 'teaches his disciples': the content of the discourse was felt to be unsuitable for a general audience. For 'opened his mouth' Luke (6.20) substituted 'lifted up his eyes upon his disciples' but omitted the mountain altogether and even, defiantly, substituted a spot on the level, τόπος πεδινός (6.17). The 'disciples', of whom only two or at the most four have yet been noted, are an anachronism.

5.3 Since it was taken into a pre-existing context, the discourse must already have existed as a separate document, a conclusion supported by the occurrence of exceptionally deep corruptions in it. To whom was that document addressed, and in what context was it created? It is demonstrable that the citation of the Christian sacramental prayer at 6.7–15 was inserted into a complex advising observance of Jewish almsgiving, prayer, and fasting but in private as contrasted with the behaviour of 'the playactors', οἱ ὑποκριταί. If, as that implies, those addressed were Jewish converts, it would account for their 'persecution' and would explain the link with 10.21 (in the other discourse introduced at the same time), which refers to family disruptions that can only be Jewish. The 'crowds' and the 'disciples' (5.1) would have been surprised to learn that they had been 'persecuted'! The original source of the material could have been in epistolary form and the addressees members of the Jewish wing of the church who have accepted that admission to 'the kingdom' is obtained by belief in Jesus and not by their own merit but who nevertheless continue to live as observant Jews. That the introduction of the discourses was due to an outbreak of persecution may be deduced from the fact that the references to persecution in 5.10–12 have been attached artificially to the pattern of 5.3–9.

The discourse is addressed in the second person plural except for passages which elaborate preceding admonitions (5.23–6, 29–30, 36, 39b–42; 6.2a, 3–4, 6, 17–18, 22–3, 7.3–5). It is couched throughout not in plain language but in cryptic terms as if intended to be understood only by those privy to a code. The audience is assumed to differentiate itself not only from 'the tax-gatherers' but from 'the gentiles' (5.46, 47; 6.32). They are warned against 'judging' their 'brother' (7.1–3) and to beware of 'false prophets' who produce 'bad fruit' and will therefore be cut down and thrown on the fire (cf. 3.10).

God is frequently referred to as 'your/our Father in heaven' (5.16, 48; 6.1, 9; 7.11), or 'your heavenly Father' (6.14, 26, 32), or simply 'your Father' (6.8, 15); but in the passages which use the second person singular God is referred to only as 'your Father' simply (6.4, 6, 18). In addition there is 'sons of God' in a 'beatitude' (5.8) and in 5.45 'in order that you may become sons of your heavenly Father'. The speaker once only (7.21) refers to '*my* Father in heaven'. Thus, with the exception of the opening (5.1–10) and the end (7.21–7), those addressed are treated as belonging already to a special company—'the sons of God'.

The discourse is absent in Luke here and in Mark altogether. In its place is a passage, closely identical in Luke 4.31–40 and Mark 1.21–34, comprising (1) a summary statement of teaching and healing, (2) a sentence, in the exact words of Matthew at 7.28, about the effect of Jesus' teaching on hearers, (3) the exorcism of an unclean spirit, and (4) the healing of Simon's mother-in-law (= Matt. 8.14ff.). Whoever composed that passage must have excised the discourse and closed up the gap. The alternative would be to suppose that whoever inserted the discourse picked the exact spot to do so immediately before a description of the effect on hearers.

It was Luke, not Mark, who performed the excision. For Luke the excision was integral to a major rearrangement which deferred substantial consecutive parts of it to form an address by Jesus to his disciples after he had chosen the twelve (6.20ff.) For Mark the omission of the discourse matched the general style of his book, eschewing as it did long spoken passages. It follows that the closest form of the discourse to the original which is available to us is that in Matthew.

The accompanying table shows to what extent and where and how the discourse was absorbed elsewhere in the text of Luke and Mark.

The analysis throws up a picture which is quite irreconcilable with any hypothesis that the discourse was culled from scattered places in Luke and Mark. For example, such a hypothesis would require the compilation to have been accompanied by the addition from elsewhere of problematical passages, long (e.g. 5.20–4,

27, 28) or short (e.g. 5.14), for the rejection of which by Luke plausible reasons can be assigned.

Matthew	Luke*	Mark
5.2–12	*6.20–6*	
13	14.34, 35	9.50
14		
15	8.16; 11.33	4.21
16		
17–19	16.17	
20–4		
25, 26	12.58, 59	
27, 28		
29, 30		9.43–7
31, 32	16.18	
33–8		
39–48	*6.27–36*	
6.1–6		
7–13	11.2–4	
14, 15		11.25
16–18		
19–21	12.33–4	
22, 23	11.34–6	
24	16.13	
25–33	12.22–31	
7.1, 2	*6.37*	4.24
3–5	*6.41, 42*	
6		
7–11	11.9–13	
12	*6.31*	
13, 14	13.24	
15		
16	*6.44*	
17–20	*6.43*	
21	*6.46*	
22, 23	[13.25–8]†	
24–7	*6.47–9*	

* Items in the same order as in Matthew are italicized.
† Linked with Matt. 25.11, 12.

The question then remains as to the mechanical processes which the authors of Luke and Mark operated.

Luke reduced the length of the discourse by major cuts before inserting the remainder in virtually unaltered order at a later point (6.20–49) as a distinct sermon in its own right. The pieces of text with which he was then left he either rejected altogether or brought in at other points. The passages rejected altogether might well present theological difficulty or have been found incomprehensible:

5.19, 20 exceeding the righteousness of the scribes etc.
5.21–4, 27–30, 33–7, 43–5 the confrontation of the Law with its extreme implications
6.1–6, 16–18 privacy of alms, prayer, and fasting
7.6 'pearls before swine'
7.15 'wolves in sheep's clothing'

Mark, who eschewed the discourse altogether, nevertheless used five graphic passages from it. Three are passages which Luke had used and where Mark is demonstrably derivative; but the remaining two involve direct use of Matthew. Curiously, all but one are connected with treatment of the puzzle presented by Matt. 5.13–16 (q.v.).

There remains one item not used by Luke for which Mark found a place. While omitting the 'Lord's Prayer' itself (Matt. 6.7–13), Mark introduced (at 11.25) the commentary about forgiving and being forgiven, attaching it to 'ask and it shall be given' (Matt. 7.7–11), which Luke reproduced in full (at 11.9–13). In doing so, however, Mark used the wording 'if you have anything against anyone', which points to Matt. 5.23, 24, a passage neither he nor Luke had used. Nor is the allusion involuntary or mechanical, for Mark has inverted the offence from ὅτι ἔχει τι κατὰ σοῦ into εἴ τι ἔχετε κατά τινος, so that there may be something to forgive.

The conclusion to which the above five items in Mark point is that, reading on from where Luke first broke off after the 'beatitudes', Mark studied with close attention the section about the salt and the lamp, noted how Luke had sought to cope with its difficulties, and made his own attempt to do better. Though not attracted by the extrapolation of the Law, he studied that section also and rescued two gnomic passages (agreeing with one's adversary and cutting off one's hand). Why he dropped the 'Lord's Prayer' itself but kept the injunction to forgiveness may perhaps never be conjectured.

In short, Mark took note of Luke but remained independent of him in handling Matthew.

Luke on the other hand found room for the items in the 'Sermon' which he had not rejected in four clusters, between cc. 11 and 16, as follows.

First, the 'Lord's Prayer', provided with a strained introduction at 11.1–4, was followed by the parable of the importunate friend, peculiar to Luke (11.5–8), and this again by 'ask and you shall receive' (11.8–13 = Matt. 7.7–11). An exorcism and the Beelzebul dialogue plus the 'sign from heaven' (= Matt. 12.22–30, 38–45) are then followed by the lamp (see above) and the 'eye the light of the body' (= Matt. 6.22, 23).

Thereafter, at an interval and after the embodiment of the bulk of Matt. 10.26–33 and the parable, peculiar to Luke, of the rich man's boast (12.13–20), are inserted 'the lilies of the field' (Matt. 6.25–33), 'treasure in heaven' (Matt. 6.19–21), and, eventually, 'agreeing with one's adversary' (Matt. 5.25, 26).

Thirdly, after the strained preface (13.22, 23) 'will there be few who are saved?', the 'narrow gate' (Matt. 7.13, 14) is prefaced to the warning of many rejected (Matt. 7.22, 23, continuing with 8.11, 12). Finally, at 16.13, 17, 18, between two parables peculiar to Luke, 'God and Mammon' (Matt. 6.24), 'jot and tittle' (Matt. 5.18), and, in isolation from its context at Matt. 5.32, the prohibition of divorce are inserted.

The pattern of these insertions reflects a recognizable policy. The guiding consideration was subject-matter and relevance to a general topic. Where necessary a leading question was devised to create relevance.

5.3 All nine congratulations—μακάριος is the term used in congratulating Peter at 16.17—except the last (5.11, 12), which is anomalous in other respects also, are in the third person plural. It may be pure freak that the first four categories begin in Greek with the letter Π. The items rely heavily upon code, which has attracted annotations ('in spirit', 'for righteousness') designed to ensure that they are understood metaphorically. 'Poor' is protected against literalism by τῷ πνεύματι, which has to be strained to mean 'spiritually', as τῇ καρδίᾳ below means 'at heart'. But while the difference between purity of body and of heart is intelligible, 'poor in spirit' is not. The addition of
5.6 διψῶντες, which can take the accusative, to πεινῶντες, which cannot, is vacuous: if 'hungering for righteousness' meant anything, it would be the same as 'thirsting for righteousness' and its recompense would be to be fed (or watered) with 'righteousness'.

Three classes of person are deprived—poor, bereaved, and

hungry—whose deprivation will be remedied. That the 'poor', those who claim no merit of their own, will possess the kingdom is notorious (19.21); the hungry are fed by the sacramental bread; and the 'mourners' are comforted by it for the loss of the bride-
5.5 groom (cf. 9.15). In contrast, four classes are characterized by qualities, and their recompense is different. Decoded, they are qualities lacking in the opponents of the Judaizing church. 'Gentle', πραΰς, is applied by Jesus to himself (11.29), in the context of not imposing intolerable obligations, and in an Isaiah *testimonium* (21.5); the reward of the 'gentle', in a reference to Ps. 37.11, will be universality, the 'earth' will be their κλῆρος. The 'merciful'—those who have acknowledged God's 'mercy', ἔλεος, in accepting the gentiles—will themselves be the beneficiaries of his mercy. There are signs of artificiality in the remaining rewards. The 'pure', who accept that Jesus can 'make clean' (see on 8.2), will 'see God', a reward which seems not to be promised else-where (but cf. on 23.39); and those who 'make peace'—between whom? rival factions?—receive no more than inclusion in the general appellation of 'sons of God', applied to the other hearers of the discourse.

Luke (6.20) not only telescoped into one the two concluding items but cut the classes of person congratulated from seven to three, namely, 'poor', 'hungry', and 'mourners'. He also composed four antithetical Woes, made up with wording culled from elsewhere ('they have their reward' from 6.2; 'false prophets' from 7.15).

5.10, 11 The two last μακάριοι duplicate each other: blessed are the persecuted. The first ends by lamely repeating 5.3, 'theirs is the kingdom of heaven'. The second—which switches to the second person plural of direct address—is savagely polemical, replacing 'because of righteousness' by 'because of me' and accusing the persecutors of 'speaking all evil' (πονηρόν, code for denying Jesus' divinity, cf. p. 102). The kingdom of heaven is not gained just by having been persecuted (perf. tense, δεδιωγμένος) but by suffering for proclaiming Jesus as saviour.

Μισθός 'wages', thus metaphorically, recurs outside the discourse itself (5.46, 6.1) only in 10.41, 42 (μισθὸς εἰς ὄνομα δικαίου/προφήτου).

Those whom their traducers persecute will have 'great reward'. διώκω 'persecute', lit. 'drive out', occurs below at 5.44, where οἱ διώκοντες ὑμᾶς is synonymous with ἐχθροί, 'enemies.' Otherwise it is found only in two passages, clearly cognate with one another, 10.23 and 23.34, in the context of being 'chased' (from one city to another). The corresponding noun, διωγμός, is coupled with θλῖψις, 'oppression' (which, in 24.9, 21, 29, characterizes a future period of stress), in the interpretation of the parable of the sower (13.21). Even when ψευδόμενοι, 'untruthfully', has been removed as an officious interpolation, the wording remains exuberant and excited: the tautology, 'rejoice and triumph', made an impression on Luke, who reproduced it in noun form (1.14 χαρὰ καὶ ἀγαλλίασις) in his nativity of John and used the verb in his *Magnificat* hymn (1.47). 'Because of me', which links the persecution to relationship with Jesus, also occurs in 10.18, 37 (=16.25) and, in the form 'for the sake of my name', in 19.29.

As the parallel with 10.30ff. confirms, the victims of 'persecution' who are promised their heavenly reward in this supplement to the list of μακάριοι were Jewish converts who get rabbled in the course of their missionary activities (10.23). They were not the first to be subjected to this treatment; but like those who suffered similarly before them, they are 'prophets'.

.13–16 The theme of persecution and its reward is developed further. Persecution enables those to whom the discourse is addressed to perform a function which they are encouraged to perceive and fulfil. The passage turns on twin metaphorical assertions: 'you are the salt of the earth' and 'you are the light of the world'. They must not shrink from the conditions on which this mission can be accomplished.

A light, in order to shed illumination, must be placed high and kept visible. The corresponding condition for the efficacy of salt has been obliterated by a severe corruption. A lamp lights, but not unless its rays are shed abroad: it must 'shine in the sight of mankind'. Salt preserves, but not unless it is sprinkled and rubbed in. Unfortunately 'unless it is sprinkled', ἐὰν μὴ ῥανθῇ, was corrupted to ἐὰν μωρανθῇ, producing nonsense that spawned further corruption, with which Luke and Mark wrestled helplessly. Salt does not 'lose its savour' (even if μωρανθῇ could mean that), nor is salt 'salted', nor if it *had* 'lost its savour', would there be any point in stamping it into the ground. However, the literal meaning has been allowed to peep through: it is not the salt but those addressed who have been 'cast out and downtrodden'. The following sentence defies emendation: the passage is not about how to 'hide' a city, but about shedding light. There is no natural sense in which the 'light of the world' can be 'set on a mountain'. πόλις at least is hopelessly corrupt; nor is the remainder of the passage free from corruption.

5.15 The unsuitable place for the lighted lamp appears in the text as 'under the *modius*' (a unit of measurement of dry capacity, of Latin origin but found in Greek of the first century BC and earlier, equivalent to about one-sixth of a bushel); but the word is pointless here, because a light put under a measure would just go out, irrespective of the capacity of the particular measure. What is required is something normally or invariably found in a low position, where a lamp could not shed light. A possible word would be 'footstool', ὑποπόδιον, which could easily generate ὑπὸ μόδιον (ΥΠΟΤΟΥΠΟΠΟΔΙΟΝ). The conclusion is wrong too: the purpose of being 'the light of the world' is not to be admired but to enlighten mankind, so that God is glorified. The analogy of 13.43, where the righteous 'shine out like the sun' in the kingdom, suggests allusion to Dan. 12.3: 'And those who understand shall appear as luminaries of heaven (φανοῦσιν ὡς φωστῆρες), and those who strengthen my words as the stars of heaven for ever and ever' (LXX), or alternatively 'And those who understand shall shine forth as the brightness of the firmament (ἐκλάμψουσιν ὡς ἡ λαμπρότης τοῦ στερεώματος) and many of the just as the stars for ever and a day' (Theodotion).

The corruptions in the passage had occurred early; for both Luke and Mark were confronted with them (see below); and the absurdity of 'salt salted' was already an object of rabbinical ridicule by about the end of the first century AD. (Answer to the question 'with what will it be salted?': 'with the afterbirth of a mule'. 'But does a mule have an afterbirth?' Answer: 'Can salt become foolish?' Strack–Billerbeck i. 236.)

Luke found it all acutely problematic. He jibbed at describing the audience either as 'the salt of the earth' or as 'the light of the world' who would 'shine before men'. Nor did he see the point of 'the city on a mountain'. However, he was unwilling to discard either the salt or the lamp. The salt he inserted at a later point (14.34) but without context. The second person being there inappropriate, he substituted, as introduction, for 'you are the salt of the earth' the insipid phrase 'salt is good'. He reduced the embarrassment of 'salting salt' by substituting ἀρτυθήσεται ('shall be flavoured') for ἁλισθήσεται ('shall be salted'). He did his best to tone down the remainder ('it is suitable neither for the earth nor for the dunghill: they throw it out'); but 'become foolish' defeated even him, and he left it.

Equally puzzled and fascinated by the lamp, Luke introduced it not once but twice, though ignoring the exhortation 'so let your light' etc.: 8.16 (in connection with 'nothing is hidden that shall not be revealed' = Matt. 10.26) 'No one, having lit a lamp, covers it with a jar or puts it under a bed, but puts it on a lamp-stand, so that those who come in can see the light'; 11.33 (in connection with 'the eye is the light of the body' = Matt. 6.22) 'No one, having lit a lamp, puts it into a hiding-place or under the *modius*, but on the lampstand, so that those who come in can see the beam.'

Luke had several shots at solving the problem of the 'bushel'. First, for *modius* he substituted a generic term, 'jar' (σκεῦος). Then he realized the required sense and suggested 'under a *bed*' (which is fair, but not so good an emendation as 'footstool'). Possibly the non-existent word κρύπτην, which is translated 'hiding-place', conceals yet another suggestion with similar meaning. As it is incredible that he would then have put back the corruption itself, the corrupt word 'bushel' is evidently a contamination from the text in Matthew. The touch 'those who come in' is due to Luke's unease with the (possibly metaphorical) phrase 'all those in the house', whereas a lamp can light only those in the same room.

Mark, confronting the same difficulties as Luke, betrays that he partially followed his guidance. The lamp he placed (4.21, 22) in exactly the same, not very obvious, setting after the parable of the sower and the seed, and acknowledged Luke's emendation σκεύει ἢ ὑποκάτω τὴν κλίνην ('with a vessel or under the bed') by writing 'surely a lamp does not come in to be put under the *modius* or under the bed' (ὑπὸ τὸν μόδιον ἢ ὑπὸ τὴν κλίνην), where the curious use of 'come in' for 'be brought in' suggests recollection of Luke's εἰσπορευόμενοι, 'those who come in'—an unconscious echo. As for the metaphor of the salt, while retaining 'salt is a fine thing', Mark found a different context as follows. He had decided to save Matt. 5.29, 30 ('cut off your hand'), which Luke rejected along with the whole of the extension of the Law from deed to thought, and had attached it (at 9.43), because it turns upon the term σκανδαλίζω, to the 'millstone around the neck', which Luke used in a different context (17.1, 2). Mark, however, added after 'hellfire' at the end of the 'cut off your hand' passage two sentences (9.48, 49). One is Isa. 66.24. The other makes the point that the whole body and not just a limb will be destroyed there by fire. The expression forced to mean this, 'for all will be *salted* by fire', πᾶς γὰρ πυρὶ ἁλισθήσεται, provided the point of attachment (9.50) of the saying about salt, to which, having substituted 'become saltless' for 'become foolish', Mark added an equally irrelevant conclusion: 'have salt in yourselves and be at peace with one another', implying a trilingual pun, ἅλς, *sal*, 'salt', שלום, 'peace'

5.17–20 The Jewish convert was confronted with the allegation that Jesus 'came' to abolish the Law and the prophets. That allegation is now to be refuted by applying the commandment which Jesus taught (19.19) must be fulfilled to enter the kingdom—to love others as one has been loved (i.e. forgiven) by God (6.12). It creates obligations in 'excess' (περισσεύειν) of the Law, which is thus more than fulfilled—a proposition which the section that follows illustrates.

However, the repudiation of the accusation (5.17 'Do not suppose that I came . . .') is severed from its logical sequel (5.20 'For I tell you that you will not enter unless') by a bitterly personalized passage (5.18, 19) incompatible with the context: the question was not who would be 'least' or 'greatest' in the kingdom of heaven but who would be able to enter it at all. The taunt implies contention over ranking ('be called') in 'the kingdom' (cf. 20.21).

5.17 The word translated 'abolish' (καταλῦσαι) is elsewhere used physically of demolishing a building (24.2; 26.61 = 27.40). That rendered 'fulfil' (πληρῶσαι) is used of 'fulfilling' a prophecy (see on 1.22) or occasionally physically of filling a net (13.48) or a measure (23.32). But though 'fulfil' might be appropriate to 'the prophets', 'abolish' is not, nor does the rest of the argument refer at all to 'the prophets', also paired with νόμος at 22.40.

5.18 This is the first of 31 occurrences, all in Jesus' mouth, of the asseverative 'Verily I say to you', followed immediately by a statement, with or without the conjunction 'that'. 'Amen', Hebrew אמן, occurs in the Old Testament only as a note of assent ('and all the people shall say, Amen' Deut. 27.15 etc.). The asseverative usage appears to be unexampled outside the New Testament. The duplication 'amen, amen' is confined to John. Though the rendering 'jot or tittle' has become proverbial, 'one iota or one stroke' is not without difficulty. 'Iota' no doubt stands for the Hebrew *yōd*, י, the smallest of the letters, while the word κεραία, lit. 'horn', 'projection', may denote the tiny stroke which distinguishes some Hebrew letters from others, e.g. ד from ר or ב from כ. Neither, however, though visually small, is unimportant for the meaning. The whole expression thus amounts to no more than a general assertion of integrity: 'not a letter' will be lost. The unusual chiasmus, lit. 'iota one or one stroke', ἰῶτα ἓν ἢ μία κεραία, strengthens the rhetorical impression.

'Pass away', παρελθεῖν, though suitable to the dissolution or disappearance of the world, is strained as applied to the loss of a letter, especially in combination with '*from* the Law'. Luke, inserting the sentence in another context (16.17), paraphrased: 'it is easier for heaven and earth to pass away than for one stroke of the Law to *fall*' (πεσεῖν). 'Until all is over' will not do either. It is impossible to co-ordinate with 'until heaven and earth pass away', and 'all things' is meaningless without qualification: *what* things? The sentence is verbally so similar to 24.34, 35, of which it might be an adaptation, as to suggest that the same hand also composed the insertion here. It is in 24.34, 35 that the verb παρελθεῖν belongs.

5.19 'Loose', λύειν, in the sense of 'break' occurs nowhere else in the New Testament except in John. The strained expression 'one of these, the least commandments' is, if taken literally, illogical, implying that breach of any but the least commandments is not punishable. It has to be understood as irony, a polemical thrust at those who claim to divide the Law into lesser and greater commandments and treat only the latter as binding, a distinction implicit in the otherwise vacuous enquiry (22.36, q.v.) 'which is the greatest commandment in the Law?'

The statement at 5.19 is intrusive: it suddenly introduces the question of ranking in the kingdom into a context concerned with who will get into (εἰσελθεῖν) the kingdom *at all*.

5.20 The other occurrences of περισσεύειν in the book are 14.20 = 15.37, where it means 'to be left over', and 13.12 (=25.29), in a unique and unintelligible passive which Mark and Luke omitted. The sense 'be in excess of', which is required here, does not fit with πλεῖον, 'more' (here only in the book used as an adverb). The phrase (the only place in the discourse where the Pharisees or the scribes are referred to expressly) has the appearance of a gloss due to π. being understood as 'abound'.

The expression '*enter* the kingdom of heaven' treats the kingdom not as something which 'comes', or is about to come (3.2, 4.17), with different consequences for different people, but as something into which entry is severely restricted; cf. 'enter into life', 19.17. The underlying notion seems to be that of a judgement (25.34, 46) of which entrance into the kingdom is one of two alternative outcomes. The term recurs in the closely connected section 7.13–21, q.v.

5.21–48 'Excess' observation of the Law beyond that of the 'scribes and Pharisees', due to applying the rule of reciprocity (7.12), is now expounded in an essay citing a series of social commandments, viz. those prohibiting murder, adultery, and perjury and those enjoining equal compensation for injury and love for one's 'neighbour'. The section has been subjected to much elaboration, often irrelevant or misconceived.

5.21 (1) 'Murder' involves harbouring ill will (anger). This demands the deduction 'But I say to you, that everyone that is angry with his brother has already murdered him in his heart' (cf. 5.28). (The expansion of the commandment with allusions to judgement and the rabbinically elaborated gradations of abuse are irrelevant accretions.) Symmetry with the following case has been breached by two added items: (1) (5.23, 24) apparently sacramental, God will not accept the offering of one whose 'brother' is unreconciled with him; (2) (5.25, 26) judgemental, God will exact the uttermost penalty from those unreconciled with their fellows (cf. 18.23–35). The passage is equivalent to a commentary upon 6.11, 12. The person addressed is presumed to be in the wrong or to owe the debt, because he represents man in the sight of God. Of the word or thing κοδράντης, *quadrans*, conventionally translated 'farthing', the smallest Roman coin—as indeed of the λεπτόν (lit. 'lightweight') which Luke (12.59) substituted—no evidence (apart from this passage) relating to Palestine appears to have been produced.

5.27 (2) 'Adultery' involves lustful desire for another's wife. Since therefore desire is involuntary, keeping of the Law justifies physical measures to prevent lust. The deduction is duplicated, making the 'eye' (the right eye!) the organ of lust, due to failure to recognize 'hand' as a euphemism for penis.* The description of the eye as a 'limb' (μέλος) betrays what has happened.

It follows that 18.8–9 was derived from this passage: see the discussion there. The conclusion that the passage originally recommended self-castration might be regarded as outlandish, however logical, if it were not for 19.12: 'there are eunuchs who made themselves eunuchs for the sake of (entering) the kingdom of heaven', which describes both the act and the motive implied here.

* In several Semitic languages יד 'hand' is a euphemism for penis; see E. Ullendorff, 'The Bawdy Bible', *Bulletin of the School of Oriental and African Studies*, 42 (1979), 427–56, at p. 441.

5.29 The word translated 'cause to fall', σκανδαλίζειν (lit. 'trip up'), first makes its appearance here. It was a technical term, denoting to cause the destruction of those who would otherwise be saved at the coming of the kingdom: see 24.10. It occurs in Dan. 11.41 (second century BC), translating כשל ('stumble').

5.31 The rider is added that all divorce, though permitted by the Law, involves adultery and therefore injury to someone else, making it unlawful.

'It was said', reducing the repetition of 'you heard that it was said to them of old' to a minimum, differentiates this dictum from the two preceding.

The quotation is a summary, rather than a citation, of Deut. 24.1–4, of which, by taking it in isolation, it alters the sense. The ruling in Deut. 24.1 relates to the case that the second husband of a woman twice divorced predeceases both her and the first husband, and is to the effect that the first husband cannot then take her back. It is not therefore so much concerned to enjoin the requirement of a formal divorce as to forbid remarriage even after the second marriage has been dissolved and the second ex-husband has died: so strong is the prohibition of remarriage that it is to hold good even when the second marriage has been doubly ended—by divorce and by death. The expression 'bill of separation' (βιβλίον ἀποστασίου) is in LXX Deut. 24.1 and below at 19.7. Here ἀποστάσιον is used by itself in the same sense. Elsewhere the word appears only to occur in the genitive, and nowhere else to mean 'divorce' but rather 'conveyance' or the like.

The qualification 'fornication apart', rather than an interpolation, appears to be a logical exclusion of circumstances in which divorce does not necessarily involve injury to another party, presupposing a distinction between μοιχεία (marital) and πορνεία (extra-marital). The second limb uses a form (μοιχᾶσθαι) of the word for 'commit adultery' different from that (μοιχεύειν) already used in this and the preceding saying.

5.33–7 (3) 'Perjury' involves by definition injury to another, who is induced to rely upon the oath. Against this result, intended or unintended, the only sure defence is 'not to swear at all'. Reasons (5.34b–37) which presuppose other grounds for the prohibition, such as avoidance of blasphemy, have been introduced into the text.

The text as cited does not occur in the Old Testament. Closest are: to the first part, Lev. 19.12 'thou shalt not swear by my name falsely', and to the second part, Deut. 23.22 'when thou makest a vow to the Lord thy God, thou shalt not delay to pay it off' (ἀποδοῦναι, the same word as ἀποδώσεις here, which is peculiar in the sense of 'perform'). Superficially similar is Num. 30.2 'if a man vow a vow unto the Lord, or swear an oath to bind his soul with a bond, he shall not break his word'. The Decalogue Exod. 20.16 (cited 19.18) has οὐ ψευδομαρτυρήσεις, 'commit perjury', for which is here substituted ἐπιορκήσεις, lit. 'be forsworn', i.e. swear and then fail to perform.

It is recorded that, early in the reign of Herod the Great, on one occasion (Jos. *Ant.* 15.368) the Pharisees of the schools of Pollio and Sameas and the Essenes refused to take an oath of loyalty to Herod, and on another (ibid. 17.42) the Pharisees in general refused to take an oath to Caesar and were punished with a fine. It may be that in these instances the objection was to swearing at all and not to swearing to the emperor or Herod in particular.

5.38–42 The citation is part only of the full prescription of Lev. 24.19 'if a man cause a blemish in his neighbour, as he hath done, so shall it be done to him—break for break, eye for eye, tooth for tooth: as he hath caused a blemish in a man, so it shall be done to him again'. Whatever the later interpretations, there is no ground in those words for taking them in the sense '(the price of) an eye', etc. 'So shall it be done to him' is conclusively literal.

'Not to resist', let alone 'not to resist evil (or the Devil)', is not appropriate as the antithesis to the terms of the Law. The three illustrative cases are suspect of being additions. The first two are both Judaic: ῥαπίζω 'strike' (etymologically implying strike with a stick) and σιαγών 'cheek' recall Isa. 50.6 ('I have offered my cheeks to blows'); the action requires much dexterity and involves a backhander. The court rule (κριθῆναι) which forbids taking a defendant's cloak is prescribed Exod. 22.26–7, Deut. 24.12–13. More startling in its implications is the allusion to Roman servitudes, defined as such by the vocabulary (e.g. μίλιον 'mile', not apparently found in Greek before the first century AD), which conveys that gentiles too are included in the duty of nonretaliation. The terminology is clearly attuned to Jewish addressees in Palestine. The concluding admonition, which changes the subject, looks like an ineffective and inaccurate attempt at paraphrase, avoiding the technicalities of the three cases.

Luke, who lifted (6.29, 30) the illustrations but left out the initial text about the eye and the tooth, as usual saw the difficulties and removed them. He omitted 'right' before 'cheek', eliminated the puzzling κριθῆναι, reversed the positions of the coat and cloak, and substituted for the injunction to lend to all would-be borrowers the more modest and relevant suggestion not to reclaim property from the person who takes it.

5.43–8 The 'excess' over loving one's neighbour is to love* one's enemy, interpreting 'neighbour' as someone by definition not an enemy. 'Your enemies' are then exemplified by the persecutors (cf. 5.11) of those to whom the discourse is addressed. How are you to 'love' them? You are to 'pray for them'. The commandment Lev. 19.18, associated with the Decalogue here and at 19.19, is interpreted, under the influence of the literal Greek translation of the Hebrew reciprocal איש רעהו 'each his fellow, one another', as if 'neighbour' were intensive, opposite to 'enemy'. See also below on 22.39.

The persecuted Jewish converts are shamed into obeying the 'excess' commandment by contrasting the behaviour of the two prime objects of Jewish aversion, the tax-gatherers and the gentiles. The commandment to love 'enemies' is in line with the general sense of this whole part of the discourse. The reason for it is not emulation of God's impartiality in the distribution of sunshine and rain. As throughout the section, the argument turns on 'excess' (περισσόν) and not, as implied in the wind-up, upon 'perfection'.

Luke (6.27, 28) multiplied examples, but significantly replaced the too specific 'persecute', which recalls the context of 5.10, 11 (on which see above, pp. 76–7), by 'abuse' (also from 5.11).

6.1–18 After an introductory summary, a symmetrical pattern is repeated: 'When you (singular 6.2; plural 6.5, 16) . . . , do not . . . as the "play-actors" do, in order that (ὅπως) they may be glorified (seen). Verily, I say to you, They have their reward. But when you (singular) . . . , do (thus and thus), and your Father, who sees in secret,† will repay you.'

As orthodox Jews, the Jewish converts 'do their righteous works', that is, fulfil their religious observances, as examples of which almsgiving, prayer, and fasting are taken. They are here

* The words ἀγαπῶ 'love' in this book and ὁ πλησίον 'neighbour' in all gospels occur only in the context of this commandment. φιλεῖν, to love a person, occurs only at 10.37 in this book, and elsewhere in the gospels only in John. ἐρᾶν occurs in the New Testament not at all.

† The expression for 'in secret' is varied between ἐν τῷ κρυπτῷ (6.4, 6) and ἐν τῷ κρυφαίῳ (6.18), unique in the New Testament.

warned not to do so publicly or ostentatiously, knowing that merit 'with God' is not acquired thereby—not, however, that there is no value in their obedience if known only to God. The passage gives a vivid insight into the life of observant Jewish members of the Church.

The behaviour required of them contrasts with that of the 'play-actors', who make a show of their piety and are rewarded by public esteem.

6.2 This is the first appearance of 'the hypocrites', οἱ ὑποκριταί, a word which occurs only in Jesus' mouth and always elsewhere in the vocative. In 23.13–29, a similarly structured passage, it is used in apposition to 'scribes and Pharisees' (see above, on 5.20); otherwise (7.5, 15.7, 22.18) it appears unqualified.

By what process the Greek word ὑποκριτής, 'answerer, actor, declaimer', came to be so used is unexplained. The derivation of 'hypocrite' in modern languages from its use in the New Testament is untrue to the contextual meaning. It was, however, used in LXX Job 34.30, 36.13 to translate חנף ('profane').

Artificially inserted into the symmetrical framework is a brief sacramental prayer 6.9–15. Irrelevant to the contrast between public and private prayer, it is introduced by a reference to 'babbling' and prolixity in prayer, which surprises because 'gentile' prayer is not notably babbled—a complaint which a non-Jew present at Jewish devotions might find hard to repress—and all prayer whatsoever is open to the objection that God must know the petitioner's needs in advance. An excuse has been manufactured for introducing the prayer.

6.3 However familiar proverbially, the expression 'let not thy left hand know what thy right hand doeth' is nonsensical in itself and does not fit the context. Why *should* the left hand 'know' (whatever that might mean) what the right is doing? The two hands may need co-ordination for some purposes, but not for throwing a coin to a beggar. The sense required is 'let not (even) the recipient know who is the donor', thus removing the last vestige of extraneous motivation or reward for the donor. Sense would be made if the left hand were proverbial for taking and the right for giving.

6.6 The antithesis is an echo, rather than a quotation, of Isa. 26.20: 'Enter into thy chambers and shut thy doors about thee' (in a different context). Luke (18.9–14) has a midrash on this passage.

6.9–15 The prayer is not part of the original texture. It interrupts the symmetry of the section and is not relevant to the antithesis between private and publicized religious observances. Nevertheless, the prayer is one specially tailored to the situation of the addressees. Jewish converts were under 'temptation' to concede, as Jesus was represented as doing, the Devil's argument against the sacrament at 4.3, a passage assumed to be familiar to the reader. The emphasis upon reciprocity between divine and human forgiveness also harks back to the argument of the section 5.20–48. The absurdity of inviting the Almighty to do his will could be due to rendering in Greek as a petition what in Hebrew/ Aramaic were tenseless participles.

6.10 'Will' (θέλημα) occurs only as an attribute of God (7.21, 12.50, 21.31 τοῦ πατρός and also probably 18.14), and exactly as here at 26.42, where, however, the sense, unlike here, is of submission to that will. The clause 'as in heaven, so on earth also', qualifying 'will be fulfilled' (not 'kingdom come'), disturbs the symmetry of the triple invocation (or description) of the deity and imports the awkward implication that the situation on earth has got out of hand. Luke (11.2) omitted.

6.11 The adjective qualifying 'bread'—ἐπιούσιος—is non-existent, but if it existed would mean 'tomorrow's', an adjective derived from ἐπιοῦσα (ἡμέρα). It cannot therefore represent a Hebrew/ Aramaic original—a non-existent word would scarcely be used in translation—but must be corrupt. 'The bread of heaven' would fit the context; as abbreviated ΕΠΟῩΝΙΟ̄, it differs little from ΕΠΙΟΥΣΙΟ̄. Some versions, e.g. the Anglo-Saxon, have actually translated 'supernatural', seeing this to be the correct sense and assuming (wrongly) that ἐπιούσιος could mean 'super-existent'. Luke (11.2–4) did not venture to change the word, though he did make alterations in the next clauses.

'Today' (σήμερον), implying an antithesis with yesterday or tomorrow, is not wanted: it could represent a gloss on ἐπιούσιον interpreted as 'today's' (σημερινόν). Luke substituted τὸ καθ' ἡμέραν 'day by day'.

6.12 Luke made two significant changes: he replaced 'debts' in the first half with 'sins' (ἁμαρτίας); and while leaving 'debts' in the second half, he changed the tense to the present: 'as we let off everyone who is indebted to us'. Forgiveness between men cannot extend to sins, which, as offences against God, only God can forgive (see on 9.2–4). The cancellation of a debt, on the other hand, is wholly within the power and right of a creditor. The term παραπτώματα (lit. 'side-slips') in the explanation 6.14 consciously tries to strike a mean between 'debts', ὀφειλήματα, and 'sins', ἁμαρτίαι. The clause may imply that the *pax* was already a normal component of the mass: reconciliation must precede communion.

6.12 The substantive petition, to be given 'the bread', is linked with the plea for forgiveness, predicated upon prior (ἀφήκαμεν pf.) forgiveness of 'our debtors': God will not forgive your offences against him unless you have forgiven men theirs against you.

6.13 The startling petition not to be led into temptation but to be saved from the Devil, with its implicit allusion to the temptation of Jesus at 4.3, may not form part of the original context or the original prayer. It would otherwise separate 6.12 from the explanation in 6.14, 15, which on the other hand may be the later addition. The 'temptation' is to doubt the reality of the sacrament.

6.16 The 'hypocrites' did not put on sour expressions (σκυθρωποί): as the antithesis shows, they disfigured themselves (ἀφανίζουσι) with dishevelled hair, ashes, dirt, etc. 'Gloomy' is an interpolation. Oiling the hair and washing the face are aspects of normality.

6.19–24 The 'store on earth' is accumulated by the 'scribes and Pharisees' through observance of the Law; the 'store in heaven' is accumulated by the Jewish converts through faith in Jesus. The former is perishable, the latter perpetual. The two are two masters whom a man cannot serve simultaneously, God and men. Between the metaphors of the 'store' and of the 'two masters' there is a third—'the eye is the lamp of the body', i.e. you go where your eye leads you. The relevance of this must be: on which will you keep your eye fixed—God or men? All three metaphors have been elaborated—and their meaning wrested—by inappropriate explanatory matter.

6.19 The only parallel in the book for the singular 'heaven' (οὐρανῷ) meaning anything but the sky is 18.18 (also opposite to 'the earth'), where, as here and at 19.21 (q.v.), it appears to mean 'in the kingdom of heaven' or, possibly, 'in the sight of God (whose seat is heaven)': 'stores in heaven' is the 'reward in heaven' (5.12) which God will give.

'Moth and corruption destroy' (lit. obliterate, ἀφανίζει, a word purloined from above, 6.16) is a strange combination of the concrete ('moth') and the abstract ('corruption')—with the verb in the singular.

6.24 The last sentence of this section is the basic statement, asserting an impossibility assumed axiomatic. It has been prefaced by a paraphrase which alters the sense from an axiom to an exhortation, so that δύνασθε has to be understood as 'can *wisely* or *satisfactorily*'. The paraphrase is both tautological and perverse. It is tautological, because the two halves of the sentence have the same meaning: there is no real antithesis between ἀνθέξεται 'cleave to' and καταφρονήσει 'despise'. It is perverse, because the impossibility of serving two masters is that they give incompatible commands, not that the servant likes one more than the other.

The opposite to 'serving God' is acquiring 'stores on earth' or, in the conventional code for self-acquired merit, 'wealth'. The context called for this antithesis to 'God' to be personalized. An anti-God to serve this purpose and represent the arch-advocate of 'stores on earth' was obtained by resort to the word *mamonas*, of unknown origin, which only occurs in one other passage in the New Testament. Luke, who transcribed this item unaltered (16.13), except for inserting 'servant' (οἰκετής) ('No *servant* can serve' etc.), introduced the word into the preceding context (16.9, 11) in a manner ('the *m.* of unrighteousness', 'the unrighteous *m.*') which suggests he was unfamiliar with it. It is found in place of χρυσίον, 'money', in the Hebrew (ninth–eleventh century) text of Ecclus. 31.8 and in the Targums (fifth century) as equivalent to various Hebrew words meaning 'wealth'.

22, 23 To the argument which it interrupts the sentence about the 'eye' which is 'the lamp of the body' has at first sight no relevance. It has to refer to the antithesis between reliance on God's mercy and merit claimed through works and observance of the Law. This is expressed by the contrast between an eye which is ἁπλοῦς and one which is πονηρός: one affords light, the other darkness, to 'the whole body', the same wording as above at 5.29. 'Simple, single' (ἁπλοῦς) is unnaturally strained to mean the opposite to 'bad' πονηρός, the conventional epithet (see p. 102) for the theological opponent. See on 18.9. The violence of the language and the use of the term πονηρός encourage a suspicion that the two 'eyes' represent teachers of truth and of wickedness, the 'whole body' being the followers who are respectively illuminated or led astray.

The exclamation τὸ σκότος πόσον, unexampled, is redolent of rhetoric.

25–34 From the possession of 'store in heaven' follows by deduction (διὰ τοῦτο λέγω ὑμῖν) freedom from anxious care. God, who feeds 'the fowls of the air' without their needing to produce food *or store it* (οὐδὲ συνάγουσιν εἰς ἀποθήκας), will nurture those addressed. The explanatory hand which was at work (6.27!) extended the argument, in order to cover clothing, to 'beasts of the field', and created the rhetorical flourish of 'Solomon in all his glory'.

The whole passage has been not only severely corrupted (see 6.28) but heavily annotated and elaborated. The corruptions occurred after the explanatory additions had been introduced but before Matthew was used by Luke.

6.25 The *a fortiori* argument from the 'fowls of the air' having been matched by a corresponding argument from the 'beasts of the field' (see below), the introductory sentence had to be extended to match anxiety 'for your life' (τῇ ψυχῇ) about nourishment with anxiety 'for your body' (τῷ σώματι) about clothing.

6.26 'Differ more' (μᾶλλον) conceals 'differ much' (πολλῷ); cf. 10.31.

6.27 Another rhetorical insertion (for τίς ἐξ ὑμῶν cf. 7.9, 12.11), implying a different line of argument. There is a dilemma: if ἡλικία means 'age', πῆχυς 'cubit' is metaphorical; but if ἡλικία means 'stature', πῆχυς must be literal. The former meets the requirement that the increase must be an obviously very small one; but it necessitates giving to ἡλικία the meaning of span of life and not its normal meaning, the age reached at a given time.

6.28 The words 'card not' οὐ ξαίνουσι—the process preliminary to spinning (as 'sow' above is preliminary to 'reap')—generated, by a slight misreading, the corruption αὐξάνουσι 'they grow', which is manifestly wrong, because it is not growing that is at issue but being fed and clothed. In addition, οὐ ξαίνουσι 'card not' has been replaced by οὐ κοπιῶσι 'toil not', which, as generic, cannot be paired or contrasted with the specific 'spin' (e.g. 'no money and no shillings'). Thus the wording we have is the product of a (wrong) variant αὐξάνουσι in the margin and a (wrong) interlinear gloss κοπιῶσι in the text.

The antithesis to 'fowls of the air' is not 'lilies of the field' but '*beasts* of the field'. The beasts are indeed 'clad' without industry or artifice on their part. To say that 'flowers' or, even more, flowers of one particular sort are 'clothed' is absurd: beautiful they may be, clothed they are not.

The alteration of 'beasts' into 'lilies' may be a corruption. Confusion between 'beasts' חית in חית השדה or חית הארץ and 'lilies' שושנים is difficult in Hebrew, whereas in Greek that between

ΤΑΘΗΡΙΑ, 'the beasts', and ΤΑΛΕΙΡΙΑ, 'the lilies', is not. Corruption would then have taken place in Greek in two stages—(1) θηρία, 'beasts', changed to λείρια, 'lilies', and (2) λείρια glossed with its synonym κρίνα. On the other hand, the rhetorical piece about 'Solomon' and the 'oven' may be an insertion prompted by objection to being clothed as 'the beasts' are clothed, viz. in skin and fur, and this may have suggested 'lilies'. Elaboration is betrayed by (1) 'lilies', for which 'grass', χόρτος, has later to be substituted (ovens are not fuelled with lilies) and (2) the absurdity of 'clothing' lilies or grass.

6.31–4 The argument has been completed, and does not admit of extension: 'stores in heaven' will prove sufficient. The summary at 6.31 is superfluous; and the addition 6.32–4, utilizing the sneer at the 'gentiles' from 5.47 and the sentence about God's foreknowledge from 6.8, shifts the argument on to different ground, where 'seeking the kingdom and God's righteousness' are thrown in, along with 'all these things shall be added to you', in order to make weight.

Luke (12.22) does not have 'or drink', which indeed is absent from one family of manuscripts here. He felt the difficulty of 'are you not more important than they?' (6.26) but left it unresolved with 'how much more do you differ from the birds'. The irrelevance of the cubit and the life-span worried him, and he tried to diminish it, not very successfully, by adding a rationalization: 'so, if you cannot do the least of things, why worry about the rest?'

When he came, however, to the 'lilies of the field', he achieved creditable results. He deleted 'they grow', perceiving it to be quite wrong, and solved the problem of 'toiling and spinning' by substituting 'spinning and weaving', which at least made sense: only a critical genius could have discovered the traces of 'card'. The 'lilies' he left, except that, to match their awkward specificity, he substituted in the other limb of the parallel the specific 'ravens' for the general 'birds', doubtless recollecting Job 38.41 or Ps. 147.9. It was perhaps uneasiness at high-flown 'grass of the field which *is* today' that caused him to write 'the grass which is in the field today'.

Luke proves an important fact: he was using this text, in exactly or virtually the form in which we have it, and he had—at this point at least—no other recourse. If 'spin and weave' had existed first, it could never have generated 'card and spin'; but the corruption of 'card and spin' uniquely explains how 'spin and weave' could come about. But more remains.

Even without the 'lilies' of the field, we should know that our text had passed through a stage at which, being in Greek, it was clumsily glossed in Greek for readers whose native language was not Greek. Unless, however, the corruption of 'beasts' into 'lilies' was not after all a Greek corruption, closely parallel to the case of 'card', but can plausibly be explained as having originated in Hebrew or Aramaic, we also know that the glossed and annotated text had already undergone in Greek major expansion and additional editing of the kind to which 'Solomon in all his glory' and 'the grass of the field' bear witness.

7.1–5 The Jewish convert must not be critical of his gentile 'brethren' for failure to obey the Law (e.g. circumcision?), because he thereby asserts an obligation which he is himself committed to repudiate. An individual, who is addressed in the singular and ironically labelled 'play-actor' (ὑποκριτά) like his own opponents (see on 6.2), is in no position to put right his gentile 'brother'. The contrast is between σκάρφος, a little stick, and δοκός, a beam; there is no basis for the translation of σκάρφος as 'mote'. Neither a σκάρφος nor a δοκός is suitable to be a foreign body in a human eye. The physical impractibility of the metaphor shows that 'beam' and 'splinter' are used hyperbolically (cf. 19.24).

7.6–12 The following two items, 7.6 and 7.7–11, are at first sight irrelevant and contradictory; but in line with the admonition at 7.1–5, a compromise is being proposed. 'The holy thing', τὸ ἅγιον, and 'your pearls', τοὺς μαργαρίτας ὑμῶν, represent the Jewish convert's sacrament. The two prohibitions which have been conflated are ironical, an irony ignored by the explanatory interpolations. There is no need, the Jew is told, to offer your sacraments to those whom you profess to regard as 'dogs' (cf. βαλεῖν τὸν ἄρτον τοῖς κυναρίοις in the closely related passage 15.27) or as 'swine'. Simply seek admission to the sacrament of the gentile churches, which will not be refused—your 'Father in heaven' will not deny 'good things' to those who ask him for them, any more than a human father would disappoint a son. The sacrament again is indicated not only by the 'bread' but by the fish emblem (ἰχθύς/Χριστός: see on 14.19), whence the rejected suggestion of 'a snake instead of a fish'. Luke (11.9–13), who perceptively attached the saying to the 'Lord's prayer', apparently found the antithesis bread–stone ~ fish–snake unsatisfactory and substituted fish–snake ~ egg–scorpion, possibly to make both of the examples positively harmful; but though a stone can be like a loaf (cf. 4.3), a scorpion is difficult to mistake for an egg. Luke also substituted 'the holy spirit' for 'good things'.

7.12 The sententious ending strikes a false note. Its concluding words are an inadequate reproduction of 22.40.

.13, 14 'Squeeze in (if you must) by the narrow gate' is intended ironically: attempt, if you will, to try to combine Christian belief with Jewish observance. The irony was overlooked by whoever composed the explanation which follows.

.15–20 The ironical advice is followed immediately, and logically, by a warning not to listen to 'false prophets' who court their own and their dupes' destruction by seeking to debar the gentiles from God's mercy; for the admission of the gentiles is 'the will of God' (cf. 21.28–31).

7.15 It was customary to protect sheep by providing them with coats (Columella 7.4.3; Varro 2.2.18–19). It would thus be possible for wolves wearing these coats to gain admission to a sheepfold. There is presumably an allusion to some fable to that effect. (A number of Fathers quote ἐν δέρματι 'in hides' instead of ἐν ἐνδύματι 'in clothes'—a well-meant conjecture, but δέρμα is not right for sheep.) 'Inside', ἔσωθεν, is unusual for 'underneath', 'while all the time being'; it is curious that ἔσωθεν and ἁρπαγή recur together in an apparently different context at 23.25.

7.21, 22 The 'false prophets' acknowledge Jesus as 'Lord' and purport to act in his name; but the result is ἀνομία, the 'lawlessness' attributed at 5.20 to the 'scribes and Pharisees', and the frustration of God's purpose for the gentiles. The crowning, bitterest paradox is that those who insisted on observance of the νόμος will be convicted of ἀνομία. Those who have used the name of Jesus, made converts, and performed miracles will at the judgement, when they start up the gentile liturgy ('Lord, have mercy', see on 15.22), be packed off to perdition, convicted as breakers of the law ('workers of ἀνομία').

7.23 The use of ὁμολογεῖν, lit. 'agree, confess', in the sense of 'declare' is highly peculiar. It is due to the eschatological use of ὁμολογεῖν declaratorily, as at 10.32.

7.24–7 The significance of 'building' on the 'rock' in allusion to Peter and Peter's Church (16.18) was unlikely to be overlooked. The exaggerated catastrophe (7.27) could be a reference to that of AD 70. After 7.23, which has the appearance of the original conclusion of the 'sermon', 7.24–7 gives it an artificial ending appropriate to a discourse.

7.26 The mirror-image is exact, with the sole verbal change of 'smote' (προσέκοψαν) in the second half for προσέπεσαν ('fell upon') in the first—unless indeed this variation is due to a gloss. The repetition was found jejune by Luke (6.47–9), who, observing it to be self-evidently better to build a house on rock than on sand, recomposed the passage in different language and incidentally eliminated the improbability of 'on sand' by substituting 'on the ground without a foundation'. The word used for 'man' is not, as in every other parable or similitude, ἄνθρωπος, but curiously ἀνήρ (i.e. male human being), as if a reference to actual individuals were hinted at. The language is extraordinary, if strained. If rain fell, why not say so, instead of using the abnormal noun βροχή and verb καταβαίνειν? (βροχή is found in LXX only twice, Pss. 67.10 and 104.32—instead of the normal ὑετός—to translate גשם.) Even more peculiar is 'the rivers came': οἱ ποταμοί means 'the rivers', and by no stretch 'the (consequent) floods'. Luke could not put up with it: he wrote instead 'there was a flood (πλημμύρα) and the river washed against the house', and omitted 'the winds' altogether. The concluding punch line is really absurd: if the house fell, then, large or small, that was the end of the matter.

7.28, 29 The 'astonishment' of 'the crowds' which greets the conclusion of the discourse 5.3–7.27 was not specially called for by any of its contents. The transitional formula after a speech is everywhere else (11.1, 13.53, 19.1, 26.1) followed immediately by an action of Jesus (e.g. μετέβη ἐκεῖθεν). This suggests that the words which intervene here before ἠκολούθησαν αὐτῷ ὄχλοι πολλοί (8.1) are not original.

8.1–13 The insertion (4.23–8.13) which contains the discourse 5.3–7.27 concludes with the narration of two healings. This can hardly be fortuitous, any more than can the fact that the healings are respectively the healing by physical contact of a Jew who is then commanded to fulfil the Law and the long-range healing of a gentile. There is an allegory of the coexistence of the Judaizing church in Palestine with the worldwide mission to the gentiles.

8.2 Leprosy is not one of the complaints listed at 4.23–5, though included below in the discourse at 10.8 and in the catalogue at 11.5. The only other leper in the book is Simon 'the Leper' (26.6).

The leper prostrated himself, προσεκύνει, the action demanded of Jesus by Satan (4.9). The term was avoided by Luke 5.12 ('fell upon his face') and Mark 1.40 ('fell on his knees'), as implying recognition of divinity.

Not accidentally, the first healing is of a Jew, whose knowledge of the Mosaic Law and of his obligations under it is taken for granted. The reference is to the leprosy code in Lev. 13–14, where the offerings after recovery are prescribed. As the code implied, spontaneous recovery from leprosy was not unusual.

8.3 Jesus signifies the granting of the man's petition simply by commanding him to fulfil the code. The man's faith, which causes him to obey, is also the means of his being cured: the cure occurs in the course of his obeying the command. Reflection upon this prompted Luke to compose the story (17.11–19) of the ten lepers who are cured on their way to the priests: the return of one supplies the necessary information, the injunction to silence is suppressed, and the grateful leper (who, however, benefits no more than the others) is a Samaritan. The occurrence of the actual cure after the departure of the sufferer raises the question of the beneficiary coming back to say thank you, which was the motive of Luke's midrash and of his rather grotesque substitution of ten lepers for one, in order to enhance the contrast between gratitude and ingratitude.

In the healing of the leper 'the priests' are confronted (8.4 εἰς μαρτύριον αὐτοῖς) with the fact that Jesus has power to 'cleanse', i.e. to render pure and permissible that which otherwise would not be so. It is part of a larger debate about ritual purity, of which the liturgical implications are taken up later (15.1ff.) and which belongs to the assertion that Jesus has power to save outside the Law.

8.4 The original has been tampered with. The actual cleansing, which appeared to be missing, was expressly inserted, thus destroying the point and pathos of the story, with the officious words 'the leprosy'—it was the man, not the leprosy, that was cleansed. (Luke 5.13 corrected to 'the leprosy left him'.) The injunction 'Be sure to tell no man', which follows the healing,* is a patent absurdity: everyone was bound to become aware that the leper had been cured, and in any case he is told in the same breath to 'show himself to the priest'. The same interpolator's hand is found at work again at 9.30 below (q.v.). An admission, if not an explanation, of the man's disobedience is provided by Luke—'but the word spread all the more about him' (5.15)—an

* Unless due to corruption. ὅρα μὴ ἐλλείπῃς σεαυτὸν δεῖξαι τῷ ἱερεῖ would mean 'be sure you do not omit to show yourself'; but the amendment is a drastic one.

embarrassed piece of composition, used and improved upon by Mark (1.45).

The same absurdity recurs in similar terms at 9.30 (q.v.) after the healing of two blind men: 'See that nobody knows', a command forthwith disobeyed. That blind men could become possessed of sight without anybody noticing is inconceivable, and the command was eliminated when the incident was repeated at 20.33.

8.5–13 The specification of Capharnaum does no more than separate this incident from the preceding one. Apart from 4.13 (q.v.) and its inclusion with Bethsaida and Chorazim in the curse at 11.23, Capharnaum recurs only at 17.24, at the beginning of another incident, with as little point as here. Josephus (*BJ* 3.519) gives an idyllic description of C.'s climate and fertility.

An 'officer commanding a hundred', ἑκατόνταρχος, is found again only at the crucifixion (27.54). Unlike κεντυρίων, which Mark 15.39 substitutes for it at the crucifixion—he omits the present incident—it does not necessarily imply a Roman officer, an implication which arises only from 8.10–12. Luke (7.2ff.) took it for granted that the officer was Roman, and composed an elaborate explanation for his encountering Jesus. Like the Jewish leper, the centurion addresses Jesus as κύριε, 'Lord'. The concluding sentence, 8.13, is expendable: the cure is presumed to be effected by the man's faith and the words of Jesus.

The occurrence proves that Jesus can heal at a distance. The necessary faith that he can do so does not need to be that of the actual sufferer. It is done by word of mouth alone (μόνον εἰπὲ λόγῳ): the gospel of Jesus is efficacious at a distance by word of mouth, and the benefit of faith can operate on behalf of others: the gentiles can be saved by receiving word of Jesus, and the salvation can be communicated by the believer to his family.

The natural (Jewish) 'sons of the kingdom' will be debarred; gentile converts 'from the east and the west' will enter the kingdom. The simile of a military commander calling up a soldier and sending him to do his bidding does not mean that Jesus sends spirit envoys to heal but represents Jesus' commissioning of his disciples to evangelize the gentiles.

8.6 'In dreadful torment', δεινῶς βασανιζόμενος, is an expression not used elsewhere; it is difficult to reconcile it with παραλυτικός, used in the mass healings at 4.24 and below at 9.2, which implies inability to move. The son was physically unable to come.

8.8 The sentence (copied by Luke) (lit.) 'I am not sufficient (ἱκανός) for you to come under my roof' is unexpected: it was not so much the unworthiness of the officer to receive Jesus in his house as the superfluity of Jesus going there at all that was the point.

8.9 The centurion's disclaimer has been in other respects distorted. If the words 'under command' are eliminated as a gloss upon 'under me', the requisite sense is restored: the point is not that the centurion has to obey his superiors but that he too can whistle up a subordinate and tell him to go to such-and-such a place and do such-and-such a thing, a meaning which has been obscured by glosses through failure to see that it is the same subordinate throughout.

The father's faith, effective vicariously on his child's behalf, perhaps refers to infant baptism in the gentile church. The bitter outburst 8.10–12, which confirms the officer not to be an Israelite, breaks the continuity of 8.13 with 8.9.

Abraham, Isaac, and Jacob will be taking part in the Messianic feast. The fact that they will be present there was sufficiently established in 'the scriptures' (22.29) for deductions to be securely based upon it. While there are Old Testament passages which prophesy the redeemed coming from both or all four points of the compass (cf. 24.31—the gentile church existed east as well as west of Palestine)—no kingdom literature which featured Abraham and his son and grandson is extant. Luke removed the passage from its context here and attached it (13.28, 29) to the eschatological prediction at 7.21–3 above.

What is obscure is the identity of those who will be cast out—the formula recurs at 24.51 to describe the fate of the ὑποκριταί. They are inadequately, and perhaps ironically, described as 'sons of the kingdom', i.e. those due to inherit it, or simply (if τῆς βασιλείας is not genuine) as 'sons'—presumably of Abraham etc. Not all Israelites will enter the kingdom, but surely not all will be excluded. Even the Baptist at 3.9 only declared that to be a 'son' was not sufficient in itself. The polemic intention is deliberately veiled—but from the context the targets should be those who deny the efficacy for non-Israelites of faith in Jesus' power to save.

8.14 The words 'came into Peter's house' were designed to follow 4.20 directly. 'Peter' is here without the definite article, which it has invariably elsewhere except at 14.29, where ὁ Πέτρος immediately precedes. The name 'Simon', apart from the list at 10.2, is used only once later, viz. in the unique combination 'Simon Peter' at 16.16. Elsewhere he is always simply 'Peter' (ὁ Πέτρος).

The phenomenon of Peter's mother-in-law is striking. Why

that particular relation, instead of a more obvious female such as sister, wife, or even mother, especially as Peter's wife or family are never alluded to? The archetypal mother-in-law in the Bible is Naomi in Ruth (1.6), who 'heard in the country of Moab that the Lord had visited his people in giving them bread'.

8.15 She has been chosen for a distinguished role. Her recovery is marked by her rising; but that she then prepared a meal—διακονεῖν means 'serve' food, cf. 4.11, 25.44—adds nothing evidential and is pointless unless it was to be the prelude to something else. 'Sitting at meat', ἀνακειμένου, refers back to it in
26.6 the original sequel, preserved at 26.6–13, where the incident of the woman and the jar of myrrh interrupts the transition from the high priests' resolve at 26.5 to the offer of Judas at 26.14. The object of moving the incident, in which Jesus feasted and was anointed,* would have been to obliterate the Messianic identification and downgrade the importance of Peter.

26.13 In the present form of the incident the acclaim given to the woman is wildly extravagant: to find anything comparable one would have to turn to the congratulation of Peter at 16.17 for having recognized Jesus to be the Messiah. The transfer necessi-
26.8 tated not only altering the identity of Simon (Πέτρος ὁ λεπρός) and the location (Βηθανία from 21.17) but composing a new dialogue—for ἀγανακτεῖν unqualified cf. 20.24—to supply a different significance to the woman's action. The altered dialogue introduced a grotesque antithesis between feeding the poor and anticipatorily embalming Jesus' body, a touch which afforded Luke (24.1) the motive he needed for the ill-explained return of the women to the tomb at 28.1 (q.v.). It also involved explicit emphasis on the expensiveness of the myrrh, which Mark (14.3) improved upon by smashing the jar itself, a feature which, if original, would have had to be retained. The lack of point in the transplanted and rewritten incident produced fascinating results: Luke (7.37ff.) took it away again from the context of Jesus' death and substituted an entirely new climax, making the woman a 'great sinner' and her action an act of contrition which procured forgiveness. John (11.2 and 12.1ff.) kept the story in the crucifixion context but linked it with that of Lazarus by identifying the woman as Lazarus' sister and the house as that of Lazarus. He dispensed entirely with a climax, but transferred the

* The anointing of the head is specifically an act of consecration, for which myrrh is used in Exod. 30.23. There is a verbal similarity (cf. p. 211) with Plato, *Republic*, 2, 398a μύρον κατὰ τῆς κεφαλῆς καταχέαντες.

anointing to Jesus' feet, taking a hint from Luke, whose 'great sinner' had wept on them.

8.16 There originally followed a night crossing of the sea under storm, allegorically representing the gentile mission, in which Peter played a prominent and dramatic role and which confirmed for the disciples the fact of Jesus' divine parentage. This episode was prepared, like the insertion of the discourse (see on 4.23), by a generalized description of healings, producing a 'crowd' which served the purpose of the narrative by motivating Jesus to stay while Peter and the other disciples crossed the sea in advance of him.

The original text was replaced by an expurgated version (8.24–7), which eliminated Peter, the water-walking miracles, and the acclamation of Jesus by the disciples. The displaced original was not, however, deleted outright but a place found for it at 14.23–36, where it breaks the intended transition between the feeding (14.13–21) and the topic of hand-washing (15.1ff.). It is significant that in its new position Mark (6.45ff.) and John (6.16ff.) both eliminated from it the Peter event as well as the recognition of Jesus as 'son of God'.

Traces of the substitution which remain here cause difficulty. (1) 'When evening was come' (8.16) was the necessary prelude to a night voyage, but those bringing their sick for healing had no need to delay doing so until late in the day; (2) Jesus in the original narrative put off departure 'until he could send away the crowds' (14.22), whereas here no sooner does he 'see a crowd around him' (8.18) than he 'gives command to depart'; (3) The term ὀλιγόπιστος (8.26), appropriately applied to Peter in the original (14.31), is inappropriate to the alarmed crew and passengers who purport not even to know who Jesus is (8.27).

8.17 The Old Testament *testimonium* is notably strained, since Isaiah's 'took' and 'bore' evidently did not mean 'took away'. The application was assisted by rendering מכאבות 'pains' in Isa. 53.3 as νόσοι, 'diseases'. (LXX περὶ ἡμῶν ὀδυνᾶται, 'suffers on our behalf', is quite different.)

8.23 'And when he had gone on board his disciples followed him' is designed to follow directly upon 8.18 'he gave the command to depart'. '*The* boat' (def. art.) means the boat implicit in 'gone on board'. There is no need to understand it to mean Peter's own boat, though the sentence no doubt gave Luke the hint which he exploited by making Jesus go aboard 'Simon's boat' (5.3) to distance himself from 'the crowds'. Between the two halves of the sentence have been inserted two brief repartees of Jesus, which should relate to departure for the mission field across the Mediterranean. Both repartees obviously convey a negative response. The second is not difficult to decode: 'quit without delay the doomed scene in Palestine'. The first repartee makes the same point in a different way: taking the fox as typical of animals which have their home in the ground—a fact missed by the gloss-writer, who balanced it with a general reference to the birds—Jesus asserts that the Messiah is not earth-bound in Palestine but can launch out across the Mediterranean.

8.20 This is the first of 29 occurrences in Matthew of 'son of man', a translation of בן־אדם, 'man, human being'. Applied always by Jesus to himself, it need nowhere be anything but a deprecatory periphrasis for the first person singular. Many of the occurrences, however, are in explicitly Messianic contexts while others, notably those linked with παραδίδοσθαι, 'be betrayed', are in the context of the Passion. The glorified and victorious figure in Dan. 7.13 is described as כבר אנש (Aram.), ὡς υἱὸς ἀνθρώπου (LXX), 'like a human being'. In consequence υἱὸς ἀνθρώπου may, in some or all of the places where it occurs, be intended, as in the Book of Enoch and some rabbinical literature (see Strack–Billerbeck i. 475–6), to signify the Messiah, with whom therefore Jesus would be identifying himself. Curiously, 'son of man', used incessantly by Ezekiel as the term with which he is addressed by God, occurs at Ezek. 13.1–4 in close proximity to 'foxes': 'Son of man, prophesy to the prophets of Israel . . . O Israel, thy prophets are like foxes in the deserts.'

8.24 An 'earthquake (σεισμός) on the sea' is unacceptable. The word may be an inadequate gloss upon some unusual word in the original for 'storm', such as λαῖλαψ, which Luke (8.23) and Mark (4.37) both have. Equally inappropriate is καλύπτεσθαι: a storm-tossed ship is at risk not of 'being hidden' but of sinking (καταδύεσθαι), which Luke (8.23 συνεπληροῦντο) and Mark (4.37 γεμίζεσθαι) both substituted. It is noteworthy that the original (14.24) also used a peculiar metaphor, 'tormented (βασανιζόμενον) by the waves'.

8.25 What did those who awoke Jesus expect him to do? They said, like Peter in the original (14.30), 'Save, Lord'; but how was he to do so without a supernatural act inconsistent with their astonishment (ποταπός etc., 8.27) when he performs it? A compensation was needed for the loss of the miracle of water-walking in the displaced narrative.

8.28 There is what looks like duplication between εἰς τὸ πέραν, 'the other coast', and εἰς τὴν χώραν τῶν Γαδαρηνῶν, 'the country of the G.' There was no need to create an alternative to the remainder of the story, with the exorcism of the lunatics and the hostility of the local inhabitants. These were not therefore repeated in the position to which the original narrative was transferred; but Gadara was altered to Gennesaret, and the now unmotivated hostility of the population was turned (παρεκάλεσαν–παρεκάλουν) into the description of a friendly welcome (14.35, 36), composed with prior knowledge of 9.20, 21 (διεσώθησαν–διεσώθη). Gadarenes, implying the place Gadara, was replaced in some ancient versions by Gerasenes and in one manuscript family by Gergesenes. In the corresponding passages of Mark (5.1–17) and Luke (8.26–37) there are the same variants, presumably as a result of comparison. None of the three names occurs elsewhere in the New Testament. Josephus knows both Gadara and Gerasa to the south-east of the Sea of Galilee, and Gergesaeus as the eponymous founder of a city destroyed by the Israelites (*Ant.* 1.139).

28–31 The narrative has been ruined by officious interpolations. The acclamation of Jesus as 'son of God' by the lunatics required no further elaboration or explanation. The exorcism was performed simply by Jesus' peremptory command 'Get you gone' (ὑπάγετε), and the destruction of the herd of swine was the proof that it had taken place.

8.33 There was no need for 'everything' to be explained; but the gloss omitted the crucial tidings which led on to the next sentence, viz. what had happened to the swine. Nevertheless, the interpolation may have inspired Luke (8.35, 39) to paint the scene of Jesus and the healed lunatic.

9.2 A series of individual healings, diversely allegorical, follows. In the first the faith which enables Jesus to heal is that of persons not apparently related to the sufferer. The healing confirms that, to be efficacious, 'faith' need not be on behalf of a family relative (a son, for example, cf. 8.8). It can equally avail on behalf of someone else: intercession on behalf of others can help to bring about their salvation.

Luke (5.18) felt more dramatic evidence of the 'faith' to be lacking. He supplied it by an incident which, if original, was not likely to be omitted. (The diminutive κλινίδιον repeating κλίνη 'bed' is characteristic of Luke; cf. ὠτίον repeating οὖς at 22.50, 51.) Luke was followed by Mark, who told the same story more tautly but, with his liking for numerical detail, added that four men were needed to carry the bed. However, the 'faith' of those who brought the sufferer, which enabled him to be healed by Jesus' command, was no more demonstrated by the trouble they took than by the fact of their decision to bring him.

9.4 The dialogue equates the salvation which Jesus affords to the gentiles with forgiveness of sins. This does not imply that the sufferers' malady was a punishment for sin or is to be cured by forgiveness: it identifies salvation with the extension of God's mercy to the gentiles outside the Law (6.11, 12). The power to save is inseparably bound up with the power to forgive, as Jesus demonstrates ('which is easier?', 9.5). To opponents who 'think evil in their hearts' (ἐνθυμεῖσθαι πονηρά—πονηρός specialized in the sense of denying Jesus' divinity) the purported absolution is blasphemy, the offence for which Jesus was executed (26.66). Jesus refutes a charge not publicly made but attributed by thought-reading: if the scribes had actually charged him with blasphemy, they would have been obliged to proceed against him forthwith. In reality, to deny Jesus' identity as the son of God is itself blasphemy, the 'blasphemy against the holy spirit' (see on 12.31).

9.8 The crowds glorify God for having given such 'authority' (ἐξουσία) to 'mankind' (τοῖς ἀνθρώποις). The expression is striking and significant. The gentile Church had to have a priesthood with authority to grant absolution. The mission to the gentiles will be exercised primarily by those who are themselves gentiles. This is underlined by the deferment of the next healings in order to relate the 'calling' to discipleship (modelled upon Peter's) of a tax-gatherer and the admission of him and his fellows to the sacramental meal which follows calling (cf. 8.15; Acts 16.34). A Judaizing challenge to this acceptance provokes the sharp and sarcastic retort at 9.12, followed by the key text from Hosea (6.6) about 'mercy and not sacrifice'.

Nowhere else in the book are 'the crowds' described as having been 'frightened' (ἐφοβήθησαν). Is there a corruption of ἐθαμβήθησαν (Mark 1.27), 'were astounded'?

Logically, Jesus' command at 9.2 ought to effect the healing. In order, however, to accommodate the refutation of 'the scribes', the effective words are deferred until a later point.

9.9 'Proceeding from thence', παράγων ἐκεῖθεν, a purely artificial connection between two events, is used again below, 9.27.

'Called M.' has to denote simply 'a man whose name was M.'

and not as elsewhere (e.g. 4.18) an alternative name. The name Matthew Μαθθαιος (cf. Μαθθαν 1.15) represents מתתיה ('gift of Yahweh'). The name recurs only in the list of apostles at 10.3. Its absence here would not be missed. The unambiguously Jewish and indeed Levitical name 'Levi' was substituted by Luke (5.27) followed by Mark (2.14). That Mark added 'son of Alphaeus' would be due to a wish to find 'Levi' on the apostles' list by identifying him with 'James son of Alphaeus'.

9.10 'In the house', ἐν τῇ οἰκίᾳ, conveys elliptically that Matthew had invited Jesus into his house to a meal, an invitation which Luke (5.29) was fain to render explicit. The meal is parallel with that above in Peter's house (see on 8.15), after his calling.

Despite its familiarity, the expression 'tax-gatherers and sinners', which recurs at 11.19, is an unnatural linkage of particular ('tax-gatherers') and general ('sinners'). In 18.17 'treat him as a gentile and a tax-gatherer' τελώνης is used to mean someone 'beyond the pale'; but the parallel 'tax-gatherers and whores' in 21.31, 32, an expression in which both terms are specific, suggests that 'sinners', ἁμαρτωλοί, may have been substituted, for decency, for 'whores', πόρναι. Curiously, the compound πορνοτελώνης is cited from Greek comedy, and τελῶναι is linked with πορνοβοσκοί 'pimps' in Aspasius (*c.* AD 110). In effect, 'tax-gatherers and sinners', or whatever it conceals, represents 'gentiles', and 'Pharisees' (see above, p. 64) their Judaizing opponents.

Three interpolations have caused grotesque distortions. (1) The Pharisees might call the guests 'tax-gatherers and sinners': the narrator must not. (2) The Pharisees put their question to Jesus' disciples outside: Jesus must not cut in and give the answer himself before they can reply. (3) Jesus equates sharing the meal with healing the sick: he 'called' only Matthew.

9.12–13 'Healthy' (ἰσχύοντες) is of course ironical, and the tone is notably acerbic. The quote from Hos. 6.6, which Luke and Mark do not have, is applied in the sense that converting the gentiles is 'mercy', which God prefers to the 'sacrifices' prescribed by the Law not observed by gentile converts. The same citation recurs at 12.7, curiously also prefaced by τί ἐστιν, governed by εἰ ἐγνώκειτε, as here by πορευθέντες μάθετε.

9.14, 15 An incident based upon the sacramental 'meal' leads naturally to raising and answering another question: why is it that the gentile church has such a meal when neither the Judaizers nor John's followers do? We know from 6.16 (q.v.) that the Judaizing church observed the practice of fasting. The general sense appears to be 'a marriage-feast is no time for fasting'; but then 'mourn' (πενθεῖν) should be 'fast', πεινᾶν, and the point that the eating will continue as long as the groom is there but stop when he has gone is superfluous. The verb 'cannot' (μὴ δύνανται) is curious: it is not so much that one *can't* fast at a wedding as that one *doesn't*.

9.15 Jesus' retort, 'You didn't expect us not to eat (νηστεύειν 'not eat', as at 4.2), did you? After all, this is a wedding!', presupposes familiarity with the identification of the Messianic feast as a marriage-feast (22.2–10; 25.1–11; Isa. 62.4) and the Messiah as the bridegroom. What is inappropriate at a wedding is not mourning (πενθεῖν)—that was not the complaint—but νηστεύειν, not eating.

The reference forward ('as long as the bridegroom, etc.'), presumably to the period after Jesus' resurrection and ascension, is irrelevant to the question. The interpolation was intended to prevent Jesus being taken to issue a lasting prohibition of fasting.

9.16, 17 The same train of thought is continued: the sacramental meal marked more decisively than anything else the novelty of Christianity and its break with Judaism and with John the Baptist's 'righteousness'. 'Of course the followers of Jesus differ (in this respect too) from those of John and from the Jews. What do you expect?'

Jesus' coming was the inception of a new dispensation (new clothes, new wine) which would be incompatible with that which it superseded.

The price of John the Baptist's recognition as Jesus' 'forerunner' was acceptance that Jesus superseded him and inaugurated a new era. This point, expanded later at 11.2–19, is illustrated here by the two similes of the new cloak and the new wine. Both have been heavily and officiously glossed. It is understandable that the conversion of the gentile world is compared to pouring 'new wine'—a common metaphor—into old or new skins. The appropriate corresponding analogy from clothing would be putting on a splendid new cloak on top of an old shirt—not a 'patch' on an old garment. But why ῥάκος, 'rag', creating the oxymoron 'new unfulled rag'? 'Rag' may be a mistranslation of בגד, which means a 'garment . . . of any kind, from the filthy clothing of the leper to the holy robes of the high priest, the simplest covering of the poor as well as the costly raiment of the rich and noble' (Gesenius–Brown–Driver–Briggs); but an 'unfulled rag' is in any case nonsense, whereas ἄγναφος χλαῖνα is found in the sense 'brand-new cloak' (see LSJ s.v.). The word ἐπίβλημα, taken to mean 'patch', has that meaning nowhere else and in LXX means 'cloak'.

8–25 'While he was thus speaking' is a purely linking device. The incident with which the series of individual allegorical healings now resumes extends the efficacy of vicarious faith so as to cover the salvation of a believer's child when already dead—though admittedly only 'just' (ἄρτι) dead—a belief implicit in the practice of 'being baptized on behalf of the dead', to which Paul (1 Cor. 15.29) appeals as support for the acceptance of personal resurrection. It also has obvious relevance to the practice of infant baptism (see below, p. 160). In the period between salvation and resurrection (ἠγέρθη 'got up', 9.25) the person saved was 'not dead but asleep' (9.24, cf. 27.52). The superfluous note that Jesus was accompanied by his disciples (9.19) is an intimation that he was about to perform a normative act: they too will be called upon to do the same in his absence. The designation of the parent, εἷς, 'a certain person' (cf. 8.19), as 'a ruler' (ἄρχων) is not functionally necessary to the narrative. Luke was puzzled by its apparent incompatibility with Roman rule and explained it away as 'one prominent in the synagogue' (8.41), a position for which Mark (5.22) produced the special term (ἀρχισυνάγωγος).

20–2 Into the incident is dovetailed a demonstration that faith in Jesus' power to save can take effect without his action or even knowledge—that is, after he has ceased to be present on earth. Luke (8.46) considered it necessary to provide some physical means for Jesus to be aware that the woman had been healed. Given the chronic nature of the woman's complaint, cure of it could not be verified instantaneously, for which reason Jesus assures the woman that it has taken place (σέσωκεν).

Innocent of the allegorical meaning, Luke (8.49), followed in greater detail by Mark (5.22), altered the narrative so that the daughter was only 'dying' when the 'ruler' made his request and did not die until Jesus was on his way. He also dramatized (similarly followed by Mark) the incident of the woman with the flux by stating that she had suffered from it 'for twelve years' (8.43), a hint which Mark (5.42) took to make the daughter twelve years old.

9.23 Flute-players (αὐλητάς) hired for mournings occur not only rabbinically (Strack–Billerbeck i.521) but also at Jos. *BJ* 3.437. As regards θορυβούμενον (here only in Matthew), the 'crowd' was surely not 'making a disturbance'. Corruption of ὀδυρόμενον or the like is to be suspected.

9.26 The transition to the next item has been contrived with the reference to notoriety (ἐξῆλθεν ἡ φήμη αὕτη = 4.24 ἀπῆλθεν ἡ ἀκοὴ αὐτοῦ), the verb παράγοντι (cf. 9.9), and the awkward 'When he entered *the* house' (which 'house'?), 9.28.

9.26–34 The two healings, 9.26–34, originally formed a single complex with 12.22–4, where the crowds' exclamation 'This is surely not the son of David' has to refer to the novel invocation 'Son of David' at 9.27 and where 12.24 repeats 9.34. The complex formed the prelude to a lengthy denunciation (12.25ff.) of those so obstinate or wicked as to deny that the power exercised by Jesus was none other than that of the holy spirit. For this purpose the sufferer healed had to be demonically possessed: this accounts for the choice of a mute. But a mute cannot shout 'Son of David!': hence two separate healings—of the blind men, whose invocation 'Son of David' is discounted by 'the crowds', and of the mute. The complex was divided by duplicating 12.22–4 with 9.32–4 and inserting 'blind' into 12.22. The duplication is betrayed by the vacuous exclamation 9.33 'Such a thing has never been seen in Israel before' to replace the pointed and vigorous 12.23 'This is no son of David', by the toning down of ἐξίσταντο 'were amazed' into the pedestrian ἐθαύμασαν 'marvelled', and by the exorcism being taken for granted ('when the devil had been cast out').

The division thus contrived of the original complex, 9.26–34 plus 12.22–4, had the effect, and no doubt the object, of creating a gap in which were accommodated (1) 9.35–10.42 containing the discourse 10.5–42, (2) the Baptist passage 11.1–24, and (3) the sabbatarian debate 12.1–13.

9.30 There is a verbal curiosity. The verb for 'admonish'—ἐνεβριμήθη, lit. 'snort upon', here passive but elsewhere found only in the middle voice—had appeared in the LXX of Dan. 11.30, referring to the Romans 'triumphing over' Epiphanes. This is its only occurrence in Matthew; but Mark introduced it (1.43) into the healing of the leper, and used it (14.5) in the anointing scene to denote the resentment shown by the disciples. John (11.33, 38) applied it in a quite different way to inward groaning.

See above on 8.4. The blind men shouted; Jesus rebuked them; but inside 'the house' he healed them. An interpolator has removed the words 'And Jesus rebuked them' to after the healing (when it was too late) and has supplied the content of the 're-buke' in the form of an impracticable prohibition, immediately ignored.

9.33 The impersonal expression οὐδέποτε ἐφάνη οὕτως, with no subject to ἐφάνη other than what is implied in the adverb οὕτως, is peculiar: it could be a deliberate echo of Judg. 19.30.

9.35 The purpose of the division of the 9.27–34 + 12.22–4 complex was to make room for the massive insertion 9.35–12.21 comprising principally (1) a discourse cognate with 5.3–7.27 (the 'Sermon on the Mount') and like it addressed to the Judaizing church, and (2) a John the Baptist passage reaffirming John's forerunner relationship to Jesus.

The first of those contents is prepared, not without artificiality, by an elaborate transition (9.35–10.5). Its first sentence is copied with minimum alteration from the introduction to the 'Sermon' (9.35 = 4.23), continued, conventionally, with 'seeing the crowds' (5.1). The rhetorical features of duplication and high-flown vocabulary (as at 4.24, q.v.) are again represented, by ἐσκυλμένοι καὶ ἐρριμμένοι. The topic of missionary effort is then introduced, under the metaphor of workers in the harvest field, at the price of illogicality by inviting the existing 'disciples' to petition 'the owner of the crop' for reinforcements. Without awaiting the outcome of the petition, Jesus himself proceeds to confer upon the existing disciples, without increasing their number, the missionary powers to exorcise and to heal. The number of the disciples, like that of the tribes of Israel (cf. 19.28), is stated as twelve, a number now first mentioned in this context. A list has then been there inserted of twelve names of persons designated, here only in the book, as ἀπόστολοι, 'emissaries', a derivative of the verb ἀποσστέλλω 'send out', about to be used in the envoi to the discourse (10.5 ἀπέστειλεν).

36, 37 The observation that 'the crowds' were 'confused and dejected' and 'like sheep that have not a shepherd' is unprepared by any part hitherto played by 'the crowds', who have been simply spectators and audience, occasionally surprised and admiring. If people are 'like sheep that have not a shepherd', the remedy must be to supply 'shepherds'; but this is evidently not the role envisaged in the discourse.

As for 'the crop being large but the workers few' (9.37, 38), the remedy must be more workers; but whether 'the owner of the crop' is God or Jesus, it is grotesque to invite the disciples to pray for him to send more workers into the harvest: Jesus is perfectly competent to do this himself, and if divine permission were indispensable, he would not need the prayers of the disciples to reinforce his own. To endow the existing disciples with special healing powers and send them out on mission (10.1) would not meet the deficiency.

Seeing the crowd and feeling compassion for them reappears in the prelude to the two miraculous feedings 14.14 and 15.32, each time with a different construction of the verb σπλαγχνίζομαι. Here the motive assigned is different. The verb σκύλλω, here only in Matthew, is used by Luke (7.6 and 8.49 = Mark 5.35) in the sense of 'bother', 'give trouble to'. It is a post-classical word not found in the versions of the Old Testament. 'Prostrate', ἐρριμμένοι, occurs here only in the New Testament. The two epithets are surprising in themselves and consort ill with shepherdless sheep ('like sheep . . . shepherd' in Num. 27.17, preparing for the appointment of Aaron by Moses).

9.37 'Beseech', δέομαι, is here only in Matthew, and ἐκβάλλειν, lit. 'throw out', is paralleled nowhere else in the book, not even at 12.35 (= 13.52), though there also the use is peculiar. The 'owner of the crop' is not quite 'owner of the vineyard', κύριος τοῦ ἀμπελῶνος, at 20.8. 'Crop', θερισμός, is elsewhere (13.30, 39) 'harvest-time'.

10.2 The first two pairs of brothers have occurred at 4.18–22, of which the word 'first' is possibly a recognition, but all the rest are also arranged in pairs. Of these, the eighth name, Matthew, has already appeared at 9.9 (q.v.); but of the remainder only Judas makes an appearance in the rest of the book. James, No. 9, is given a patronymic because there is another James, and Simon, No. 11, is given an epithet because there is another Simon: only Judas has a description not apparently needed for differentiation.

The same list (of course without Judas Iscariot) occurs in Acts 1.13 (where also it appears to be a later insertion), but following
10.4 Luke 6.15 Simon is called 'the zealot', deriving Καναναῖος (with κ) from קנא 'be zealous', because כנען 'Canaan' is invariably transliterated with χ (see on 15.22), and Judas 'son of James' replaces Thaddaeus. Of the seven names not previously mentioned, one (Philip) is Greek (like Andrew), and one (Bartholomew) is an Aramaic patronymic (Bar-Tolmai). Only four of the twelve—Simon Peter, James and John, sons of Zebedee, and Judas—play any part in the narrative of the book. Philip, however, and Thomas have substantial roles in John and Thaddaeus-Judas appears once in John (14.22), suggesting that John laid the list

under contribution to provide named interlocutors. All the rest reappear nowhere in the New Testament.

10.5 The word for 'charge', παραγγέλλω, occurs elsewhere in the book only at 15.35: in 11.1 διατάσσω, unique in the book, is used for variety.

The introduction of the discourse (9.35–10.5) created two problems which Luke took drastic measures to solve. First, there is no increase in the number of 'workers'; and secondly, those sent out never come back to report but simply reappear at 12.1 as if nothing had happened. Luke spread the available material over two separate missions (9.1–6 and 10.1–20), the latter six times more numerous than the other, and arranged a formal return (10.17) with an enthusiastic report.

5b–42 The discourse comprises a mass of absurdities and switches backwards and forwards between one line of argument and another, as if a bare skeleton had been padded out to create a speech.

The discourse is aimed at the same audience as the longer one at 5.3–7.24, with which is has in common the asseveration 'Don't imagine that I came . . .' (10.34 = 5.17). The 'wolves' whom the hearers will encounter (10.16) are none other than the 'wolves in sheep's clothing' of 7.15 (q.v.). Their audience is destined to incur Jewish hostility (10.17, 18) and be troubled by intrafamilial feuds. Many of the same phrases and motifs will be taken up again in the discourse over Jerusalem, 24.3ff. An advanced state of persecution of Jewish Christians with gentile co-operation is presupposed: the general situation is similar to that experienced by Paul (Acts 21.27ff.), which resulted eventually in his 'appeal to Caesar'.

The practical object of the discourse is to encourage the recipients to steadfastness by reassuring them that they can expect divine observation, approval, and reward.

5b–15 The discourse is an extraordinary concoction. It comprises two main themes, which are interwoven: (1) instructions for a mission to 'the cities of Israel' (10.5–15, 23, 40–2), and (2) a warning not to be alarmed by family divisions or by persecution (10.16–22, 26–39), with the promise that an all-seeing Father will reward staunchness. The treatment of the two themes, however, is characterized by portions of text, not of the nature of glosses or interpolations, which misinterpret or contradict the remainder. The second theme is more appropriate to a wider audience than the ἀπόστολοι; it is in fact applicable to all

Jewish believers. Hence the possibility arises that an original text addressed (like the 'sermon', 5.2–7.27) to the Judaizing church has been converted and expanded by intrusive matter, often unusual in thought or diction, into a missionary 'charge' to the ἀπόστολοι.

10.6, 7 The only reference in the book to Samaria or its inhabitants. The wording was obtained from 15.24, plus 4.17.

10.9 The reason for the warning against getting 'gold or silver' is already implicit in δωρεὰν ἐλάβετε, δωρεὰν δότε. It is no reason for going without ready cash, a stick and shoes, and a change of clothing; nor are those items of τροφή, of which 'the labourer is worthy'.

10.10 'Stay till you leave' is absurd. The following sentences are mere repetition; and 'if it be not worthy' contradicts the foregoing.

The word ἄξιος, which here denotes the opposite to not receiving the apostles or listening to their words, is used below (10.37) with μου, 'worthy of me', and (in the negative) at 22.9 of the 'undeserving' guests who did not come when called. It appears to be an in-word for a predestined category who heeded, or would heed, warning. Cf. Wisd. 3.5 'God proved them and found them *worthy* of himself (ἀξίους ἑαυτοῦ).' 'Greet', ἀσπάζεσθαι (cf. 5.47), is used to mean 'bless', 'speak peace', —Luke (10.5) spells this out.

10.14 The operation of shaking dust off one's feet is a difficult one. It was perhaps to meet this difficulty that Mark 6.11 substituted 'soil' (χοῦν); cf. Luke 10.11 ('wipe off').

10.15 The relevance of Sodom is that there will no longer be left 'in that city' a minority whose presence would save it (Gen. 18.32). The comparison ignores the difficulty that Sodom has already been punished and so will not, like 'that city', come up for judgement. The saying recurs at 11.24 (q.v.).

10.16, 17 The warning 'I am sending you out like sheep in the midst of wolves' requires no sequential admonition. 'Men' is too general a description of opponents. 'To be witness to them' comes from 8.4.

With the corresponding passage in Mark (13.9), this and Acts 22.19 are the only known references to corporal punishment administered in synagogues; cf. 2 Cor. 11.24. See, however, 21.35.

10.22 A direct import from 24.9, 13.

10.23 There is no point of reference for ἡ πόλις αὕτη, nor is ἡ ἑτέρα (πόλις) 'the other city (of two)' right; nor is it any reason for flight that the son of man will come before those addressed have 'finished' the 'cities of Israel'. 'Complete the cities' is a remarkable term; elsewhere τελεῖν, 'conclude', occurs in the book only in the formula 'finished these words' etc. (7.28, 13.53, 19.1, 26.1), apart from the conclusion in 11.1, 'finished instructing', which is no real parallel. Nor is there any to 'the cities of I.' (unlike 'the cities of Judah'). The term ἔλθῃ ὁ υἱὸς τοῦ ἀνθρώπου is used as equivalent to 'the end', on the basis of e.g. 24.30, 25.31: see on 8.20.

There are two major logical difficulties. If the apostles were not going to get around all the cities in time, the object of the exercise, to give due warning, would have been defeated. Secondly, while it is sense to say 'Hurry up, because otherwise you won't finish', it is nonsense to say, 'Hurry up, because you won't finish anyhow'.

10.24, 25 The argument—dependent for 'Beezebul' on 12.24, 27 and for οἰκιακοί on 10.36 below—'why should you expect to be treated better than I?' is out of line with the train of reasoning which follows at 10.28ff.

10.26 The meaning of 'all will be revealed' (i.e. at the judgement), as confirmed by 10.29 'God's omniscient eyes and ears will be watching and hearing you', is obliterated by the futile explanation at 10.27, which implies that Jesus is keeping part of his doctrine secret.

10.27 What will be revealed is how the accused behaves when put on trial, not some arcane doctrine committed to him by Jesus which he will disclose. Luke (12.3), with a brutality more akin to forgery than to conjectural emendation, rewrote: 'what you say in the dark will be heard in the light, and what you speak in the ear will be proclaimed on the housetops'.

10.28 'Fear from', φοβεῖσθαι ἀπό, is as impossible in Greek as in English. It is the appropriate construction for προσέχετε, 'beware', as above, 10.17. The expression φ. ἀπὸ προσώπου in the LXX, but only with God as the object, translating וייראו מפני or יראו מלפניו in Hag. 1.12, Eccles. 3.14, 8.12, 'fear before (from before) God', is not a parallel, and there is none in the New Testament. The form of the verb 'kill', ἀποκτεννόντων, here is unique (apart from the equivalent passage Luke 12.4) in the gospels. The words τὸν δυνάμενον, extremely awkward if they mean God, are an interpolation due to failure to recognize that ἀπολέσαι has the same sense of 'lose' as below (10.39).

10.31 The point is not that an all-seeing God saves the sparrow from falling but that he observes its fall: no believer is so obscure or unimportant that his fortitude under persecution will be overlooked or unremembered.

The composer of the similes of the sparrows and the hairs of the head was dominated by recollection of two Old Testament passages, regardless of the different context in which he was placing them. The passages are 1 Sam. 14.45, where the people demand that no harm shall befall Jonathan: εἰ πεσεῖται τῆς τριχὸς τῆς κεφαλῆς αὐτοῦ ἐπὶ τὴν γῆν. The other verbal echo is from Amos 3.5, εἰ πεσεῖται ὄρνεον ἐπὶ τὴν γῆν ἄνευ ἰξευτοῦ, where the 'fall' of the bird points to the activity and purpose of the bird-snarer. The mention of sparrows, by recalling 6.26–30 to the writer's memory, led him into the absurdity 'you are worth more than many sparrows'.

In his paraphrase (12.6) Luke omitted the sparrow falling to the ground and substituted lamely 'not one sparrow *is forgotten*'. He saw the relevant price was that of *one* sparrow and so, there being no half-*as* coin, substituted five for two *as*. Elsewhere (12.7) he left the sparrows out and inserted 'not a hair of your head shall be lost'.

The word translated 'farthing', ἀσσάριον, Latin *as*, *assarius* (*nummus*) (here only in the Old or New Testament), is unambiguously Roman. It was a bronze coin, minted locally in the Empire.

10.32 The word 'acknowledge', ὁμολογεῖν, occurs in only two other places in the book: literally, as 'promise' a reward, at 14.7, and at 7.23, q.v. There is also ἐξομολογεῖσθαι at 3.6, 'confess' sins, and at 11.25 (q.v.), 'thank'. There is no parallel to the construction here, ὁ. ἐν, lit. 'acknowledge *in* me (him)'. Luke 12.8 did not change it but substituted 'the angels in heaven' for 'my Father in heaven' (for which in Jesus' mouth see 7.21) and the passive ἀπαρνηθήσεται, 'shall be denied', for ἀρνήσομαι, 'I will deny', but probably merely for stylistic variation of the second limb, as also when changing ἔμπροσθεν into his favourite ἐνώπιον. (It is a strange coincidence that the words 'Father in heaven' immediately precede at 5.16 the same words which follow here, 'think not that I came'.) The word ἀρνεῖσθαι, 'deny', is only used elsewhere at 26.70, 72 of Peter denying an accusation. So far, however, as 'acknowledgement before my Father' is concerned, there is a certain parallel at 7.23 (incidentally the only other relevant occurrence—and a peculiar one—of ὁμολογεῖν), where 'I know you not' from Jesus is the sentence of condemnation at the judgement. But there those whom Jesus does not 'know' are not those who have not known (acknowledged) him but those who have claimed falsely to act in his name.

10.34 The word βάλλειν 'throw' for 'bring', though also used as 'put', e.g. 9.17 ('pour'), 25.27 (money at interest), may have been chosen because of 'sword'. 'Divide', διχάζειν, here only in the New Testament. The quotation from Mic. 7.6, 'son shall dishonour father, daughter rebel against her mother, daughter-in-law against her mother-in-law, and a man's enemies (shall be) those of his house', has been slightly adapted to follow 'divide'.

This passage and 10.13 (where the context is different) are the only occurrences of 'peace', εἰρήνη, in the book.

10.37 The unusual vocabulary underlines the unconditional nature of the believer's commitment to Jesus. φιλεῖν 'love' a person—not 'like' a thing (6.5, 23.6) or 'kiss' (26.48)—occurs here only in the book. Elsewhere 'love' (God, neighbour, etc.) is ἀγαπᾶν (5.43 etc.). To 'love' relatives more than Jesus must in the context mean to avoid family dissension by not becoming or not remaining his follower. No one who does so can be 'worthy' of Jesus, ἄξιός μου (cf. 10.11 above), which has to mean fit to be acknowledged by him at the judgement.

10.38 The second sentence (10.38), loosely attached by καί 'and', is an intrusion out of line with the clauses which precede; but the genuineness of the word σταυρόν, any more than the reference to the crucifixion of Jesus, is not open to doubt. (For crucifixion and σταυρός, of which this is the first occurrence in the book, see on 27.26.) The meaning of the sentence must be one applicable to all sincere converts, no less than preferring loyalty to Jesus before family ties. Whatever the meaning of αἴρειν τὸν στ. at 27.32 (q.v.), λαμβάνειν τὸν σταυρόν cannot mean 'be crucified': Jesus himself did not 'carry' his cross; 'carry one's cross' would be a pointless circumlocution for 'be crucified' if every victim was obliged to do so; and no follower, however loyal, can guarantee to get crucified. These considerations equally exclude any feeble metaphorical sense such as 'tribulation'. λαμβάνειν represents either 'be given' or 'pick up', e.g. in the hand (so ἄρτον 14.19, 15.36, 26.26). The only conclusion which remains is that the allusion is to a badge which was (at the time of composition of the intrusive words) customarily taken up, possibly at baptism, as a sign of conversion.

10.40 The logic of the conclusion is consequent upon ψυχή representing both 'life' and 'soul'. εὑρίσκειν, 'find', though Luke (17.33) and John (12.25) thought it necessary to paraphrase it, is used to mean 'save, avoid losing'.

10.40–2 The wind-up paragraph, 10.40–2, appears to revert to the theme in the first section (10.14) of missionaries being 'received' or not 'received'. The first sentence, reproduced by Mark (9.37) and Luke (10.16), made a great impression on John, who paraphrased it repeatedly (5.23, 12.44, 13.20, 14.21).

The conclusion of the discourse introduces a fresh line of thought akin to 10.14, namely the rewards of those who 'receive' them 'as prophets' or 'as righteous'. Then, incompatibly and separately, there follows a contrast with 'one of these little ones' given a cup of water; but by now the scale of rewards has run out. A 'disciple' does not have to be 'received' but only given a cup of water.

Though in 15.24 Jesus describes himself as 'sent', 'receives the Father' is difficult, and not present in the equivalent passage 25.35–40, 42–5. The original need have been no more than 'he that receives you, receives him that sent you' (i.e. me), the corruption having been caused by ἐμέ glossing τὸν ἀποστείλαντα. There seems to be no clear parallel for εἰς ὄνομα used, as here, for ἐν ὀνόματι. ψυχρόν 'cold', by itself, without ὕδωρ 'water', means 'cold water'.

11.1 The end of the discourse is followed by the next large Johannine insertion. The insertion has its own transition and mini-introduction, in the manner of 4.23 and 9.35, beginning with wording identical with that of 7.28. μετέβη ἐκεῖθεν 'removed thence' (cf. 12.9, 15.29) is intentionally indeterminate. '*Their* cities' echoes '*their* synagogues', 9.35.

11.2 'Sent *by* (διά) his disciples' conceals δύο 'two', which Luke (7.18) appears to have read or conjectured. It was normal to have two witnesses, cf. 18.16. For John's 'disciples' see 9.14.

'The prison' must be presumed implicit in the arrest reported at 4.12 (q.v.); but the transition is strained—why was the prison not mentioned at 9.14?—and the whole is inconsistent with 3.14. 'Is coming' has to be understood as in 'comes after me', 3.11; but it is not a recognized formula. This is the only passage in the book where Χριστός is used simply for Jesus (apart from 1.17: see p. 53).

The addition of the words 'or are we to await another?' is not entirely natural, whether προσδοκῶμεν is subjunctive ('are we to await?') or indicative ('are we awaiting?'), and Jesus' reply does not fit. It was because he 'had heard' of the doings of Jesus that John sent his disciples. So Jesus could hardly reply: 'Go and tell John what you hear and see', where the words 'hear and' exclude even the evasion that John was wanting eyewitness confirmation. Anyhow, John's disciples are not represented as 'seeing' any of the doings.

The passage fulfils, for all its difficulties, the purpose of establishing that John was contemporary with Jesus and subordinate to him. It had to wait until after the relation in 8–9.34 of the 'doings' on which the argument is rested.

11.5 The reply of Jesus consists in citing two passages from Isaiah: 35.5, 6 'Behold, God himself will come and save you', followed by a list of healings, most, if not all, of which have occurred in the preceding narrative; and 61.1 'The spirit of the Lord is upon me, for which reason he anointed me'. In both citations the point lies in the preceding words, which are either not quoted, as familiar to the hearers, or have been deleted: God has come, begetting Jesus by the holy spirit to be the anointed one, the Messiah. There have been blind (9.27), lame (9.2, paralysed), a leper (8.3), and dead (9.25); but though κωφός means 'deaf' or 'dumb' or 'deaf mute', the κωφός at 9.32 has speech, not hearing, restored. The comparable list in Isa. 35.5, 6 (blind, deaf, lame, dumb) distinguishes 'deaf' from 'dumb' as well as omitting lepers and the dead: חרש 'deaf/dumb' is translated by κωφός in LXX, but אלם 'dumb' by μογιλάλος, lit. 'hard of speech'. This latter is the word in Mark 7.32—the unique Marcan 'miracle' not in this book—where a 'deaf mute', κωφὸς καὶ μογιλάλος, is given his hearing and speech: the concluding sentence (Mark 7.37) has τοὺς κωφοὺς καὶ ἀλάλους. The desire to supply a dumb healing was possibly the motive for the one 'miracle' added in Mark.

πτωχοί, lit. 'beggars', means 'poor' in general, the classical πένης being disused. There has been no specific indication that those to whom Jesus delivered the message were the 'poor', either as such or amongst others. The term is taken esoterically; see on 'treasure' at 6.19ff. The verb בשר (Isa. 61.1) is translated (LXX) εὐαγγελίσασθαι. That word, which occurs here only in the book, is put into the passive to match the preceding clauses, as if εὐαγγελίζω were a transitive verb with the recipient of the good news as its object.

11.6 The meaning of σκανδαλίζω is to 'corrupt' or 'lead astray' those who would otherwise inherit the kingdom; but in combination with ἐν ἐμοί etc. it comes to mean 'dissuade from believing in me', e.g. 26.33. The sentence conveys a sharp admonition to John's followers to accept the Christian theology. 'Blessed', μακάριος, meaning 'deserving of congratulation', is also an esoteric term; see on 5.3–11.

11.7 'As they went away' and 'proceeded' are purely marks of transition; cf. 28.11. This auxiliary use of ἤρξατο, lit. 'began', i.e. 'proceeded', is uncommon in Matthew (possibly 11.20 and 26.22, 37) but massive in Luke and John.

The threefold question is curiously lacking in point or climax. The motive of watching a reed in the wind is too absurd to serve the purpose, and the implicit reference in the second question to John's clothing (3.4), even if the interpolated sentence, which spoils the symmetry, were genuine, would not produce a contrast with 'prophet'. In any case, it was not to 'watch' or 'see' John but to be baptized that the crowds went out (3.5); and incidentally, the variation θεάσασθαι . . . ἰδεῖν . . . ἰδεῖν is curious in so consciously iterative a passage. It is equally awkward, after having elicited that the crowds went out 'to see a prophet', to add 'and more than a prophet', unless they too accepted in advance that he was the subject of Mal. 3.1. καὶ περισσότερον 'even something more': περισσότερον here only in the book (apart from the variant at 23.13).

11.10 The first person in Mal. 3.1 ('before *me*') has been altered, making the words a promise from God to the Messiah.

11.11 The word γεννητός occurs in the New Testament only here (= Luke 7.28); 'man born of woman' is used simply for human beings in Job 14.1, 15.14, 25.4, but with the association of inherited uncleanness and (as γεννήματα γυναικῶν) in apposition to ἄνθρωποι in Ecclus. 10.18. 'Arise' is a term appropriate to prophets (24.11, 24, cf. 12.42). For being 'least' and 'great' in the kingdom of heaven see 5.19: μικρότερος, the comparative, is used for the superlative μικρότατος (not found in the New Testament) or ἐλάχιστος, as the positive μέγας or the comparative μείζων (18.1, 4) is used for the superlative μέγιστος (only found in the New Testament at 2 Pet. 1.4).

11.12 The sentence is massively and incurably corrupt. 'From the days of John the Baptist until now' cannot follow John's personal intervention; and βιάζεται, which is perverse, has provoked an unintelligible attempt at explanation ('violent men lay hands on it'). Nothing is wanting between 11.11 and 11.13: 'All the prophets and the Law (were) until John, who is no other than Elijah (the forerunner of God's intervention).' Luke (16.16), while paraphrasing, 'everyone forces his way (βιάζεται) into it', produced intelligibility by substituting εὐαγγελίζεται 'is proclaimed'. 'Prophesied', ἐπροφήτευσαν (which Luke apparently did not read), is inappropriate to ὁ νόμος. The order of 'the prophets' before 'the Law' is unique: Luke reversed it.

11.14 εἰ θέλετε δέξασθαι, not 'if you will believe it': 'receive' is used, as at 10.14 etc., in the sense of giving credence to the bearer of a message. John's followers do not reject him by following Jesus. When John announced the kingdom to be imminent, he was acting the part of Elijah (Mal. 3.23) implicit in the quotation above of Mal. 3.1, and his prophecy has been fulfilled by the appearance of Jesus. The reconciliation of the Johannines with the Church is neatly effected: μετάνοια 'repentance' (see on 3.2) has received a new import. The 'ears' that 'hear' are those which decode the inner meaning of John being 'Elijah' (cf. 13.9, 43, on the decoding of a parable), which the gloss ὁ μέλλων ἔρχεσθαι endeavoured to spell out.

6–12.21 The remaining space after Jesus' answer to John and words to 'the crowds' and before the resumption at 12.22 of the narrative artificially interrupted at 9.34 is occupied by material which is connected to that answer by a detectable logical train of thought: the present generation has failed fatally to realize that John's 'mightier' successor has arrived and a new era thereby opened. The logic has been obscured and overlaid by a series of officious explanations and elaborations. The style is distinctively rhetorical, characterized by artificial questions and oratorical flourishes.

11.16 'To what shall I compare this generation?' is a rhetorical question: why pose it when the answer is to follow immediately, and to whom is it addressed? The phraseology is repeated (perhaps imitated) by Luke (13.18, 20). No such preface is necessary for the simile of children playing Follow-my-Leader, where one team fails to obey a command mimed by the other; nor is it clear why the children have to be described as 'sitting in the squares'.

There was one great difference between the followers of John and those of Jesus, which had already been discussed at 9.14. The latter, not the former, had a sacramental meal at which they ate and drank, and which they shared with gentiles. The illustration of the difference is composed with an eye to 9.10–12; but the reader (who knows from 3.2 of John's asceticism) is unaware of John being accused of 'having a devil': it is not the same as the charge levied against Jesus (9.34 = 12.24) of using demonic assistance. 'This generation' (ἡ γενεὰ αὕτη; cf. 12.41, 42, 45, or 23.36) is placed in antithesis to both Johannines and Jesus-followers. It had been willing to listen to neither.

11.19 'So much', the diatribe ends triumphantly, 'for all the good their cleverness (σοφία) has done them'. This jibe at the expense of the 'wise', with whom Jesus' 'childlike' followers (νήπιοι) are contrasted, was designed to be followed immediately by 11.25, where Jesus thanks God for having confined his 'revelation' to the latter but where the contents of the revelation, 'all this' (ταῦτα), remain undefined.

The only other occurrence of δικαιοῦσθαι in the book is 12.37 with ἐκ τῶν λόγων σου, 'be judged on one's own words'. It is construed with ἀπό at Acts 13.38 in the same sense as ἐκ elsewhere (e.g. Gal. 2.16).

11.20–4 Between 11.19 and 11.25 is interposed, with the aid of the transition 'At that time Jesus lifted up his voice and said' (11.25), a section, 11.20–4, which bears all the marks of being spurious, a rhetorical exercise, inspired by 10.15 and designed to bridge the gap between 11.19 and the exultation at 11.25 over the σοφοὶ καὶ συνετοί. It is in any case fatuous, as no δυνάμεις (for which cf. 14.2) have been recorded in the named cities.

Luke (10.13–15) did a competent editorial job to iron the difficulties out. Observing that 11.24 had already occurred above at 10.15 and that Capharnaum cannot be cursed twice, once by 'thou shalt descend into Hell' and again by comparison with Sodom, Luke omitted the passage here and tacked 11.21–2 (Tyre and Sidon) on there, leaving Isaiah's curse on Capharnaum free-standing.

11.25 The wisdom of 'the wise' has not proved sufficient to penetrate the true meaning of John's announcement. Only 'revelation' by God's grace (cf. 16.17) could disclose the crucial fact of Jesus' identity to those conscious of their own helplessness (νήπιοι).

'At that time' is an articifial linkage; cf. 12.1, 14.1. 'Answering' here is purely pleonastic with 'said'; but a real parallel, where no question is stated or implied, would be hard to find.

The word ἐξομολογεῖσθαι (see on 10.32) occurs elsewhere in the book only at 3.6, where it has its natural meaning 'make a clean breast'. However, the meaning 'give thanks to' is well established in prayers: LXX 2 Kgs. 22.50 and especially Ecclus. 51.1, beginning 'I will give thanks to thee, O lord king . . . I give thanks (ἐξομολογοῦμαι) to thy name', followed as here by ὅτι 'because'. The elaborate title 'lord etc.', not specially called for by the context, suggests that the words may have been a regular exordium to a prayer (cf. 6.10). The expression κύριε τοῦ οὐρανοῦ καὶ τῆς γῆς, 'lord of heaven and earth' (= Luke 10.21), is unique in Matthew. With the repetition 'Yea father', and the superfluous and circumlocutory 'because so it was pleasing in your sight', it reinforces the impression of a liturgical framework.

'Clever', συνετῶν, here only (= Luke 10.21) in the gospels, may be an interpolated gloss to restrict the scope of 'wise', σοφῶν; but the hendiadys may be a Hebraism, cf. Isa. 29.14 'the wisdom of the wise and the cleverness of the clever'. There is no corresponding hendiadys, however, to νήπιοι, here only (= Luke 10.21) in the gospels except at 21.16 citing LXX, on the technical sense of which and of παιδία see on 18.1.

11.26 'Yes' (ναί), as a mark of repetition (unlike 11.9 above), the use of ὁ πατήρ as vocative instead of πάτερ as above, and the circumlocution for 'this was your good pleasure' are redolent of liturgy.

For οὕτως used almost as a noun, cf. 9.33. A close parallel is at 18.14. εὐδοκία 'good pleasure' occurs here only (= Luke 10.21) in the gospels, apart from the angelic song at Luke 2.14.

11.27 The identity of Jesus, known only to the father, is a matter of revelation by God (cf. 16.17); but it can be revealed by the son, to whom that power has been devolved (cf. 28.18). This logic, which is impeccable, is interrupted by interpolation with an irrelevant statement about knowledge of the father, which is not in question.

11.28 Knowledge of the identity of the son is what makes possible that relief from the obligations of the Law in which the passage culminates. The promise of 'surcease' (ἀνάπαυσις) is to all persons who can be described as 'toiling and burdened'. The surcease is obtained by accepting Jesus' 'yoke', presumably in substitution for that under which they 'toil and are burdened'. Their present yoke is a hard one (opposite to χρηστός 'comfortable') and attached to it is a load which is heavy (opposite to 'light' ἐλαφρόν). The 'yoke' metaphor implies a person carrying a load on a shoulder attachment, and not a yoke of draught animals pulling a weight.

The invitation to 'take my yoke' is an abbreviation for taking my yoke *and the lighter burden which I attach to it*; for there are two separate sources of discomfort—the yoke itself, which is uncomfortable, and the load, which is heavy. If the yoke and burden complained of are the obligations imposed by 'the Pharisees' (cf. ch. 23) and Jesus offers converts less onerous obligations, the invitation is strongly anti-Judaizing.

The 'gentle Jesus meek and mild' interpolation is irrelevant and conflicts with the invitation. Those addressed cannot be relieved by 'learning' a milder and more inoffensive behaviour; they are not burdened because they are cruel (opposite to πραΰς) or proud (opposite to ταπεινός) but because of what has been put upon them by others.

The language, but not the sense, recalls Ecclus. 51.26–7 in praise of 'instruction' (παιδεία): 'put your neck under the yoke (ζυγόν) . . . see that I toiled (ἐκοπίασα) little and found for myself much relief (ἀνάπαυσιν)'. The quotation from Jer. 6.16 has 'surcease', as in the Hebrew (מרגוע 'rest, repose'), not 'sanctification' (ἁγνισμός) as in LXX.

12.1 The insertion of the discourses on the missionaries and on John, like that of the 'Sermon on the Mount' (see on 8.1), does not conclude without an illustration or two in allegoric narrative form. They turn on the sabbatarian commands and prohibitions sought to be imposed upon gentiles. 'Pharisees' are produced to object when the disciples prepare and eat food (bread) on the Sabbath. On the face of it, the plea that King David committed sacrilege too is no defence. But there is allegory: it was loaves presented as a sacrifice to God in the Temple which David and his companions in breach of the prohibition ate to save their lives. In any case, runs the alternative answer (which would have been superfluous if the first were conclusive), the Law exempts work done on the Sabbath by priests in performance of their priestly duty. In short, the priest who gives communion to the gentiles on the Sabbath does not break the Law.

The objection of the Judaizers ('the Pharisees') to the communion liturgy being performed in the gentile church on the Sabbath is rebutted first from Scripture and then separately by practical example. The passage belongs to a period when the Jewish Sabbath had not yet been superseded in the gentile churches by the Christian Sunday, κυριακή, 'the day of the lord', who is 'lord of the Sabbath' (12.8). Had objection been taken literally to the disciples plucking and eating ears of corn on the Sabbath, it would have been irrelevant to refer to David and his followers eating the shewbread—not on the Sabbath!—or to the priests—and no others!—being permitted to go about their duties as such on the Sabbath. The scriptural confutation is neat and conclusive:

the 'bread' of the communion is an offering which has been presented to God, and those who administer it to the worshippers are 'priests'. The setting in the cornfield, where the workers reap the harvest of converts (cf. 9.37), is an encoded reference to the gentile mission field. In the practical example (12.13) the 'healing' represents the salvific effect of the communion, bread of salvation, which heals and saves, and the superfluous command 'stretch out your arm' may well be an allusion to the reception of the sacramental bread.

Luke (6.3), not suspecting allegory, jibbed at making 'the son of man is lord of the Sabbath' the logical reason (γάρ) and turned the sentence into a separate observation ('and he said to them . . .'). Mark (2.27), adopting that phrase, went further and wilfully misinterpreted 'son of man' to mean mankind.

12.4 The absence of a counterpart to 'something greater than the Temple is here' (cf. 12.41, 42) arouses suspicion that the first argument too was originally clinched by 'a greater than David is here', which fell victim to deletion. It would account for the awkwardness of describing Jesus as τοῦ ἱεροῦ μεῖζον. Reference to the gentile churches is confirmed by the Hosea tag about 'mercy' and 'sacrifice' (see on 9.12–13).

2.9–14 Connected by purely formal transition (cf. 11.1, 15.29), the second incident is modelled upon that of the paralytic at 9.2–8 (τότε λέγει 12.13 = 9.6). The selection of a sheep as the animal at risk and the (not strictly relevant) emphasis on 'one' conform with the application of 'lost sheep' (18.12) to salvation. It may be intentional that the word used for 'lift it out' (ἐγερεῖ) is not really right for e.g. ἐξελεῖ, but is the term for 'raising up' from the dead. The insipid conclusion (12.12) is a more than usually officious interpolation.

12.10 The received text describes 'them' ('the Pharisees', presumably) as 'asking' Jesus 'if it is permitted to heal on the Sabbath'; but ἐπετήρουν 'watched', which Luke (6.7, followed by Mark 3.2) either read or conjectured, is evidently right. Its corruption into ἐπηρώτησαν 'asked' resulted in 'if he will heal' (θεραπεύσει) being altered into 'if <it is permissible> to heal' (θεραπεῦσαι). If the interlocutors had wanted to denounce Jesus, they would not have started by asking if what he intends to do is permissible. Jesus, as elsewhere, answers an unspoken thought. That the day was the Sabbath is treated as implicit in the reference to 'their synagogue'.

.14–23 What follows provides the transition back to the main narrative after the insertion 9.35–12.13; but the text has been seriously perverted, with the result that Jesus is made uncharacteristically to seek to conceal himself and his activities. Upon the face of it, the Pharisees' 'plot' to 'destroy' Jesus anticipates the plot (26.4) of 'the high priests and elders of the people' at Jerusalem which introduces the arrest and trial. If the text here were sound, something of that sort, namely measures to 'destroy' Jesus, would have had to follow directly. We know, however, what did have to follow, viz. the accusation of healing by demonic assistance (12.25). In any case, the successful 'plot' against Jesus' life, when it came, was not by 'the Pharisees'.

In order to regain the main narrative, what 'the Pharisees' must do is to accuse Jesus falsely of healing with demonic help, a charge which he rebuts below but which does not amount to 'destroying' him. The clue lies in the parallel passage 22.15, where 'the Pharisees' set a trap for Jesus, ὅπως αὐτὸν παγιδεύσωσιν ἐν λόγῳ. The word ἀπολέσωσιν has been substituted for some such word as διαβάλωσιν, 'accuse falsely'; and then in order to explain why the 'plot' was not carried out, Jesus was made to resort to self-concealment—an action so curious that a prophetic text was inserted to justify it (12.17–21).

12.16 The expression φανερὸν (here only in the book) ποιεῖν, 'make public', is peculiar; ἐπιτιμᾶν 'charge' recurs at 16.20. There is a weakness in that, if Jesus healed 'all', the 'many' must all have been sick.

12.17–21 As usual, the citation of Isa. 42.1–4 corresponds closely with neither LXX nor M, and there is some suspicion of deliberate adaptation. Apart from minor verbal variations, 'son' is substituted for 'Israel' (LXX) or 'servant' (M), the gift of the spirit is moved from past to future, and 'gentiles' hoping on his name (LXX) is preferred to 'isles (איים) waiting for his law' (M).

12.23 For μήτι 'surely *not*' cf. 7.16. Something has happened not continuous with the past of Israel. That something is 'the son of God' inaugurating a new dispensation.

12.24 ἐν, translated 'by', suggests 'in the name of' (cf. 7.22), presumably implying the (vocal or silent) invocation of the demon king's name.

The name is supplied as 'Beezebul', but probably by interpolation, since the name divides the definite article τῷ from ἄρχοντι, which requires it. Beezebul occurs in the New Testament only here (and in the derivative passages of Mark and

Luke) and in 10.25 (q.v.). It may be formed vituperatively from Baal and זבל 'dung', as Beelzebub (e.g. 2 Kgs. 1.2) is formed from Baal and זבוב 'flies'; but alternatively it may be Baal and זבל 'height'. The word Baal בעל itself means 'master'.

12.25 'Knowing their thoughts' implies that, as at 9.3, the critics had not spoken. But there would be little point in refutation of an unspoken (and unattributed) charge. The sentence is borrowed from 9.4 (q.v.), a passage already exploited at 12.10ff.

2.25–9 The argument has been subjected to heavy glossing, which resulted in further interpolations:

1. The unusual οὐ σταθήσεται, 'will not stand', was glossed ἐρημοῦται, 'is ruined', which generated the duplicate 'every city or house divided against itself'.
2. 'How therefore shall his kingdom stand?' spelt out the deduction already implicit in 'is divided against himself' and incidentally attributed a 'kingdom' to Satan.
3. 'If Satan is casting out Satan' was glossed 'if I cast out the devils by Beezebul', leaving, when inserted, an apparently incomplete sentence, which was then completed by οἱ υἱοὶ ὑμῶν . . . κριταὶ ἔσονται ὑμῶν.
4. 'And then he will plunder his house' is otiose after 'enter the house' at the beginning of the sentence.

12.28 It is assumed as acknowledged fact that Jesus, the son of God, acts by virtue of the holy spirit. For the conferment of the 'spirit of God' on Jesus see 3.16. Luke 11.20 substituted 'finger of God', perhaps recalling the exclamation of the Egyptian sorcerers at Exod. 8.19. Unusual are 'Satan' (cf. 4.10), 'kingdom of *God*' (see on 3.2), the use of ἄρα for 'then', and φθάνειν, here (and Luke 11.20) only in the New Testament.

2.30–2 Acknowledgement of the identity of Jesus as the son of God being a matter of revelation, the absence of objective evidence presented a continuing problem. In the appalling commination which now follows, it is solved by treating failure of recognition (i.e. rejection) of the fatherhood of the holy spirit as due to inherent badness, πονηρία. Such perversity is of course fatal because it bars access to salvation 'in this world and the next'. It is consequently unforgivable and irremediable. Argument is replaced by abuse. Those who are not 'with' Jesus, are *ipso facto* 'against' him, not recognizing him for who he is, and can have no part in the proclamation of his salvation.

12.30 The first half of the saying is a prosaic gloss on the aphoristic second half. In the context—especially with the emphatic διὰ τοῦτο λέγω ὑμῖν (cf. 6.25) following—the meaning has to be that acceptance of the operation of the holy spirit is indispensable to the work of salvation.

At 25.24–6 συνάγω 'collect' and σκορπίζω 'scatter' are equated respectively with θερίζω 'reap' and σπείρω 'sow'. Applied here, this would point to the original having been inverted: for example, ὁ μὴ σκορπίζων μετ' ἐμοῦ οὐ συνάγει, 'he that does not sow with me does not reap', if the οὐ were lost after ἐμοῦ, could be amended by inversion into ὁ μὴ συνάγων μετ' ἐμοῦ σκορπίζει, with σκορπίζω misunderstood in a bad sense, 'squander'. Luke (11.23) left the sentence as it stood; but in a different context (9.50), by what looks like deliberate contradiction, he reversed it: 'who is not against us is with us', in which Mark (9.40) followed suit.

12.31–7 A passage of bitterly repetitive invective, in which those who deny Jesus' identity are described as committing a blasphemy to which they are naturally prone, being πονηροί, 'bad'. Nothing better can be expected from them. In the end they will be punished for what they have said. It was denial of Jesus' divine sonship which made Israel 'unfruitful'. Significantly, the threat is finally narrowed down to a second person singular (12.37).

12.31 The second sentence (12.32) is an expansion or explanation of the first (12.31), where 'and blasphemy', which may have originated as an alternative to 'sin', destroys the antithesis. Later, the word 'holy' is betrayed as interpolation by being attached to 'spirit' only at its second mention.

'Blasphemy' (βλασφημία), here equated with 'saying a word against', occurs in LXX only in the plural Ezek. 35.12 in the sense of boastful threats. The verb (βλασφημεῖν) is in Dan. 3.96 'whoever blasphemes against the god of Shadrach etc.' and 2 Macc. 10.34 'blasphemed exceedingly and uttered forbidden words', cf. 9.28 'murderer and blasphemer' (of Antiochus). In this book the word occurs in three other passages. At the trial of Jesus his implicit self-identification with 'the Christ, the son of God' is hailed by the high priest as inculpation of blasphemy (26.65). In another (15.19) the word is the last in a list of six sins (murder, adultery, etc.) which are bracketed with 'evil thoughts' as 'proceeding from the heart' and 'defiling man'. The third passage is 9.2, where Jesus' statement 'your sins are forgiven' is treated by scribes as 'blaspheming'. The polemic here boldly reverses the charge: it is 'blasphemy' to deny or to dispute Jesus' sonship, which endows him with 'the spirit' of God. The declaration that forgiveness is not only not available 'in the age to come', i.e. at the judgement, but 'in this age' would convey, if strictly interpreted, that there is to be no forgiveness for, or reconciliation with, those holding the opposite Christology.

Luke (12.10) transferred the whole passage into the context of 10.32–3.

12.33 'Making' a tree 'good' or 'bad' is a strained expression. Those who deny Jesus' divine sonship condemn Israel to 'unfruitfulness' (cf. 7.17). The familiar tree and fruit metaphor has been severely corrupted. The alternative is not between a decision to 'make' a tree and its fruit good or bad but between the tree being one or the other.

12.34 'Progeny of vipers' occurs, likewise in the vicinity of a tree metaphor, at 3.7, attributed to the Baptist; and it recurs in the Woes at 23.33. Evil thoughts 'overflow' (περίσσευμα, cf. περισσεία Jas. 1.21) from 'the heart' in words in the same way at 15.19. The metaphor of the store is the same as at 13.52.

36, 37 An 'idle (ἀργόν) saying' in this context must be equivalent to that previously designated 'evil' or 'blasphemy'. ἀργός, lit. 'unemployed' (20.3, 6; 1 Tim. 5.13), is being used, rather like 'foolish', by deliberate litotes or euphemism for 'false, scandalous'. The concluding sentence, which unlike the foregoing (12.31, 34) is in the singular, has a proverbial ring ('condemned out of your own mouth'). Words spoken now will be a sufficient ground for final condemnation. καταδικασθήσῃ, a gloss on δικαιωθήσῃ (cf. 11.19), has generated a duplicate.

.38–42 In the absence of proof, the opponents demand a 'sign', which is refused: belief is a matter of faith.

Continuity with the foregoing is perhaps implied by 'answered', ἀπεκρίθησαν, though the request may be no more than a device to elicit the response. In 24.24 'false Christs and false prophets' will authenti-cate themselves by 'giving signs', σημεῖα, an expression from Deut. 13.2, where the persons who thus authenticate themselves urge 'going and worshipping other gods whom you do not know'. Jesus here abruptly refuses a σημεῖον, describing those who request it as 'an evil and adulterous generation', an expression which, apart from the doublet 16.4 (q.v.), occurs at Mark (8.38) 'this adulterous and sinful generation'.

Those who insist on a sign are put to shame by the gentiles, who accept Jesus on the strength of verbal tidings. The gentiles are typified by the Ninevites, who believed Jonah's preachment and repented without any sign. (Jonah's whale and his gourd, if signs at all, were signs to him, not to the Ninevites.) The Queen of Sheba came all the way to Solomon's court on the basis of mere report. (The sense requires ἀκούσασα, corrupted to ἀκοῦσαι.)

12.39, 40 Misunderstanding of the argument resulted in two successive interpolations: (1) it was assumed that Jonah *did* give a sign; and (2) that sign was then identified with the crucifixion. 'Stand up (rise up) at the judgement with' means to bear hostile witness which convicts. Jesus is 'greater' (cf. 12.6) than Jonah or Solomon, who were merely prophet or king. In the later narrative Jesus does not spend 'three days and three nights' in the earth. (The substitution of καρδία 'heart' for κοιλία 'belly' appears to be due to καρδία θαλάσσης, 'depth of the sea', in Jonah 2.4 (after Ezek. 27.4), but the variation tends to spoil the point.) 'The men of N.', ἄνδρες N., where ἄνδρες adds nothing to the sense, is not a locution used elsewhere in the book. It may be due to ἄνδρες Νινευη at Jonah 3.5.

The interpolators' efforts were no more desperate than that of Luke (11.30), who substituted the explanation that Jonah was a σημεῖον to the Ninevites as Jesus 'to this generation'.

12.43–5 There is a logical, if unstated, connection of thought with the preceding context. Only Jesus' divine nature enables him to vanquish the gods of the gentiles (δαιμόνια), so much so that the gentile convert who has been freed from an 'unclean spirit' must not remain without a replacement for his former belief: he must not σχολάζειν, 'be left unoccupied'. In the context, it is by faith in Jesus as the son of God by the holy spirit that the place of the old error must be occupied.

12.43 'Unclean spirit' as at 10.1 and Zech. 13.2 ('I will extirpate the false prophets and the unclean spirit'). In these two places and 8.16 πνεῦμα, 'spirit', is used instead of δαιμόνιον. The vocabulary of the whole passage is exceptionally luxuriant, viz. 'waterless places' (ἄνυδροι τόποι) instead of e.g. 'desert' (ἔρημος), σχολάζειν in the sense of 'be vacant', and 'vacant, swept, and tidied'—all choice words, matching the humorous exaggeration of *seven* others '*worse*'.

12.45 The concluding sentence is an attempt to forge some sort of link with the immediately foregoing passage. Luke (11.24–6) had the same object when he transplanted the section to follow 12.30.

The foregoing emphatic asseverations of Jesus' divine parentage are shortly followed by a collection of parables (13.1–52), which centres upon the annihilation of the 'enemy' (13.28) who teaches contrary doctrine. The collection is preceded and followed by two duplicate incidents (12.46–50 and 13.53–8) which dispose of the implicit contradiction of that parentage offered by his putative family circumstances.

12.46 The last occasion where Jesus was expressly described as speaking 'to the crowds' was 11.7, since when much has happened. The phrase, however, is only designed to create a transition and frame a setting—not very successfully, because 'outside' (ἔξω) implies standing outside a building or hall rather than on the (surely visible?) fringes of a crowd. Luke (8.19–21) did his best to put this right by explaining that 'because of the crowd' a message had to be sent 'in'!

12.50 The interpolated explanation at the conclusion destroys the force of the incident. Deductions as to the ultimate size and composition of Joseph's family obviously do not arise: the omission of reference to the human stepfather was inevitable and carries no implication that Joseph was already dead.

13.1 'Out of the house' reflects the assumption that the preceding incident occurred when Jesus was inside a building. The parables are formally signed off at 13.53.

'On that day' is purely a link, as at 22.23 (cf. on 3.1). It appears that two 'sat down' sentences have been combined, a sitting by the sea and a sitting in the boat. The latter created an allegory of the Mediterranean or worldwide mission: it was the only way Jesus could reach so many people. As at 5.1 and 24.3 on the mountain, Jesus teaches sitting, implying authority. Luke (5.1–11) neatly worked the picturesque touch into the calling of Peter etc. (See on 4.18.)

13.3 παραβολή in the sense of an allegoric story appears to be confined to the New Testament.

13.3–50 The long parabolic discourse which follows contains two sequences each comprising (1) a major parable, (2) an explanation for speaking in parables, and (3) a private interpretation of the parable for the disciples. One of these sequences (the darnel) is a virulent attack upon a teacher who leads converts astray. The other (the sower) is comparatively innocuous and deals with the diffusion of the gospel. It is natural to deduce that the latter sequence was composed to replace the former.*

The shorter parables, which have no connection with the main themes, will have been inserted (in two blocs 13.31–3 and 13.44–8) in order to provide a reason for explaining why Jesus spoke 'only in parables'.

The natural, and original, rounding-off was 13.51: 'Have you understood all these things?' . . . 'Yes', followed by what is not really one of the parables, viz. 'So you now understand why a scribe, in order to become a disciple of the kingdom', has to get rid of 'new as well as old possessions'?—his Judaism first and then his adherence to the Judaizing faction.

Luke (8.4–15) handled all the problems in a characteristic manner. Having changed the tell-tale plural 'parables', 13.3a, into the singular, he took over 13.3b–33 entire. Then he dropped altogether, as duplicates, the darnel and its interpretation and the wind-up at 13.34–5, but used the 'mustard-seed' and the yeast together elsewhere (13.18–21). He also dropped the treasure, the pearl, and the net. All these are alterations which could not have occurred in the opposite direction.

13.3 'Behold', ἰδού, belongs with the event, not at the beginning. '*The* sower', ὁ σπείρων, is wrong: ἄνθρωπος is normal at the commencement of a parable (cf. 13.24), and ὁ could represent ἄν̅ο̅ς absorbed between -εν and σ-, with τοῦ σπείρειν a gloss (albeit a correct one) on σπείρων.

13.5 Whatever the implied method of sowing—presumably broadcast—it must have secured that the seed, except on the road, was immediately covered up with soil. Otherwise the birds would have eaten the rest too. With this covering of soil above, the seed sank roots as it germinated; but where the ground was stony, the blade no sooner sprang up, εὐθέως ἐξανέτειλεν (the verb so used in LXX Gen. 2.9 and Pss. 103.14 and 146.8), than it withered, because it had struck no root. The shoot would not appear 'immediately' after sowing, nor would sunrise (ἡλίου ἀνατείλαντος) be the necessary condition of it withering. The sense has been obscured by interpolations.

13.7, 8 The 'thorns' or 'thistles' are a mystery. They cannot at the time of the sowing have been at all advanced, i.e. they had not

* The Translation has been rearranged to correspond with this hypothesis, but the Commentary follows the traditional order.

yet 'come up' (ἀνέβησαν), as otherwise the seed would not have reached the ground and been covered with soil. The use of cardinal numbers in the sense of 'a hundred*fold*' etc. is unusual.

13.11 'Mysteries', μυστήρια (= Mark 4.11, Luke 8.10), is not found elsewhere in the gospels. Common in the Epistles, it recalls the striking expression οἰκονόμοι μυστηρίων θεοῦ in 1 Cor. 4.1. It is a term which has liturgical implications. ἀναπληροῦται and προφητεία (13.14) are similarly unique.

The paradoxical proverb 13.12 (cf. 25.29) breaks the connection of thought between 13.11 and 13.13.

.13, 14 The references to 'seeing' here and below, irrelevant in the context, are due to the endeavour to conform with the wording of the Old Testament citation.

The Isaiah passage (6.9–10)—its text here, exceptionally, corresponds precisely with LXX—was a pointed irony at the expense of the Judaizers: 'But you have always been determined to shut your eyes and stop your ears to what it behoved you to know.' 'Because', ὅτι, is correct, rather than the expected final 'in order that' (ἵνα) which one family of manuscripts has substituted: Jesus' disciples are now to 'hear', in the sense of understanding the meaning of, the parable.

13.17 The 'prophets' and the 'righteous', linked again at 23.29, are the same two superseded categories as at 10.41 (q.v.).

13.19 Since the first convert has 'not understood', it is strictly superfluous for the birds to gobble him up or the Devil to snatch (as in the interpolation) 'what has been sown in his heart'. It is the meaning peeping through which causes illogicality: the Devil is the Judaizing missioner who steals converts who have not grasped the pro-gentile gospel. The 'persecution' which causes the new convert to 'defect' (13.21) is Jewish persecution (cf. 5.11, 10.17). It follows that the 'care of the world' and 'the snare of wealth' which 'choke' the third convert and prevent him from passing on the gospel have correspondingly theological meanings (for μέριμνα cf. 6.25ff.). The fruitful seeds (13.23) are the converts who make others.

13.24 The insertion of the alternative parable begins with a jolt, introduced by a formula obtained from 13.31 (cf. 13.33) below. In this formula, παρέθηκεν, 'propounded', though correct in the sense of putting forward a philosophical or other proposition, is peculiar: elsewhere in the gospels (e.g. Mark 6.41, Luke 9.16) it is used of 'serving up' food.

'Is likened', ὡμοιώθη, though it recurs introducing parables at 22.2, is not strictly equivalent to 'is like', ὁμοία ἐστίν (13.31 etc. below). The point of using the past of the verb is not clear.

13.25 One would expect 'When *he* slept, his enemy . . .'; and the original may have been ἐν τῷ καθεύδειν αὐτὸν ἦλθεν ἐχθρός, since 'the men' is not the natural equivalent of 'the servants', and the master would be asleep as well as the servants. But then, God,
13.28 whom the master represents, never sleeps! 'Some enemy', ἐχθρὸς ἄνθρωπος, has the force of ἐχθρός τις. Darnel-seeds, if eaten with the wheat, are poisonous but could not be separated out by primitive winnowing processes; hence the need to reap the darnel separately if it had not been eradicated by hand earlier. 'Good', applied to the 'seed', means 'wheat', not 'clean' in the sense of free from admixture. The order to the reapers implies a field intersected by numerous paths.

13.31, 32 σίναπι means 'mustard' and κόκκος means 'seed'; but a mustard-seed is not particularly small and does not grow into a tree in the branches of which birds roost. The words are therefore wrong. Luke 13.18, 19 kept the parable but omitted the statement that the seed is the 'smallest' and the plant the 'largest', and he planted the seed in a 'garden', not a 'field'. To make things worse, the expression recurs in equally puzzling circumstances at 17.20, apparently signifying a microscopic quantity.

The largest (tallest) trees are pines, which have also a notoriously small seed; but how was πίτυος corrupted into σινάπεως, and in two places (unless the one was altered by comparison with the other)? If the original was πίτυος, 'is the largest of plants' would probably have been added after the corruption to σινάπεως. There is here a recollection of the visionary tree in Dan. 4.12, 21, and especially of Ezek. 17.23, 31.6, and Ps. 103.12 (where κατασκηνοῦν 'pitch their tents' also occurs)—all three referring to 'cedars'.

13.33 The point is lost unless the (small) quantity of the yeast is stated or implied: a measure of quantity corresponding to σάτα τρία has fallen out. The word represented by ἐνέκρυψεν, 'hid', must have indicated a process of 'mixing' (ἐνέμιξεν), which is persisted with until the dough rises.

13.34 The brief replacement for the answer at 13.11–17 to the question 'Why in parables?' finds a less wounding Old Testament precedent. The first line of the citation of Ps. 77.2 is verbally as in LXX; but in LXX the second runs 'I will utter riddles from the beginning', ἀπ' ἀρχῆς, M 'from ancient times' (מני קדם).

13.36b 'Interpret', διασάφησον, is used elsewhere in the New Testament only at 18.31, 'report'. One family of manuscripts has φράσον, 'show', which may be the original; but δ. is used in LXX Gen. 40.8 of 'interpreting' dreams. The parable 'of the man who sowed' (13.18 τοῦ σπείραντος aor.) had to be specified because of the three lesser parables intervening.

The interpretation equates the seed not with 'the word' but with the various persons who hear it: the sower is sowing potential converts.

13.38 'Sons of the kingdom', a Hebraism meaning those who will enter the kingdom, is chosen as an antithesis to 'sons of the Devil', his followers.

3.41–3 The eschatology is closely related in thought and language to the commination at 7.23 (q.v.). This passage and 25.41 are the only appearances of ὁ διάβολος in the book except 4.1–11 (q.v.). Apart from Heb. 9.26, the expression συντέλεια τοῦ αἰῶνος, the 'ending of this (pre-judgement) world' (for αἰών cf. 12.32), for 'the end' τέλος (see 10.22) is unique to this book (here, 24.3 and 28.20). τὰ σκάνδαλα, lit. 'stumbling-blocks', are what cause converts σκανδαλίζεσθαι 'to fall away' (see on 11.6); but it is awkward to equate them with persons, 'those that do unrighteousness'. The phrase occurs in Zeph. 1.3, where it is a later insertion, found in M but not in LXX, and thus presumably third century BC or later. The terminology of σκάνδαλον etc. and ἀνομία is virtually unique to this book in the New Testament, while the Hebrew equivalents והמכשלות את־הרשעים are mainly 'post-exilic'. 'The furnace of fire' (κάμινος here only in the New Testament—κλίβανος 6.30—except in Revelation) is tautological and peculiar.

'The righteous will shine out . . . in the kingdom of their father' does not conform to the picture in 25.34, nor correspond with any feature in the parable itself. It strongly recalls 5.16 (q.v.).

13.44 A man, presumably while digging (as an employee or tenant) in a field not his own property, finds buried treasure. He has thus (like 'this last' in the vineyard at 20.14) obtained it for a trifling outlay, and, again like the gentiles, in someone else's plot. He buries it again, ἔκρυψεν, and lays out whatever sum is necessary to buy the field.

13.45 ἐμπόρῳ, 'merchant', is suspicious, as elsewhere the actor in the parables is 'man' ἄνθρωπος (or γυνή, v. 33!), which one group of manuscripts inserts here. If the man was a pearl merchant, his action would be pointless. If he was a merchant in anything but pearls, his profession is irrelevant. The sense requires that he be an amateur pearl-fancier who acquires one fine pearl in preference to all other possessions.

13.47 σαγήνη 'net', ἀναβιβάζω 'pull up', ἄγγος 'container' are found only here in the New Testament. σαπρός 'bad' (lit. 'rotten'), in antithesis to καλός 'good', is used of trees (7.17) and fruit (12.33).

The parable of the net and the fish is out of line with the preceding parables, which allegorized the kingdom as an inestimable prize. The specialized terms πονηρός and σαπρός give the allegory away: at the end of the world the 'good' and the 'bad' will be sorted out and dealt with accordingly. The code of catching fish for making converts (cf. 4.19) has enforced awkwardnesses (e.g. 'burning' bad fish) upon the piscatorial analogue. The gloss has (correctly) copied the conclusion (13.49) from the interpretation of the darnel parable (13.40, 41).

13.52 'Become a disciple to the kingdom' is an expression not paralleled by 'became a disciple of Jesus' at 27.57, one of the only two other occurrences of μαθητεύειν in the gospels—the other is at 28.19.

13.53 The same formal transition is used again—also, as it happens, after a parable—at 19.1.

13.54–8 The incident is based upon, and intended to confute, that related at 12.46–54, the derivation being evidenced by the appearance of 'sisters' as an afterthought (like 'sister' at 12.50). That Jesus is the son of God was asserted at 12.45ff. by denying that he has any mother or siblings other than his disciples. That argument is confuted here by confronting Jesus with a father, with a mother 'called' Mary, with four named brothers, and with an indefinite number of (unnamed) sisters.

'Home town', πατρίς, in the gospels only in this story; strictly, '*father*'s town or country'. In 9.1 ἰδία 'own country'; but the event there does not depend on the location. Elsewhere (7.28, 22.33) the crowds are 'amazed' (ἐκπλήσσονται) 'at his teaching' (ἐπὶ τῇ διδαχῇ αὐτοῦ); the reason is not stated. What it was that Jesus 'taught' 'in their synagogue' (cf. 4.23, 9.35) is pertinent but not reported—Luke (4.17) supplied the missing information.

Neither ἡ σοφία αὕτη 'this wisdom' nor αἱ δυνάμεις 'the miracles' is a suitable summary of the implications of Jesus' teaching: the sentence arose out of a gloss on 'whence has he *all this*?' below.

13.55 'The carpenter's son' is impossible when it has nowhere been stated that Joseph was a τέκτων ('artificer' in stone, wood, or metal). Any temptation to transpose the τ, making τεκόντος, 'the son of the man who begat him', must apparently be resisted: τίκτειν is normally used of the *mother*; and although it is not unexampled for the father in fifth-century Greek (Aeschylus, *Choephori*, 690; Sophocles, *Oedipus Coloneus*, 1108), the argument requires an unambiguous word such as γεννήσαντος. To treat the sentence as a colloquial statement, 'this is no carpenter's son', would run counter to the drift of the context. Luke was right to substitute 'Joseph' (4.22).

13.57 'And house', καὶ ἐν τῇ οἰκίᾳ, is irrelevant to the context,
and may have originated in τῇ πατρίδι αὐτοῦ τῇ οἰκείᾳ, 'his
13.58 *own* country', cf. τῇ ἰδίᾳ πατρίδι in John 4.44. Curiously,
ἀπιστία, 'lack of faith', occurs nowhere else in Matthew; elsewhere ὀλιγοπιστία (see on 6.30) is used.

The conclusion is intolerably lame, the incident having already served its purpose. The people of the place may have been 'turned against' Jesus, but we are not told that they did anything about it. This lack Luke (4.28–30) dramatically remedied with the attempt (miraculously foiled) to push Jesus off a cliff. The proverb-like statement about the prophet is a devious way of saying that a prophet is never honoured in his own town (cf. John 4.44); but is that true, and is it true that a prophet is honoured everywhere except in his own town? Luke (4.24) eliminated the double negative, but Jesus has been made to downgrade himself into 'a prophet'. Mark (6.6), who stayed with Matthew, did his best by having Jesus 'wonder' at the people's ἀπιστία.

14.1–12 The passage 14.1–12, clumsily constructed and artificially linked at the end into the subsequent narrative, confutes the allegation (which was incompatible with Jesus being the 'son of God') that Jesus was John 'resurrected from the dead'. Grossly inconsistent with the Baptist's other appearances as a contemporary of Jesus, the allegation is here attributed to Herod. In order to sustain it, it would be necessary to show how (1) John had been killed and (2) Herod had verified the disappearance of his body. The story, which is incompatible with whatever explanation of John's arrest must originally have been given at 4.12, excluded (2) by explicitly leaving Herodias in possession of John's head (14.11) and relating that Herod surrendered the trunk to the disciples (14.12).

That the Herod–Salome passage is an insertion is proved by its defective reconnection with the continuing narrative (14.12 'and they went and informed Jesus'), which confuses current with past time; but it differs radically from the other Baptist insertions. Their purpose was to represent John as having acknowledged Jesus as his destined 'mightier' successor. On the contrary, if Herod's assertion here was even rational, let alone true, he would know that he had already killed John before Jesus' public acts began. The Salome story, which Luke (9.7–9) rejected, is not strictly necessary to explain ἐκ τῶν νεκρῶν 'from the dead'—that only needed a bald statement that Herod had put John to death in prison—but it supplied apparently corroborative detail and incidentally removed two difficulties, explaining why Herod did not put John to death upon his arrest and why he was unable to verify the disappearance of his corpse, having relinquished it to John's disciples.

The insertion tends to call in question the contacts described elsewhere of John with Jesus. The editorial endeavour (14.12, see above) to make the killing of John appear a contemporary event was probably an unsuccessful attempt to counteract the damage. Luke (9.7–9) sidestepped the problem: Herod only *hears* 'some say that John had risen from the dead, others that Elijah had appeared, and yet others that one of the old prophets had arisen'—material obtained from 16.14. Herod himself then denies John's identity with Jesus: 'As for John, I decapitated him—so who can this be?' (i.e. it cannot be John)—this, although Luke does not relate the decapitation at all!

Sensing that the matter could not be left there, Luke added 'and he (Herod) sought to see Jesus' (9.9), and was careful to arrange such an interview after Jesus' arrest (23.7).

Mark (6.14–16) got into a mess. He began by writing: 'And king (not tetrarch!) Herod heard—for his (Jesus') fame became public—and they said, "John the Baptist has risen from the dead, and for that reason the mighty powers are at work in him".' At this point Mark observed how Luke had coped, and copied him: 'But others said that it is Elijah, and others said that it is one of the prophets.' He then altered Luke's conclusion into a question: 'Has John, whom I decapitated, risen again?', omitting the indispensable reference to further enquiry. Mark's dependence upon Luke is also betrayed by his retaining the accusative Ἰωάννην ungrammatically after ὃν ἐγὼ ἀπεκεφάλισα.

The Salome tale, with its unique wealth of dramatic detail, which anchors John firmly in secular history, is remarkably isolated. Whatever were the circumstances surrounding John's arrest at 4.12, there was no room in the narrative there for anything to do with Herodias. The Salome story made John a martyr to his principled denunciation of the Herod–Herodias marriage and explained how Herod's reluctance to execute John came to be overcome.

14.1 'At that time' is purely transitional (cf. 11.25, 12.1). Herod 'the tetrarch' (as opposed to Herod 'the king', 2.1), not previously mentioned, is assumed to require no introduction to the reader. Also called Antipas, he was King Herod's youngest son, whom, after Herod's death in 4 BC, Augustus appointed in accordance with Herod's will to be ruler of that portion of Herod's dominions—hence tetrarch, ruler of a fraction—which comprised Galilee and
14.2 Peraea (Transjordan). He had no sons, a difficulty which cannot be removed by taking παῖδες to mean 'courtiers, pages', meanings only possible where the context dictates: εἶπεν 'said' called for an audience. The second part of Herod's exclamation is curious. The expression αἱ δυνάμεις elsewhere (7.22, 11.20–3, 13.58) means 'mighty works, miracles'. Why should 'he does miracles' be expressed by 'the mighty powers are at work in him'? The clause may be designed to supply a reason for Herod's otherwise unmotivated assertion.

δυνάμεις here may be due to its occurrence in the immediately preceding context (13.58).

14.3 The language of the narrative is in many particulars curious. 'Put him away' (ἀπέθετο), here only in the gospels, is peculiar for 'imprisoned'; so is 'for the sake of' (διά) Herodias; and so is 'have her' (ἔχειν), which leaves it open whether John was speaking before or after Herod took Herodias, an event which is implied
14.6 rather than stated. γενεσίοις γενομένοις is not really right for ἐν γενεσίοις, nor is there any point in the feast being a birthday-feast, as there might be, for instance, in a marriage-feast (γαμηλίοις).

The key to Herodias' revenge is the meaning of ἤρεσεν 'took his fancy'. Herod's sworn promise would be an extravagant form of applause after a dance, and Herodias could not have foreseen it so as to have her daughter primed with the answer. 'Took Herod's fancy' is euphemistic abbreviation: Herod persuaded her to do his pleasure by promising her whatever reward she wanted afterwards. Having performed her part of the bargain, as counselled by her mother, she exacted the ghastly price.

14.7 Again the language is peculiar: ὅθεν, here only in the gospels in the sense 'for which reason', not quite the required conjunction; ὁμολογεῖν as 'promise' here only in the New Testament (cf. on 10.32); likewise προβιβάζειν 'coach' and ἀποκεφαλίζειν 'decapitate' (= Mark 6.16, 27, Luke 9.9). The girl's request was that the head be given to her there and then, not that it be given to her 'on a plate'. The brutal force of δός μοι ὧδε (cf. φέρετέ μοι ὧδε at 14.18, perhaps the model) is diminished by the addition of ἐπὶ πίνακι. The next sentence, which construes with difficulty, is defective. Herod 'the tetrarch' would hardly now be called 'the king', and the obligation upon him did not need explanation by reference to 'the oaths' and the witnesses. The command that the head be given to the girl cannot be duplicated by the command to behead John. Without the sentence the presentation of the Baptist's head would take place in private. Its sole effect in the narrative is to introduce, what would otherwise be lacking, an indication of reluctance upon Herod's part to perpetrate the deed. The graphic subtlety of the original has been destroyed by interpolations, which Mark (6.27) already found.

The passage 14.1ff. is the first to be encountered since Chapter 2 which contains references to what purport to be historical personages; but there is no correspondence between the contents of the passage and our other information about those persons. That other information is almost exclusively derived from Josephus.

According to Josephus (*Ant.* 18.109) Herodias was previously married not to 'Philip'* but to the tetrarch's half-brother Herod, and Herodias' daughter by her former marriage, Salome, here apparently still a girl, was married at an unspecified date to Philip (*Ant.* 18.137). The arrest and execution of the Baptist in *Ant.* 18.117—a passage apparently an insertion in its context—bear no resemblance to the account here. Josephus explains Herod's decision to eliminate John as intended to forestall a potential rebellion owing to John's popularity.

14.13 As the narrative approached the definitive declaration of Jesus' identity (16.16, 17) and the climax at Jerusalem, room had still to be found for the original lake-crossing and water-walking incident (14.24–36) and for the duplicate feedings (14.14–21 = 15.32–8). They are now inserted, loosely attached with similar formulae of transition, viz. 14.13 ἀνεχώρησεν ἐκεῖθεν; 15.21 ἐξελθὼν ἐκεῖθεν ἀνεχώρησεν; 15.29 μεταβὰς ἐκεῖθεν.

* The name is here omitted, perhaps for this reason, in one MS group: its presence in some MSS in Luke 3.19 may be due to contamination from here. In the same group of MSS the dancer is Herod's own daughter, another Herodias.

Jesus does not react at all to the news of John's death and burial. Instead there is a transitional passage of which the embarrassments are due to its paving the way for the insertions which follow, viz. the duplicate feeding (14.14–21) and the original lake-crossing and water-walking (14.24–36, see above on 8.18). The 'boat' is an awkward and apparently superfluous feature which creates the ludicrous picture of Jesus sailing away for privacy and the 'crowds' pounding after him along the shore like a coach along a towpath. The result, however, was to provide (1) 'the' boat (and by implication the lake), (2) the separation of the disciples from Jesus, which was necessary for the lake-crossing episode, and (3) the crowds, which were necessary for the feeding.

14.14 The unheralded healing of the crowds is due to 15.29–31, where the mass healing is preliminary to the mass feeding.

14.15 The duplicate feedings (14.14–21 = 15.32–8) resemble one another so closely as to exclude the possibility of their being reports of two separate actual events: the one has been composed on the basis of the other, with the intention, therefore, of replacing and not standing alongside it. Mark (6.31–44, 8.1–9) transcribed both feedings; Luke (9.12–17), more conscious of literary style, contented himself with the first. The main difference between the two alternatives, which is numerical, must be intentional and significant.

The analogy between the feedings and the 'last supper' (26.26) suggests that the narrative is an allegory of the communion—a ceremony in which bread is blessed and broken by a priest, distributed by assistants, and received by worshippers seated as if at table, perhaps by separate sexes in view of the expression 'men, besides women and children', which is common to both alternatives but illogical, in so far as it diminishes the total of persons reported to have been fed.

A striking feature of the narrative, common to both alternatives, is its emphasis upon the left-overs—not a natural indication of how many people had been fed, which is in any case stated specifically. The meaning seems to be that the bread, once blessed and broken, may be or should be kept. Both alternatives accept this duty of retaining—'reserving' is the later liturgical term—the residue. The symbolism of the number of containers required for the surplus must have been considered crucial and its alteration have been deliberate and polemical—in particular the replacement of the number of the seven churches of Asia (Rev. 1.11) by the number of the twelve tribes of Israel. It assisted the alteration if the number of loaves (from seven—they started with seven loaves and finished with the same number of boxes of fragments!—to five) and the number of those fed (from 4,000 to 5,000) were also altered.

On this assumption the original feeding would have been the gentile-oriented 'seven' alternative, with the Jewish-oriented 'twelve' alternative based upon it. This is consistent with Jesus saying in the 'seven' alternative (15.32), possibly by way of allegorical allusion to the 'three' days between crucifixion and resurrection, 'the crowd have been attending me for three days now, and if I let them go away hungry, they may collapse on the way'. So startling, improbable, and unprepared an assertion could scarcely replace, but might well be replaced by, the clumsy, rationalistic motivation in the 'twelve' alternative, where the disciples ask Jesus to send the crowds away to buy food in the villages and he retorts, 'They have no *need* (χρείαν ἔχειν, cf. 3.14) to go away; *you* feed them.' It passes belief that ἡ ὥρα παρῆλθεν, 'the hour is past', means 'it's past dinner-time': neither Mark 6.35 (ἤδη ὥρα πολλή, 'a late hour') nor Luke 9.12 (ἡ ἡμέρα ἤρξατο κλίνειν) accepted it. Why should those who went back to their villages have to *buy* (ἀγοράσωσιν) comestibles (βρώματα)? Luke, substituting 'find provender' (εὕρωσιν ἐπισιτισμόν), transferred the buying to the disciples' ironical remonstrance, 'Surely you don't expect us to *buy* provisions for them (ἀγοράσωμεν βρώματα)?'

It may also not be accidental that the 'seven' alternative uses the term εὐχαριστεῖν 'give thanks'—cf. 26.27—(instead of εὐλογεῖν) and that the 'twelve' alternative describes the 'celebrant's' attitude—'looked up to heaven'. Even the substitution of κόφινος 'box' in the 'twelve' alternative for σπυρίς 'basket' could conceal a liturgical allusion: the *cophinus* is mentioned by Juvenal (Rome, *c.* AD 100) 3.14 and 6.542 as a cultic implement of Jews. The vocabulary of the 'seven' alternative is more choice in at least two cases: the use of ἀναπίπτειν (instead of ἀνακλίνεσθαι), the specific word for sitting down to eat ('reclining'), and of παραγγέλλειν (instead of κελεύειν) 'instruct'. Where the 'twelve' alternative has χόρτος 'grass' instead of γῆ 'ground' for sitting on, there may be a hint, which John 6.10 followed up, of an allusion to Ps. 23.2, 'green pastures'.

14.17 The fish, which feature in both alternatives, are a nuisance and do not fit—who ever thought of breaking and distributing fish? They must therefore have been allegorically indispensable, prompting, this being an allegory of the communion, the conjecture that the practice of impressing upon the host the fish-sign ΙΧΘΥΣ for Christ already existed (cf. 7.10).

.22–33 The original water-walking episode, transferred from 8.16 (q.v.). Its introduction here is awkward because the feeding has been presented (14.15) as an alternative to 'sending the people away'. There may be an allusion to the formula of dismissal at the end of the communion.

14.23 The ascent into the mountain to pray is a device to allow time for the disciples' boat to reach a sufficient distance from the shore. It should have dispensed with ὀψίας γενομένης, derived from 8.16.

4.34–6 A welcome is substituted for the rejection of Jesus at 8.34 (q.v.).

15.1 The dialogue which now follows would have come immediately after the first alternative feeding (14.15–21), had not the lake-crossing intervened.

Suddenly, without apparent occasion, 'Pharisees and scribes' make the journey from Jerusalem to complain that the disciples do not perform ablution before eating 'bread'. Hitherto the 'Pharisees' have always obligingly been on hand wherever Jesus was (cf. on 9.10). Mark felt the difficulty and made only the 'scribes' come from Jerusalem; but this does not help, as the 'scribes' too have hitherto been around, usually in the reverse order 'scribes and Pharisees' (5.20, 12.38, 23.13ff.). As at 9.11 (introduced by a similar form of words), the reference is to the feeding, or communion, which has just been recorded: the disciples have distributed the 'bread' (ἄρτος) to the crowd apparently without prior ablution. An opposing party, defined as Judaizers by their provenance 'from Jerusalem', is in liturgical dispute.

When Jesus' answer to the objection comes at last, at 15.11ff., it is that people are defiled not by what goes into them but by what is 'in their hearts' and comes out in word and deed. The retort has been boldly broadened into the equivalent of a sweeping repudiation of the Jewish dietary Law, a repudiation so bitter and emphatic as to show that the issue was of more than minor importance, as though the attempt to impose Jewish dietary rules threatened to undermine the mission of the gentile church: the unity and survival of the church itself would be put at risk by those who (on whatever ground) asserted that the communion of the gentiles was 'unclean'. The ruling which Jesus gives is promulgated expressly to 'the crowd' (15.10); it is accompanied by an exceptionally strident assertion of unique orthodoxy (15.13) and bitter denunciation of opponents; and it ends with a scathingly worded repetition given to Peter (15.15, 16).

Into all this has been embodied (15.3–9), irrelevantly to the objection and illogically, a counter-attack by way of retort that the 'tradition' to which the opponents appeal is (in a quite different context) no better than a fraudulent means of evading the rigour of the Mosaic Law. The way is paved for this counter-attack by the reference of the 'Pharisees and scribes' to 'tradition', and it is rounded off by Jesus being represented as turning away from them to 'the crowd'.

The proposition (see above on 8.3) that 'Jesus purifies' has been boldly broadened into a repudiation of dietary purity: the 'body of Christ' which the gentile church administered knew nothing of the law of dietary purity. Indeed, the impurity is in what comes out of the 'hearts' (15.19) of theological opponents who 'blaspheme' against the identity of Jesus: their 'wicked' (πονηροί) 'thoughts' (διαλογισμοί, see 9.4) and the βλασφημίαι (see 12.31) are key accusatory words.

15.2 The 'tradition' appealed to has proved difficult to identify. It was the Law (Exod. 30.20), not 'tradition', which enjoined ablution before sacrifice; but in any case the 'Pharisees' are unlikely to have contended that the Eucharist was a sacrifice. The 'tradition', too, against which the counter-attack is launched at 15.3, relating to the fifth commandment of the Decalogue, is otherwise unknown and obscure. δῶρον, no doubt, can, as at 5.24, mean an offering (to God); but ὃ ἐὰν ὠφελήθης cannot mean 'whatever benefit you may be entitled to', nor can οὐ μὴ τιμήσει, 'shall not honour', mean 'shall not be obliged to honour'. The treatment of 'honour' as exclusively material is surprising.

15.7 The Isaiah citation (Isa. 29.13) is closer to LXX (though not identical) than to M. Only the concluding words are directly relevant; but the allusion to 'the heart' in the second sentence may have commended its inclusion.

15.10 The command to 'listen' is logical; the command to 'understand' is not. The words appear to be chosen as a foil for the reproachful reply to Peter below, and use συνιέναι as in 13.13.

15.12 The choice of the term σκανδαλίζεσθαι 'be turned away, defect' (see on 11.6), which proves the 'Pharisees' to be dissentient followers, is deliberate. The disciples argue that to insist will split the church. Jesus brushes this aside: the opposing doctrine will die out anyhow, and the result would have been to lure others to destruction. He accepts the consequences of breaking with the Judaizers: ἄφετε αὐτούς, 'say goodbye to them'. There is the same collocation of 'blind leaders' with ὑποκριταί (= Pharisees) at 23.16, 24 (ὁδηγός in these two passages only in the gospels).

15.15 Peter repeats the formula from 13.36 (where one group of manuscripts has φράσον as here for διασάφησον, the only other occurrence of φράζω in the New Testament), though the similitude explained is not 'a parable'. ἀκμήν, 'still', here only in biblical Greek; Mark 7.18 substituted οὕτως. ἀσύνετος here (= Mark 7.18) only in the gospels.

.18, 19 The very act of querying the identity and authority of the son of God is a sign of an 'evil' (πονηρός) 'heart' (καρδία). The thought, the vocabulary, and the bitterness are closely related to 12.30ff. and 9.2, 3. If 'evil thoughts' emanating 'from the heart' issue in defilement, it is curious that evil *deeds* are then included in the list—murder, adultery (doubled with πορνεῖαι 'fornication'), theft, and also perjury (cf. 19.18). Unless there is an interpolation determined to have the whole Decalogue or nothing, the implication may be intended that the 'blasphemy' (12.31) of the opposing party puts them on a level with murderers etc.

15.20 The concluding summary restatement of the argument can hardly be original.

5.21–8 The next incident is based upon the healing of the centurion's son (8.6ff.), converted for variation into the healing of a mother's daughter. The commencement and conclusion are closely similar:

'My son lies at home terribly tormented.'	'My daughter is badly possessed.'
'Get you gone: as you had faith, so be it with you.' And the son was healed in that hour.	'Woman, your faith is great: be it with you as you desire.' And the daughter was healed from that hour.

The curious adverb '*badly*' possessed (15.22 κακῶς δαιμονίζεται, cf. 'dreadfully tormented', δεινῶς βασανιζόμενος, at 8.6) and the stress on coincidence of time, less relevant to the daughter's recovery, betray the direction of the derivation.

Jesus is taken to 'Tyre and Sidon' solely for the incident of the 'Canaanite woman'. She did not 'leave that region' but 'came out (of her house)' there. Like the centurion (8.8) and the blind man (9.27ff.), the Canaanite woman presses and wins her argument. The gentile members of the local church in Syria have demanded and secured admission to the communion, at the price of acknowledging their inferior status (κυνάρια). The incident is so contrived that Jesus sanctions and confirms the decision. The woman significantly identifies Jesus as 'son of David'.

Unless the 'widow of Nain' (Luke 7.11–15) was a substitute for it, Luke ignored the whole passage. Mark (7.24–30) took Jesus actually to Tyre and made the woman 'a Syrophoenician Greek'; and he changed the saying about the dogs: 'let the children be fed *first* . . . the dogs eat the *children's* scraps'.

'The region', τὰ μέρη (lit. 'the parts'), here with cities, as at 16.13 (Caesarea)—cf. 2.22 τὰ μέρη τῆς Γαλιλαίας—serves as a means of blurring precision.

15.22 'Canaanite' with χ (Χαναναία) here only in the New Testament (for the word as spelt with κ (Καναναῖος) as the epithet of the disciple Simon, see on 10.4). In the Old Testament Canaan, כנען, invariably transliterated with χ in LXX, generally means the whole territory west of Jordan seized by the Israelites, but in this passage apparently is the coastal strip comprising Tyre and Sidon.

15.25 βοηθεῖν 'help', in the woman's second appeal, occurs nowhere else in Matthew.

15.26 Possibly the superfluous '*take* and *throw*' conceals a corruption due to the common variant readings βαλεῖν 'throw' and λαβεῖν 'take'. On the other hand, λαβεῖν may be intentional liturgical allusion ('take' the bread, cf. 26.26).

15.27 ναί 'yes' has to mean 'oh yes, it *is* fit . . .'.

15.29–39 The composition of the framework for inserting the second alternative feeding (15.32–8) was strongly influenced by the lake-crossing episode which had followed the first alternative (14.15–21). It dilates upon the 'sick' (ἄρρωστοι) of 14.14 and reuses the 'mountain' of 14.23, which has point there (Jesus could see the boat with the disciples in the distance) but not here, and at the end takes for granted 'the boat' (15.39), which conveys Jesus to a destination for which an unknown name is supplied, though nothing happens there.

15.31 It is probable that βλέποντα, agreeing with τὸν ὄχλον, should be read rather than βλέποντας.

16.1 The interval before the definitive identification of Jesus by

Peter (16.16, 17) and the commencement of the Jerusalem narrative is occupied by two items.

The first item (16.1–4) is a verbally identical duplicate of the request for a 'sign' at 12.38, 39, made here by 'the Pharisees and Sadducees', perhaps for variation, instead of by 'some of the scribes and Pharisees'. Its refusal demands a reason, such as that provided in 12.41, 42 by the references to the gentile Ninevites and the Queen of Sheba. Those references are omitted here, leaving Jesus' abrupt refusal (16.4) unexplained, which no doubt prompted the interpolation contrasting ability to read weather-signs with inability to read 'the signs of the times'. The interpolation, which occurs in one family of manuscripts only, is betrayed as such by its irrelevance: the issue, which will be decided by faith without σημεῖα, was not what was going to happen next but the true identity of Jesus. Not reproduced by Mark (8.11), it must have been of early date because read by Luke, who adapted it as a cloud in the west foretelling rain and a south wind presaging hot weather (12.54–6).

It appears that a version simply omitting the Ninevites and the Queen of Sheba was not regarded as constituting a duplicate qualified in its own right for reinsertion. The composition of the interpolation is characterized (cf. on 4.23) by high-flown language: στυγνάζων 'wrathful'; 'the face of heaven'; γιγνώσκειν διακρίνειν, 'know *how to* distinguish'.

This and the next following passage (16.6, 11) are the only appearances of the Sadducees in the book, apart from 3.7 (in the Baptist narrative) and 22.23 (where their denial of the resurrection is allegedly the material point of the incident). They are mentioned in Mark only in the context of resurrection (12.18) and, apart from that context, once only (20.27) in Luke, never in John, which suggests that their absence at the corresponding points in Mark (8.15 and 8.21, where 'Herod' is substituted) was deliberate.

16.5 The next item (16.5–12) follows directly upon 15.30. When the disciples made the crossing, they forgot to take loaves; and when they were saying to one another, 'We have no loaves', Jesus overheard and said, 'Why do you of little faith say among yourselves that you have no loaves?' Surely they understood the significance of the miraculous feedings and the surplus bread which was collected?

All this would be plain sailing, were it not for 16.6: 'Jesus said to them, "Be sure to beware of the leaven of the Pharisees and Sadducees"', and the conclusion (16.11): '"How do you fail to understand that it was not about loaves that I said, 'Beware of the leaven of the P. and S.'?" Then they perceived that he had told them to beware not of leaven in loaves but of the doctrine of the P. and S.'

A logical commentary upon the meaning of the miraculous feeding has been wrecked by the intrusion of a reference to leaven and to the P. and S., resulting in a lame and fatuous conclusion. The intrusion could be connected with a dispute over the use of unleavened bread in the communion (1 Cor. 5.7). Luke ignored the item but showed knowledge of it elsewhere (12.1), while Mark, who paraphrased and expanded the incident, observed that the mass feedings were multiplication, not creation, of bread and accordingly allowed the absent-minded disciples just one loaf in the boat (8.14).

16.13 Caesarea Philippi was a refoundation of Paneas, by the springs of the Jordan (Jos. *Ant.* 18.28; *BJ* 1.168). It had a mixed Jewish and Syrian population (Jos. *Vit.* 52, 74). The choice of this real place, not elsewhere mentioned in the New Testament, for the location of Jesus' declaration of his true identity must have an encoded significance, the key to which is lost; but Caesarea Philippi was the only place in northern Palestine containing the title *Caesar* in its name.

'To the region', εἰς τὰ μέρη, is surprising in relation to a single place. It is used in 2.22 of Galilee and in 15.21 of Tyre and Sidon. In Mark 8.10 εἰς τὰ μέρη Δαλμανουθα stands in the place of εἰς τὰ ὅρια Μαγαδαν at 15.39. Mark (8.27) was so puzzled by the expression that he made Jesus and his disciples 'go out *into the villages* of Caesarea Philippi', the dialogue taking place 'on the way'. Luke (9.18), on the other hand, simply replaced the location by a description of Jesus 'praying alone'.

The use of 'men' οἱ ἄνθρωποι, in Jesus' first question anticipates the contrast between 'men's' assumption and the revealed answer of God himself which is to follow.

'Son of man' (see on 8.20) is proved by the repetition of the
same question (16.15) as 'say that I am' to be pure periphrasis for
16.14 'me', devoid of Messianic implication; otherwise Jesus' question
would contain his own answer to it. For the identification with John the Baptist (risen, of course, from the dead) see on 14.1; for the identification with Elijah see on 17.10–13. 'Jeremiah or one of the prophets' presents difficulties: why Jeremiah, and how

does 'one' mean 'some *other*'? Luke 9.19 (= 9.8) substituted 'one of the ancient prophets'. Jeremiah (cited 2.17 and 27.9) is mentioned nowhere else in the New Testament. Was the original ἢ ἕνα τῶν ιε ἄλλων προφητῶν, 'one of the other (fifteen) prophets', and the numeral ιε taken for an abbreviation of Ἰερεμίαν? Jeremiah, however, appears in 2 Maccabees (first century BC), quoted at 2.1–12 and seen in a vision at 15.14 offering a divine sword.

The initial question and answer were composed to motivate and enhance the subsequent exchange between Jesus and Peter. However, the answer attributed to the disciples could only be proffered about someone who had appeared 'from nowhere'. It is scarcely reconcilable with e.g. 13.53–8, though it is of course consistent with the assertion of Herod at 14.1.

16.16 'You are the Christ' presupposes a general, established assumption that someone, called ὁ χριστός without further qualification, will 'come', as do the questions of King Herod (2.4), of the high priest (26.63), and of Jesus to the Pharisees (22.42), and as do the warnings against impostor Christs (24.5, 23, 24).

Apart from 11.2 (q.v.) and the mockery (26.68), Jesus is only referred to as 'Christ' in the introduction (1.1, 18, q.v.) and, as '*called* Christ', at 27.22 (23.10 is manifest interpolation). It is a translation of משיח 'anointed', used, similarly without explanation, in Dan. 9.26, which John (1.41) Hebraized (see below on Kephas) as Μεσσίας. The apposition, 'the son of the living God', here and in the high priest's question (26.63), is no more than was implicit in Jesus' reference to '*my*', as opposed to '*your*, Father in heaven', and had been anticipated at 14.33. The 'living God', אל־חי, frequent in the Old Testament, means the real, true, existing God, cf. Hos. 2.1, where Israel, as God's people, is called 'sons of the living God'.

16.17 'Blessed' as in 5.3ff.—'congratulations'. 'Revealed', as at 11.25, which, construed with this passage, intimates that none other than the will of God the Father chose Peter as the channel of this communication. 'Flesh and blood' as periphrasis for humankind again at Gal. 1.16 (a deliberate allusion to this passage?), 'blood and flesh' at Eph. 6.12, Heb. 2.14. The use of the word 'revealed' also implies that the true identity of Jesus is knowable *only* by inner illumination being vouchsafed.

Peter has answered Jesus' question (16.16), and Jesus has implicitly accepted his answer as right (16.17). Anything further is then supererogatory. It does not follow that Luke (9.20) and Mark

(8.29), who omit Jesus' answer and the following sentences, did not read them here: for those not disposed to accord Peter the accolade of 16.18 and 16.19 there was a strong motive for omission. Nevertheless, 16.18 and 16.19, introduced by the words 'and I on my part say to you', read like an afterthought. They are characterized by peculiarities of expression: whether αὐτῆς refers to πέτρᾳ or to ἐκκλησίαν, the phrase 'gates *prevail*' over a 'rock' or a 'church' is strained and unnatural.

16.18 The words 'you are (εἶ) Peter' cannot bear the meaning 'you shall (henceforth) be called Peter'. They necessarily imply that the person addressed was already 'Peter': a name cannot be invented in order there and then to make a pun upon it. In fact, prior to this point in the book this individual has never been called Simon, let alone Simon-bar-Jonah, but initially 'Simon called Peter' (4.18 and in the list of apostles at 10.2), and elsewhere invariably simply 'Peter'.

The implication is that Simon himself had assumed the fictitious name 'Peter', either at his conversion or 'calling' or at the outset of his gentile mission, and that Jesus here acknowledges it with no greater anachronism than is involved in the use of the word ἐκκλησία or in the theological and liturgical issues already confronted.

No doubt Peter, a previously non-existent name—in Jos. *Ant.* 18.156 it is no more than a variant reading of Πρῶτος—was manufactured out of πέτρα 'rock'; but that does not enable 'and on this rock' to mean 'and upon you'. Rock is a recurrent Old Testament metaphor for God, especially in Psalms. The 'rock' upon which 'my church', i.e. the 'church' of Jesus, will be 'built' is the fact of his identity as the Messiah, the son of the living God, which Peter has just declared and which he inculcated as vital to the gentile church. The transition 'and on this rock' would scarcely be possible unless the already notorious reason for Simon's adoption of the name Peter was his insistence upon the fundamental fact of the incarnation. Jesus is thus acknowledging not just the name but the meaning of it.

'Congregation', ἐκκλησία, קהל, found in the gospels only here and at 18.17, though denoting originally, whatever else it meant, a body of persons, is associated with οἰκοδομεῖν 'build' and οἰκοδομή 'building' in 1 Cor. 14.4, 12. There may be some allusion to this in 7.24. The expression ἐκκλησία τοῦ θεοῦ is found in 1 and 2 Corinthians and Galatians. 'The gates of hell' (ᾅδης, cf. 11.23, where representing שאול in Isaiah) have the function of keeping the dead *in* or, at most, frustrating any attempt to let them *out*. At the resurrection they will not be strong enough to do this to the son of God and his 'church'. Hades has 'gates' (plural) in Homer and classical Greek, in which the plural is normal even of one gateway, apparently indicating the two leaves. The plural πύλαι, however, occurs here only in the New Testament—elsewhere, πύλη. Like hell, the kingdom of heaven, which has to be 'entered' (cf. 5.20), has gates, to the plurality of which corresponds the plurality of its 'keys'. On the other hand, since the words τῆς βασιλείας τῶν οὐρανῶν are dispensable, it is possible that 'the keys' given to Peter were originally the keys of Hades and that the following words, which 16.18 introduces, explained how.

John (20.23) understood 'binding' and 'loosing' to refer to the retention or remission of sins, albeit transferring the authority, as does 18.18 below (q.v.), to the disciples generally; but a meaning for δέειν and λύειν is required which flows from inculcation of the true identity of Jesus. One consequence of that doctrine was freedom from the old Law, and λύειν 'loose' has been used, in the relevant passage 5.19, for 'waiving' a commandment of the Law. Given λύειν in this sense, its converse δέειν 'bind' would mean 'declare to be binding', and in that context 'on earth' and 'in heaven' would mean respectively 'in this world' and 'as a condition for entering the kingdom of heaven'.

The *obiter dicta* of Jesus in 16.18, 19 are not so much a conferment of ecclesiastical authority upon Peter as an authoritative validation of the doctrine of the gentile church where it differed signally from that of the Judaizers.

16.20 The authoritative identification of Jesus as the Messiah created two problems, which are immediately confronted. Since he was not about to, and in fact did not, proceed to inaugurate the kingdom, his identity must be concealed in order to avoid creating expectations only to be inexplicably disappointed. Hence the injunction to silence on the part of those who witnessed the identification. It is a kindred device to that adopted in Dan. 12.4 to explain why alleged past events and prophecies, now published to meet a current need, had not been common knowledge all along. The other problem which the injunction to silence resolved was to explain how, in the light of this declaration by Jesus in the presence of the disciples, there could be continuing division over the nature of his identity.

16.21 The affirmation of Jesus' identity at 16.13–20 has been the climax of a narrative in which his divine parentage was submitted to repeated challenge. At this point, therefore, must commence (ἀπὸ τότε ἤρξατο) the Jerusalem narrative which is to end in the final proof of Jesus' divinity by his resurrection. That is why the predictions marking the approach to Jerusalem at 16.21, 17.23, and 20.10 all include a resurrection which the hearers consistently, and embarrassingly, ignore.

The verb of motion in the repetition at 20.18 is the more natural 'go *up*' (to Jerusalem), suggesting that ἀνελθεῖν 'go up' was the original here rather than ἀπελθεῖν ('depart'). The expression δεικνύειν ὅτι, 'indicate that', is without parallel in the New Testament; it avoids stating directly, as in the equivalent passages (see below), that Jesus actually 'said' this. πάσχειν ἀπό, 'at the hands of', instead of ὑπό as at e.g. 17.12, is highly abnormal. The 'elders and high priests and scribes' are all found together at 27.41; 'elders' is omitted in the parallel passage 20.18; otherwise there is 'high priests and elders of the people' at 21.23, 26.3, 47, 27.1, 'high priests and elders' at 27.3, 12, 20, and once (26.57)—in the high priest's house—'scribes and elders'. The passive form for 'be killed', ἀποκτανθῆναι, is confined in the New Testament to this sentence (= Mark 8.31, Luke 9.22) and Revelation. Specific reference to crucifixion is absent (see on 20.17–23).

16.22 The signal distinction which has just been conferred on Peter is nullified by a violently anti-Petrine passage which, not content with making Jesus call him 'Satan', insinuates that he will jib at sharing his master's fate. Composed with 16.13–20 in view, as shown by the reuse of ἐπιτιμᾶν 'strictly charge' (16.20) in the sense of 'upbraid', it is closely similar to 10.37–9, from which, rather than a common source, it appears to be derived, because (1) at 10.37–9 it is relevant to the context (behaviour when on trial), unlike here, (2) the curious expression ἀπαρνεῖσθαι ἑαυτόν, 'deny himself', is under the influence of the previous discussion of ἀπαρνεῖσθαι (10.33), and (3) the conclusion about saving one's life and losing it begins with σῶσαι 'save' but reverts to εὑρίσκειν 'find', under the influence of 10.39.

In fact, the counterblast against Peter is composed with material from the inserted discourse at 10.5ff., with which it has in common (16.28) belief in an early date for the second coming (see 10.23). The implication is that Peter will deny Jesus. The dictum about gaining the world but losing one's soul (16.26) is a palpable thrust at the world mission of the gentile church.

προσλαβόμενος, here only (= Mark 8.32) in the gospels. No exact parallel has been found for the construction here of ἵλεως, '(God) be merciful to you', meaning 'God forbid', a euphemistic phrase as in 1 Macc. 2.21 ἵλεως ἡμῖν καταλιπεῖν νόμον καὶ δικαιώματα, 'God forbid we should abandon the Law and the judgements', 1 Chr. 11.19 ἵλεώς μοι ὁ θεὸς τοῦ ποιῆσαι τὸ ῥῆμα τοῦτο, 'God forbid I should do this thing', 2 Sam. 20.20 ἵλεώς μοι εἰ καταποντιῶ καὶ εἰ διαφθερῶ, 'shame on me if I drown and destroy'. οὐ μὴ ἔσται here and 26.35 (also in Peter's mouth) are the only secure instances out of twenty cases of οὐ μή in the book—at 15.6 τιμήσει is interchangeable with τιμήσῃ—where the future indicative is used instead of the aorist subjunctive. The expression ἔσται σοι in the sense of 'happen to you' is also unusual. στραφείς, 'turning', 'rounding on him', is the regular accompaniment of rebuke, cf. Luke 9.55. σκάνδαλον ἐμοῦ, that which σκανδαλίζει με, 'causes me to defect', is highly peculiar; for the technical meaning of σκάνδαλον see on 5.29.

With 'Satan' came, from 4.10, the dismissive command ὕπαγε, 'get you gone'; but the words 'behind me', although used at Peter's own 'calling' (4.19), do not fit: Satan is as dangerous behind as in front.

16.24 Peter's words were omitted by Mark (8.32, 33), and the whole exchange by Luke (9.23). Having responded to Peter, Jesus proceeds to address to his disciples a series of statements inherently applicable to any hearer. This is no doubt why Luke (9.23) awkwardly interposed πρὸς πάντας ('he said to *everybody*'), and Mark (8.34) made him 'summon the crowd with his disciples' before speaking. The word ἀπαρνεῖσθαι occurs elsewhere in the New Testament only applied to Peter's denial of Jesus at 26.34, 35, 75; but ἀρνεῖσθαι is used in 10.33 of 'denying' Jesus as opposed to 'confessing' him (ὁμολογεῖν). There is no natural meaning for 'deny oneself', nor can the expression mean, apart from any question of relevance, 'undergo privation'. It is intelligible only as ironic allusion to Peter's denial of Jesus, contradicting his announcement (16.16) on which he has just been congratulated. Luke (9.23) tried to water the sentence down by inserting καθ' ἡμέραν and thus inadmissibly reducing cross-carrying to daily penance. There is evidently an allusion to Peter's actual behaviour in the sequel: he 'follows' Jesus (ἠκολούθει, 26.58), denies him ('I know not the man', οὐκ οἶδα τὸν ἄνθρωπον, 26.72), and (assuming 'of Cyrene' to be a disguise) 'takes up' (αἴρειν) his cross (27.32).

16.25 The warnings which follow in 16.25, 26 are justified by 16.27, 28, the imminence of 'the kingdom' when everyone will be dealt with 'according to his deeds'. ψυχή is used in a double sense—'life' in this world, and 'life' in the next, 'the kingdom'. Two distinct cases are taken: (1) those who deny Jesus to save their lives under persecution (which was the context at 10.28, 39); and (2) a person who 'gains the whole world' but will be sentenced to lose his eternal life for so doing. This latter is a clear reference to those, of whom Peter is the leader, who purport to 'win' (cf. κερδαίνειν, 18.15) the gentile world by waiving the Law but thereby incur loss of eternal life (ζημιωθῆναι implies judicial sentence) at the judgement, which will be based upon actual behaviour (πρᾶξις). The Judaizers' threat is in line with 5.19.

16.26 The second limb of 16.26 presents the same threat in converse. It does not ask what a man would *take* as compensation for forfeiting (eternal) life, but what he will *give* (δώσει) to ransom his soul, as ἀντάλλαγμα 'fair exchange' for it. The gentiles were being taught that Jesus will be their ransom, which is refuted by a text affirming that men will be judged on their own actions. Mark (8.36) blurred this by substituting the present ὠφελεῖ, ὠφελεῖται for the future (of the judgement) ὠφεληθήσεται and Luke (9.25) by omitting the second limb.

16.27 The scene is in 25.31ff., except that here the δόξα, 'glory', is that of the father, and the summary of the judgement is cited from Ps. 61.13 (ἀποδώσεις ἑκάστῳ κατὰ τὰ ἔργα αὐτοῦ) = Prov. 24.12, cf. Rev. 22.12. The expression 'taste death' (γεύεσθαι θανάτου), not found in LXX, was used again, apart from the equivalent passages Mark 9.1 and Luke 9.27, in John 8.52 and Heb. 2.9. The imminent 'kingdom' recalls 10.23.

17.1 Peter's privileged 'revelation' (16.17) is further downgraded by a theophany to the same effect in which James and John share. In the course of it Peter is snubbed when a proposal of his (17.4) is studiously ignored.

'*Six*' days can hardly be right in the absence of any precise moment from which time can be counted forward. Mark (9.2) transcribed unaltered; Luke (9.28), perceiving but not solving the problem, attempted to cope, with 'about eight days after this discourse'. Apart from the list of disciples at 10.2, and the 'calling' (4.21), this is the first reappearance in the narrative of the sons of Zebedee (not here so called). They are to recur at 20.20 and at 26.37, where, similarly to here, they share an experience as additional witnesses.

The next event (the 'transfiguration') had the effect of making James and John witnesses along with Peter of an irrefutable confirmation of Jesus' divine sonship. To that purpose the apparition of Moses and Elijah contributes nothing: all they do is 'talk' to Jesus, eliciting from Peter a curious proposal, to which effect is apparently not given. If their appearance was intended to allegorize the compatibility of the 'Law and the prophets' with the incarnation, the object failed to be realized.

'Carried them up', ἀναφέρει, does not naturally mean 'led them up' but, physically or supernaturally, 'bore them up'. In the gospels it is used only here (= Mark 9.2) and (in the passive) at Luke 24.51 (of the ascension). Even παραλαμβάνει, 'took along', is used at 24.40, 41 of the elect who are 'taken' at the coming of the kingdom. 'By themselves', κατ' ἰδίαν, where Jesus goes off 'alone' (14.13, 23) or is approached 'in private' (17.19, 24.3), and exactly as here at 20.17; but ὄρος ὑψηλὸν λίαν at 4.8, also the setting of a supernatural event, suggests the possibility of λίαν here.*

17.2 The nature of the transformation ('change of shape') is not specified, unless it consisted in the shining of the face. Light is not 'white', nor do garments resemble light. 'White as snow' (ὡς νιφάς?) would be more natural;† so 28.3, Mark 9.3 (var.), and Dan. 7.9 (Rev. 1.14).

17.3 It is not explained how the identity of the two figures was known. Luke (9.32) cleverly rewrote the passage so that their identity was revealed in a dream to the sleeping disciples (borrowed from Gethsemane); for in a dream the identity of characters is known without their being visually recognized. Moses and Elijah, though they 'talk with' Jesus, say nothing. Luke found it necessary (9.30, 31), following the hint of 17.9 (ἕως οὗ . . . ἐγερθῇ), to specify the content of the conversation.

17.4 'Tents', σκήνας, and especially '*making* tents', is nonsense, while 'it's nice *to be here*' is bathos. The word required is 'pillars', στήλας, which were erected at the places of encounter with the supernatural or divine (Gen. 28.18, 22; 31.13; 35.14). The original would be ὧδε ⟨θ⟩εῖναι, εἰ θέλεις, [ποιήσω ὧδε] τρεῖς στήλας, the words ποιήσω ὧδε having been inserted to supply the missing transitive verb after the θ of θεῖναι had been lost between -ε and ε-. Luke (9.33), followed by Mark (9.6),

* This conjecture was made in antiquity, and appears in the Codex Bezae.
† This conjecture was also made in antiquity: χιών in Codex Bezae.

found Peter's behaviour so irrational that he concluded he was delirious.

17.9 Following the model of 16.20 (q.v.) and for the same reasons, the revelation had to be held secret.

17.10–13 The reasoning of the disciples appears to be: if Jesus is the son of God, then God has visited his people, the 'great and manifest day of the Lord', which, according to Mal. 3.23–4 (= 4.4–5), must be preceded by the return of Elijah. The problem which the disciples respectfully put forward as posed by 'the scribes' is easily resolved, says Jesus. The sharp retort, 'Elijah came already, and they did not recognize him', has been blunted by superfluous additions—it was unnecessary to quote Micah (ἀποκαταστήσει) and irrelevant that John was done to death by the same people who will do likewise to Jesus.

17.14–21 To accommodate a saying of Jesus about the missionary power of faith in his identity and purpose, an incident is created in which the disciples have been unable to perform exorcism upon a gentile child, that is, allegory apart, to achieve a gentile conversion. Possession by an evil spirit (δαιμόνιον) represents as usual belief in a pagan deity, 'the crowd' represents (cf. 15.10) general humanity, and the child's father uses the gentile appeal (like the Canaanite woman, 15.22) 'Lord, have mercy'. The composition has borrowed from 13.31 the corrupt 'mustard-seed', which helps to heighten the violent reaction attributed to Jesus. It has also mistakenly imitated the concluding words 'from that hour' from long-range healings (8.13, 15.28) where they had a real point. The disciples have nowhere else, despite 10.1, been portrayed as attempting healing on their own account.

The saying thus accommodated (17.21) is a duplicate of 21.21 (q.v.), where it occurs in the course of the second of Jesus' two entrances into Jerusalem and where the command to the mountain, instead of being 'move from here thither', is 'rise up and be cast into the sea'. It has to be an allegorical saying; for if literal, the claim to be able to move mountains by faith, even though the author of 1 Cor. 13.2 affected to take it at face value, would demand a performance which is nowhere offered. There is allegorical significance in commanding a mountain to 'be cast into the sea', but none in telling it to 'move over'. It follows that, of the two duplicates, the original is 21.21 and the derivative based upon it is 17.21.

The allegory, which is transparent, plants the original saying firmly in Jerusalem. 'This mountain' is the Temple Mount or

Sion, and the 'sea' is as usual (see on 4.13 above) the gentile world across the Mediterranean. In the gentile church, converted by the faith of missionaries, the Judaizing church, or perhaps the Jewish dispensation as a whole, is to be submerged.

Luke (9.43) retained and elaborated the healing but omitted the saying itself altogether, replacing it with an anodyne expression of public astonishment. Mark (9.28, 29) retained the disciples' question, but substituted a wholly different and inappropriate reply, viz. 'this sort can only be exorcised by prayer'. Suggested by 21.22, it is inappropriate since Jesus is not reported to have used prayer on this occasion. If original, it could not conceivably have been displaced.

17.15 'Be subject to fits', σεληνιάζεσθαι, occurs elsewhere in the New Testament only in the general catalogue 4.24 (also, as here, with κακῶς ἔχειν 'be in a bad way'). 'Frequently', πολλάκις, is used nowhere else in Matthew.

17.17 The severe denunciation, derived apparently from Deut. 32.5, 'twisted and perverse generation', γενεὰ σκολιὰ καὶ διεστραμμένη, where Moses attacks the future apostasy of the Israelites, intimates that the rebuke goes beyond the disciples to the opposing party, signalled by γενεά (see on 23.33). 'How long shall I be with you?', which the following interpolated question purports to explain, conveys that Jesus expects his mission to the gentiles to be carried on after his own departure.

17.18 The rebuke (ἐπιτιμᾶν again, which keeps recurring since 16.20) ought to be addressed to the evil spirit (as to the wind and waves at 8.26) rather than to the boy possessed by it: Luke (9.42) and Mark (9.25) adjusted accordingly.

17.21 The devastating anticlimax of 'nothing shall be impossible for you' betrays an explanatory gloss.

17.22 The mention of Galilee in the connecting link, 'while they were gathered together etc.', indicates consciousness of a forthcoming departure from Galilee (19.1). συστρέφεσθαι, here only in the gospels, looks as if it should be ἀνα- or συναναστρ. (common in the Epistles in the sense of 'going up and down together'), which is in fact found here in some manuscripts. For the surprisingly general term ἀνθρώπων, cf. 10.17.

The polemic against Peter continues. Jesus' prediction of being handed over to be killed and rising again is repeated without evoking any protest from Peter. (The reaction of the other disciples, καὶ ἐλυπήθησαν σφόδρα, is shown by its lameness to be interpolation.) Indeed, in agreeing to pay the two-drachma tax on behalf of Jesus and himself (17.24), Peter is convicted of contradicting his own assertion that Jesus is the son of God.

The repetition of 16.21 substitutes μέλλει 'is going to' for δεῖ 'needs must'; replaces 'elders and high priests and scribes' by the vacuous 'men'; and, influenced by the subsequent narrative, introduces the theme of 'betrayal' (παράδοσις) by παραδίδοσθαι.

17.24 The 'two-drachma tax' was a half-shekel poll-tax, four drachmae equalling one shekel or *stater*, payable by each adult for the maintenance of the Temple (Jos. *BJ* 7.218). Capharnaum is presumably selected as the scene for the incident because 4.13 implied it to be Jesus' place of residence: he is supposed to be staying there with Peter.

17.25 'Anticipated', προέφθασεν, here only in the New Testament. As Peter has been trapped by his hasty 'Yes' into inconsistency with his revelation at 16.16, Jesus ironically addresses him again not as 'Peter' but, for the first and only time since 16.17, as 'Simon'. The implied contrast is between 'earthly kings' and the king of heaven, and 'their own (αὐτῶν) sons' and 'other people's (ἀλλοτρίων) sons'. τέλη 'taxes', doubled with φόρος at Rom. 13.7, is here doubled with κῆνσον (Lat. *census*), apparently unexampled elsewhere in this sense.

17.26 For the deductive question 'Then . . . ?', ἄρα γε, cf. 7.20.

17.27 To pay the tax would be to mislead, σκανδαλίζειν (see on 5.29), as to Jesus' true identity. It is not therefore paid by Jesus and Peter as taxpayers: instead, Peter, exercising his function as 'fisher of men', quits the obligation by offering the oblation of Christ (see on 'fish' at 14.17). It is left to be inferred by the reader that Peter obeyed and that the fish duly produced the sum to be handed over in lieu of the tax. Luke and Mark omit the passage.

18.1 The inferential question 'who *then* is greatest in the kingdom of heaven?' follows upon the humbling of Peter and masks a return to the crucial issue of the admission of the gentiles, debated under cover of the allegorical equation παιδίον = gentile. The difference between 'receiving' or 'not receiving' a child, despite the superficial resemblance to 10.40, is to be understood accordingly; and the ferocious punishment, worse than drowning by millstone, is for placing obstacles (σκάνδαλα) in the way of the admission of gentiles.

'In that hour', purely as a link, is used elsewhere in the book only at 26.55 (where it is even less appropriate). 'Then', ἄρα, appears to be merely an adjunct to the interrogative 'who?', without illative significance: somewhat similarly at 19.26, 27; 24.45 (q.v.). For μείζων superlative, 'greatest', cf. 13.32.

The unspoken question, 'If Peter is not pre-eminent, who is?', introduces a series of items denouncing the Judaizers, apparently directed at an identifiable individual. Entry into the kingdom is gained not by the acquired merit of Law-fulfilment (of which the gentiles are as such destitute), but through faith in the identity of Jesus and his propitiatory act. Thus a 'child', which by definition can have no acquired merit of its own, becomes the encoded equivalent of a gentile believer. The argument is *a fortiori*: you cannot enter the kingdom (at all) without becoming like a child. Therefore the greatest is he who abases himself. Insertions, and especially the absurd production of an actual child, as though the disciples would not otherwise know what a child is like, enabled the incident to be taken literally, instead of giving to 'children' its allegorical, pro-gentile meaning.

18.3 στρέφεσθαι 'turn' is nowhere else in the book used as here. It represents שוב, normally rendered μετανοεῖν 'repent'.

There is a bitter personal polemic against those (or the individual) who, claiming leadership in the church, reject the salvation offered to the gentiles. Dire punishment awaits the (identifiable) person who is responsible for the loss of a single gentile convert.

18.4 To 'abase oneself', ταπεινῶσαι ἑαυτόν, is the extremity of 'becoming as a child', and so confers the highest place in the kingdom. A child, however, does not 'abase himself': the words 'as this child' are intrusive.

18.5, 6 The two halves of the antithesis are not symmetrical. The opposite to 'receiving' is 'not receiving' (see 10.41, where εἰς ὄνομα equates with ἐπὶ τῷ ὀνόματί μου here: see there also for the force of '*one* of these little ones'). The second half anathematizes those who do not merely not 'receive' the 'little ones' but actually cause them to lose their salvation.

There is no obvious reason why the *upper* millstone should be specified, and this was perhaps Luke's motive in substituting (17.2) λίθος μυλικός, 'millstone' or perhaps 'nether millstone'. For μύλος see on 24.41. ὄνος by itself meant an upper millstone and thus millstone generally. Was perhaps the original ὄνος or ὀνικός (sc. μύλος), then glossed with μύλος? (There is apparently no evidence for the term meaning a donkey-mill as opposed to a hand-mill.) συμφέρειν ἵνα as at 5.29, 30, likewise with reference to the judgement. πέλαγος, the 'deep', apparently significant but replaced by θάλασσα in Luke (17.2) and Mark (9.42). The expression πιστεύειν εἰς 'believe on' is unique in the first three gospels, though common in John.

The παιδία are now equated with 'these little ones who believe on me'. There is a sharp personal edge to the polemic: some particular individual has been causing defections by insisting upon conformity with the Law.

18.7 οὐαί, apart from 11.21 (q.v.) and 24.19, occurs in the book only in the series of 'woes' at 23.13–29 and in οὐαὶ τῷ ἀνθρώπῳ ἐκείνῳ at 26.24. The construction 'woe from', οὐαὶ ἀπό, is apparently unique. The clause, which is not compatible with οὐαὶ τῷ ἀνθρώπῳ κ.τ.λ., lifts clear and may be intended as a substitute for it, designed to palliate the imprecation. The sense is: 'Defections may be inevitable; but that does not excuse the person who causes them.' ἀνάγκη 'needs must' appears in the book here only.

18.8, 9 A quotation from the 'sermon' (5.30), presumably intended to be recognized as such, is used to advise expulsion from the church of whoever is turning away gentiles. For 'eye' see on 6.22.

The quotation is not integrated into its new context, the second person singular being retained despite the plural in the surrounding discourse. But minor adjustments have been made: the 'eye' is no longer the 'right' eye; the 'foot' is added to the 'hand'; 'Gehenna' is replaced by 'the G. of fire' (5.22) or 'the everlasting fire' (25.41), and the alternative to it is specified as 'life' (cf. 25.46).

18.10 'See that you do not despise', ὁρᾶτε μή + aor. subj., the same construction as at 8.4; at 9.30 and 24.6 there is an imperative instead of the aorist. The word 'despise' is straight out of a debate: it is not 'despising' that is at issue but leading astray (σκανδαλίζειν) so as to bring to destruction.

18.11 The daring image, for which no satisfactory parallel has been produced, whereby each convert has an assigned guardian 'angel' gazing fixedly at God, evoked the insertion below of a pedestrian paraphrase (18.14), in which the tortuous Hebraism 'will in the sight of'*—ἔμπροσθεν representing לפני —endeavours to rationalize the 'angels', 'my' is replaced by 'your' father in heaven, and the neuter ἕν τῶν μικρῶν τούτων takes account of the one sheep (πρόβατον) above.

* Perhaps Ps. 16.8 (cited Acts 2.25) was in mind.

18.12 The question 'does he not leave . . . ?' is not the preface to a parable but to an argument from analogy, and as such it uses the formula τί ὑμῖν δοκεῖ; 'What do you think?' (cf. 17.25, 21.28). The principal verb, 'does he not leave', has to be in the present tense to match 'looks for' (ζητεῖ) and 'is glad' (χαίρει): ἀφίησι pres. has been corrupted into ἀφήσει fut. 'To the mountains' is a gloss on 'go', inserted in the wrong place after 'leave': there would be no sense in leaving the ninety-nine 'on the mountains'—they would no doubt be 'left' in the fold—nor in any case can ἐπὶ τὰ ὄρη mean 'on the mountains'. Luke (15.4) was careful to correct it (as he supposed) to ἐν τῇ ἐρήμῳ 'in the wilderness'.

The purpose of the argument in the context is to illustrate that possession of a hundred items does not make their possessor indifferent to the fate of any single one of them. That the single one, if lost, is valued *more* than the rest is strictly extraneous to the case; but that paradox was dilated upon by Luke (15.7), who found in it a means of bringing in an allusion to 'the angels in heaven' from the foregoing passage.

18.15 The conclusion of the discourse concerns how to deal with an 'erring' or 'offending' brother. The nature of the 'error' or 'offence' is not explicitly stated; but if relevant to the context, it has to be the Judaizing error which results in gentiles being turned away, the σκάνδαλον of 18.7. How should the advocate of such an error be dealt with? The answer, still addressed in the singular, appears to reflect an actual event, in which, expostulation having failed, one or two other like-minded persons were taken along, to add to the pressure, and finally prevailed. If the words 'tell the congregation; and if he disregards the congregation', are genuine, no indication is given as to how 'the congregation' should arrive at its conclusion. Instead the outcome is validated by the misapplication, which must surely be conscious, of two citations. First, Deut. 19.15, 'let every point be established on the word of two or three witnesses', is wrested from its intended application to forensic evidence of fact. Secondly, the assertion that God allows whatever two persons agree upon is based on the allegation that Jesus himself promised to be present wherever 'two or three are gathered together in his name', which is misapplied as if 'are gathered together' (συνηγμένοι) meant 'are agreed'.

18.17 By a bitter irony, the expelled Judaizing brother is to be treated as if he were one of those very 'gentiles and tax-gatherers' whom he has erred in seeking to exclude (see on 5.43–8).

18.18 'Bind', δήσητε, means, in the context, as at 16.19, 'declare to be obligatory' and 'loose', λύσητε, the reverse. The authority apparently conferred on Peter alone at 16.19 has been (silently) transferred to 'you' ('the congregation').

18.19 The original meaning has been destroyed by the irrelevant insertion of οὗ ἐὰν αἰτήσωνται, 'that they ask', after περὶ παντὸς πράγματος. πρᾶγμα, 'thing', occurs nowhere else in Matthew nor, apart from Luke's preface, in the gospels.

18.20 The illogicality of the reason, as well as the addition 'or three', casts doubt on the authenticity of this concluding sentence. The paradox of decision by two or three consenting voices, reflecting no doubt an actual event, was felt to call for explanation.

18.21–35 The ensuing parable is irrelevant to the repetition of human forgiveness; it is about God's forgiveness: God has offered to Israel forgiveness, but the Judaizer seeks to withhold the same forgiveness from the gentiles, who have been less favoured in the past than Israel, so that their 'debt' stands to Israel's 'debt' in the minuscule ratio of 100 denarii to 10,000 talents. The parable, which embodies the clue words πονηρός 'wicked' (18.32), for which see on 9.4, and ἐλεεῖν 'have mercy' (18.33), for which see on 9.13, does not fit in all respects, because the debt of 100 denarii is owed to the fellow servant, not to God; but it is at the complaint of the first debtor's fellow servants that the master takes action against him. The severity of the moral of the parable has been palliated by an introductory dialogue (18.21, 22) and a concluding summary (18.35) which ignore the allegorical meaning and relate the parable instead to wrongs done by one human being to another.

18.21 One cannot both ask the question 'how often?' and in the same breath offer a suggested specimen answer, 'up to seven times?' Interpolation was due to failure to see that Jesus picks 'seven' as an apparently high number in order then to raise it much higher. Luke (17.4) saw the difficulty, omitted the question, and substituted 'seven times *a day*'. In Gen. 4.24, which may have been in mind, שבעתים ('seven times'), contrasted with שבעים ושבעה ('seventy-seven'), is rendered (LXX) as ἑπτάκις and ἑβδομηκοντάκις ἑπτά ('seven times' and 'seventy times and seven'), which suggests that the same expression here was intended to mean 77 times, not 490 times.

18.23 For ὡμοιώθη, lit. 'was likened', see on 13.24.

The apposition of 'a king' to 'a man' is inappropriate, and inconsistent with the subsequent references to the 'master' (κύριος) of the servants (δοῦλοι). The servants have to be supposed to be of a superior kind, to whom the management of affairs is entrusted and a certain affluence allowed (so in the parable at 25.14ff.) but who can still be sold at their master's pleasure.

18.27 The servant asks only for time; but his request is met by full cancellation.

18.30 One slave cannot sell another; hence the recourse to a sponging-house (cf. 5.26) to secure payment.

18.31 'Signified', διεσάφησαν (probably from 13.36, q.v.), is a curiously pompous word for 'told'. The interposition of the fellow servants is structurally superfluous: 18.32 could perfectly well follow directly upon 18.30.

19.1–12 The wording does not presuppose the previously announced decision to go to Jerusalem (see on 16.21). The question of divorce, as is known from 1 Cor. 7.7ff., was a live one in the gentile Church. Jesus here, not unlike Paul there, achieves a rough-and-ready reconciliation with 5.31, where the 'excess' righteousness required for entry into the kingdom excluded divorce as involving adultery. In doing so he accepts the implications of Gen. 2.24 as overriding the implications of Deut. 24.11, which are blamed upon the Jews' σκληροκαρδία, 'incorrigibility'. Luke omitted the ruling altogether; Mark (10.1–12) omitted the conclusion on celibacy.

19.1, 2 A purely bridging passage framed on e.g. 11.1, 13.53 (also after parables), and cf. 12.15, also 15.39–16.1. The change of scene marks a change of subject; but none of the material between here and 20.17 requires a location in Judaea, and the wording sits uneasily with 'being about to go up to Jerusalem' at 20.17. 'The other side of Jordan' does not fit syntactically with the rest of the sentence: it seems to be an attempt to get Jesus from Galilee to Judaea without traversing Samaria (cf. 10.5). For 'confines', ὅρια, cf. 15.22; the word is elsewhere used only of a town. 'There', ἐκεῖ, has no satisfactory point of reference: as at 27.36, the question arises if it is not a duplication of the καί following.

19.3 An antecedent for αὐτοῦ, 'his' wife, is indispensable: some such word as ἀνθρώπῳ or τινί has fallen out.

19.4 Misunderstanding of ὁ κτίσας as a periphrasis for God, 'the Creator', left 'male and female' apparently without a verb, which was supplied by interpolating ἐποίησεν αὐτοὺς καί. The reference to 'the beginning' is possibly a means of citing Genesis (בראשית, ἐν ἀρχῇ).

19.8 'It was not so', with the perfect γέγονεν, could yield the meaning 'it has not been so from the beginning' (cf. 24.21, citing Joel 2.2); but the perfect is used for the simple past (cf. 25.6) in the standard citation formula 1.22, 21.4, 26.56.

19.9 The summary conclusion, which may not be original, has a close relationship with 5.31, 32, of which it is in effect a citation, marked as such by the prefatory words 'but I say to you', which belong to the repetitive pattern there but are superfluous here.

19.10–12 The query of the disciples and the reply to it, both omitted by Luke and Mark, are perverse: prohibition of divorce is not an argument in favour of celibacy, and the conclusion that celibacy, if practicable, is to be preferred does not follow from the foregoing. The embarrassment and vagueness of the question (e.g. the use of the word αἰτία, the 'matter' of a man and a woman) suggest that the opportunity was taken to annex to the dialogue on divorce a dictum in favour of celibacy.

19.11 After 'not all can be continent' the words τὸν λόγον τοῦτον have been interpolated due to failure to construe χωρεῖν as intransitive, thus requiring it to be given the meaning 'bear, accept'.

19.12 The disquisition on the three sorts of castration not only separates the conclusion 'let him that can be continent' from the statement that not all can but is inconsistent with the proposition that continence is a 'gift'. For self-castration on religious grounds, see on 5.27.

19.13–15 The defence of the non-converted marriage partner is followed, not presumably by chance, by an item dealing with the admission of children. An incident has been constructed to convey approval for a sacrament in which, to the accompaniment of appropriate prayers, hands were laid on children 'presented' to Jesus. The sacrament must have been sufficiently familiar to be recognized from the description but still the subject of controversy. Its acceptance was a corollary to the doctrine that only those as devoid of acquired merit as infants can enter the kingdom (18.3). Adult converts, by whose faith their children are saved (8.5–13; 9.18–25; 15.21–8), must be entitled to 'present' them to Jesus—not, apparently, in infant baptism but in a rite corresponding to confirmation. 'Laying on hands with prayer' occurs in Acts in connection with ordination (6.6) and with baptism (19.6).

19.14 'Allow to come', ἄφετε ἐλθεῖν, has been glossed μὴ κωλύετε, 'do not prevent'.

19.16–26 The theme of acquired merit not admitting to the kingdom is continued under the metaphor of 'wealth'; see on 'stores in heaven', θησαυρὸς ἐν οὐρανοῖς, 6.19 (an expression used with apparent deliberation in the course of the dialogue, 19.21, almost as if it were an allusion or cross-reference). A situation is constructed where a person's claim to have fulfilled the Law all his life is not disputed; but what he still needs is to relinquish all claim of merit and follow Jesus, in whom he has seen no more than a 'teacher'.

19.16 'A man', εἷς, here only has not been provided with an epithet such as 'scribe' (8.19) or 'ruler' (9.18), which Luke (18.18) inserted here. The question, having been designed merely to launch the dialogue, is vacuous. Hence the attempt to make it specific by interpolating ἀγαθόν ('what *good* thing?'), which invited the irrelevant and barely intelligible 'one only is good' in the reply, interpolations which spoil the intended brusqueness of the retort. Luke (18.19–20) adapted the text to accommodate ἀγαθόν by making the enquirer call Jesus '*good* master', a form of address which Jesus then disclaimed. Mark (10.17) was happy to follow Luke's lead.

19.18 The article τό in front of the six commandments indicates a recognized standard list. It is the same list as formed the framework of 5.21ff., with two explicable differences: because 5.21ff. is concerned with mental breaches, it omits 'Thou shalt not steal', as covered by the prohibition of covetousness, and 'Honour thy father and thy mother', as being itself an attitudinal commandment. All but the last of the six occur—with 'Honour thy father etc.' first instead of last—in Exod. 20.12ff. and Deut. 5.16ff.

19.19 A citation of Lev. 19.18 is attached to the foregoing extracts from the Decalogue. As its significance depends on the parallelism with Deut. 6.5, as below at 22.37–9 (q.v.), the association must already have been a familiar one.

19.20 'The young man', ὁ νεανίσκος, is a description which, if genuine, would have had to appear at the outset. It conceals (as Luke 18.21 perceived) the significant words ἐκ νεότητος 'from the days of my youth'.

19.21 'If you want to be perfect' is interpolated, perhaps with an eye to 5.48, the only other occurrence of τέλειος in the gospels. Apart from implying that some of those who 'enter life' are less 'perfect' than others, it is irrelevant: the enquirer asked not how to be perfect but how to get life everlasting. The interpolations again destroy the starkness of the reply.

The command 'get rid of your possessions' means 'cease imagining that you can get to heaven by your own deserts without faith in my atoning action'.

'Come hither', δεῦρο, only here (= Mark and Luke, locc. citt.) and John 11.43 in the gospels; cf. δεῦτε at 4.19. For 'follow', ἀκολούθει, cf. 8.22, and see on 16.24.

19.22 'Possessions', κτήματα, here (= Mark 10.22) only in the gospels.

19.23–4 The camel simile is ironic hyperbole, denoting impossibility, as the dialogue implies; but there is an awkwardness, in that both halves of the comparison share the verb 'enter', εἰσελθεῖν, which is not really appropriate to the camel and needle. The feeble paraphrase, which softens the absoluteness of the negative, cannot be original. For 'kingdom of *God*' (instead of 'heaven') see on 3.2. In τρῆμα ῥαφίδος 'needle's eye' Luke (18.25) replaced ῥαφίς by βελόνη, which Phrynichus Atticista 72 commended as 'more Attic', and Mark (10.25) replaced τρῆμα by τρυμαλιά, known to LXX.

19.25 The disciples do not ask 'how then can *a rich man* be saved?', which would be a contradiction of Jesus, but go behind the metaphorical sense of 'rich' and enquire, by *a fortiori* reasoning: '(if a possessor of merit cannot be saved), who *can*?' This incomprehension of his central doctrine provokes the mild irritation of Jesus implied by ἐμβλέψας and the reply: not humanly (i.e. by merit) but divinely (i.e. by God's mercy).

Apart from 10.22 (= 24.13) σώζεσθαι, 'be saved', is nowhere else in the book used as equivalent to entering the kingdom.

The expression παρὰ θεῷ, '*with* God', is due to its use in Gen. 18.14 (LXX μὴ ἀδυνατεῖ παρὰ τῷ θεῷ ῥῆμα;), where παρά represents מ (היפלא מיהוה דבר). Zech. 8.6, where there is a similar antithesis between God and men, may also have been in mind. 'Looked upon', ἐμβλέψας, is used by Luke (20.17) to preface an answer. Presumably it is what prompted the characteristically pathetic touch introduced into the story by Mark 10.21.

19.27–30 The reward of all who 'follow' Jesus and cast aside their 'possessions' (i.e. their own acquired merits) is one and the same—'life'. Peter uncomprehendingly enquires: 'What about *us*? We abandoned *all* our possessions to follow you. What shall *we* get?' Jesus' reply is heavy irony: 'Oh, you will sit on twelve thrones judging the tribes of Israel'; and the irony is underlined by the absurd promise of multiple replacement for lost relatives and property. The substantive reply, however, follows in the parable (20.1–16), which intimates that the last 'follower' will be on an equal footing with the first. It is never too late to 'follow' Jesus.

19.28 ἡ παλινγενεσία (here only in the New Testament except at Titus 3.5 ἔσωσεν ἡμᾶς διὰ λουτροῦ παλινγενεσίας, 'he saved us through the washing of regeneration', an explicit reference to baptism) is remarkable in the unique sense of general resurrection (ἀνάστασις). Its position before the words with which it has to be construed casts doubt upon its authenticity.

The situation envisaged is not the moment of the judgement—what would the disciples then be doing 'judging' the twelve tribes separately?—but the continuing organization of the kingdom after its establishment (20.22 'in your kingdom'). As in the related passage 20.21, the twelve will be the satraps of King Jesus. The ten 'lost' tribes have taken their place alongside Judah and Benjamin, as if nothing had happened. It is a purely Israelite kingdom: contrast Wisd. 3.8 κρινοῦσιν ἔθνη καὶ κρατήσουσιν λαῶν, καὶ βασιλεύσει αὐτῶν κύριος, 'they shall judge nations and govern peoples, and the Lord shall be their king'.

19.29 The absurdity of promising a plurality of fathers and mothers and a multiplication of siblings betrays the words as ironical. 'For the sake of my name', ἕνεκεν τοῦ ἐμοῦ ὀνόματος, here only for 'for my sake', ἕνεκεν ἐμοῦ (5.11; 10.18, 39; 16.25; cf. 'upon my name' at 18.5 etc.).

.1–16 The parable is adapted, as far as practicable, to its allegorical meaning. It is the owner (God) who makes a covenant ('I will give') with the workers; but the pay-out is entrusted to his steward, ἐπίτροπος (here only in Matthew), who without being expressly told knows and carries out the wishes of the owner, until at the end the owner appears in person to justify his action and rebuke the envious. The justification is delivered not to all the complainants but to an individual, which makes possible a livelier retort involving unrealistically the presence of a single one-hour worker at the owner's dialogue with the representative of the full-day workers.

The text of the parable has been severely disfigured by superfluous glosses. 'Owner', οἰκοδεσπότῃ, is suspicious; see on 13.45 ἐμπόρῳ. ('Owner' below at 20.11 is required as the antithesis to 'steward'.) 'Standing', ἑστῶτας, was sufficient in itself to convey 'idle' or 'unemployed', so that probably 'in the market-place' as well as 'idle' is a gloss. The owner's original instruction to the

steward ended 'starting with the last ones': those who 'came' (ἐλθόντες) were therefore 'the last', but the officious ἕως τῶν πρώτων has necessitated the inadequate expression οἱ περὶ τὴν ἑνδεκάτην ὥραν, 'those about the eleventh hour'. In τὸ ἀνὰ
20.10 δηνάριον, ἀνά is repeated from above: 'the first' received not 'one d. each' but '*the* (i.e. the stipulated) d.' 'Did (ἐποίησαν) one hour' cannot mean 'laboured', which would be an original ἐπόνησαν.
20.12 The words 'and the heat', despite their proverbial familiarity, look like a gloss on βάρος (here only in the gospels) in 'the *burden* of the day'.

20.15 'Evil eye' occurred in a different sense at 6.23 (q.v.); but 'evil eye' in the sense of envy or grudge is well attested (Deut. 15.9, Ecclus. 14.10).

20.17–23 The announcement is incompatible with the forecast at 17.22 and with the actual entry into Judaea at 19.1. 'On the road', ἐν τῇ ὁδῷ (which acknowledges 19.1), is contradictory with 'being about to go up' (μέλλων ἀναβαίνειν), evidently obtained from 17.22.* This, the last of three forecasts, is the only one to allude to the Roman trial and crucifixion as well as to the condemnation etc. by 'the high priests'. A clumsily executed passage, designed to foreshadow that trial and execution, of which the previous forecasts were innocent, separates the incident of 'the mother of the sons of Zebedee' (which portends the event related at 27.38, q.v.) from the dialogue with Peter (19.27–20.16), which it presupposes.

20.20 Apart from the designation of his sons, James and John, the father Zebedee never appears; but the mother, who makes the application here, is the last named of the women who at 27.56 witness the crucifixion. The mother's request relates to the reply to Peter at 19.28, not understood as irony but taken literally. It presupposes the crucifixion narrative and would more naturally have followed directly after the dialogue with Peter and the end of the parable (20.16).

20.21 In the otherwise verbally exactly similar question and answer below at 20.33 θέλω directly governs ἵνα, which suggests that εἰπέ here is an interpolation.

20.22–3 Jesus replies not to the mother but directly to the two sons. The response 'you do not know what you are asking' is appropriate to a request of which the actual fulfilment will prove

* 'Took aside by themselves', borrowed verbally from 17.1, is in conflict with 'on the road', as if Jesus took the disciples on to a sidetrack.

disagreeable to the recipients. Two persons were to be crucified, 'one on the right and one on the left' of Jesus (27.38), but they are there described, without further explanation, as 'robbers' (λῃσταί). If that was an ironic fulfilment of the mother's request, a crucifixion narrative once existed in which James and John played a prominent part. Jesus does formally promise (πίεσθε, fut. indic.) that the two brothers shall share his fate. What he disclaims authority to promise are the arrangements which will be made in the future kingdom. There was therefore a narrative, embodied within the present book, in which James and John were arrested and crucified with Jesus, a narrative from which they have been eliminated, 27.38 remaining (like this passage) as a vestige of that narrative and of their elimination from it.

0.24–8 The incident is neutralized by a counterblast, which turns out to have to do, not with the request for pre-eminence in the kingdom, but with precedence here and now (ἐν ὑμῖν) among the followers of Jesus. It is thus not an answer, as at 18.1, to the question about being 'greatest in the kingdom'. Rather, a controversy is being carried on over a question of ecclesiastical jurisdiction between the Judaizing upholders of central authority and those content to 'serve' (including sacramentally) dispersed and independent gentile churches. The key is in the reference to 'the gentiles'. *All* rulers (ἄρχοντες) bear authority: rulers rule, which is what makes them 'rulers'; and that is true no more of the 'rulers of the gentiles' than of King Herod or King David. 'Gentiles' is being used as a tauntingly ironical designation for opponents, in particular for the Judaizers and their claim to 'lord it over' others. Hence the difficulty of interpreting the antithesis literally: it is possible to say, 'If you want to be great, you must serve *first*'; but to say, 'If you want to be great, you must be a servant *at the same time*' is a contradiction in terms. Moreover, all cannot be servants of one another; and if they could, is *one* to qualify as μέγας or πρῶτος by being more so than the rest? The conundrum was resolved by the addition of a clause invoking 'the son of man', whose death is here described for the first time as 'ransom' (λύτρον).

The passage is exceptionally rhetorical, with its overblown vocabulary and double tautology: 'the rulers of the gentiles lord it over them, and their great ones use authority over them', a tautology echoed in the following sentence, of which the second limb differs from the first only to the extent of substituting 'first' for 'greatest'. κατακυριεύω is of substantial usage in LXX; but κατεξουσιάζω is not found previously, and not subsequently until Julian (fourth century AD), who may have had it from here, whereas ἐξουσιάζω is frequent.

Mark transcribed the passage with minimal alteration (10.42–4), viz. οἱ δοκοῦντες ἄρχειν for οἱ ἄρχοντες and <u>πάντων</u> δοῦλος for <u>ὑμῶν</u> δοῦλος. It was on the other hand greatly puzzling to Luke (22.24–6), who transplanted it to the 'Last Supper', and undertook two major changes: 'The rulers of the gentiles lord it (κυριευόντων instead of κατακ.) over them, and those who bear authority (ἐξουσιάζοντες) over them are called "benefactors"', thus removing the tautology. He continued that 'among you' all are to be on an equal footing, the greater and the junior, the leader (ἡγούμενος) and the table-server; 'for who is more important, the table-guest or the waiter?' He then proceeded to apply διακονεῖν (see on 4.11) to the sacramental meal.

20.28 The concluding clause, in which διακονεῖν is treated (uniquely, in this sense) as transitive and given a passive, is detachable. It is related—as the words 'for many', ἀντὶ πολλῶν, superfluous here, show—to the formula at 26.28, which affirms the propitiatory interpretation of Jesus' death.

20.29–34 The individual healing which follows—the text may at some stage, as 'when they were departing from Jericho' suggests, have run directly on after 19.2—is a duplicate of 9.27–31, but improvements have been made. (1) More naturally, the two blind men, instead of 'following', are 'sitting by the road'. (2) The unheeded adjuration to silence is deftly transferred to 'the crowd' hushing the complainants, with ἐπετίμησεν (16.20) substituted for the peculiar ἐνεβριμήθη (9.30). (3) The superfluous enquiry 'What do you want?' is prompted by 'this thing' (9.28). (4) ἅπτεσθαι is again used for 'touching' eyes. (5) The men 'follow' Jesus (20.34 ἠκολούθησαν) after, not before, their sight is restored.

Mark (10.46) introduced a bald reference to previous arrival at Jericho; but Luke (18.35–43) placed the incident itself before the entry to Jericho and, perceiving that something had to happen at Jericho to cause it to be mentioned, provided the story of Zacchaeus (19.1ff.). He also eliminated the earlier alternative and reduced the two blind men to one, whose name Mark (10.46) discovered.

20.34 The 'faith' of the sufferers (9.28, 29) is significantly replaced by Jesus' 'compassion', making this the only place in the book where it motivates a single healing, the other occurrences (9.36, 14.14, 15.32) being directed to the 'crowd' generally. Luke (18.42) put 'faith' back into the incident again. The duplication here of the self-consciously (see on 9.27–34) Davidic healing has the purpose of preparing for the Davidic entry into Jerusalem.

21.1 There are two alternative accounts of Jesus' entrance into Jerusalem, viz. 21.1–11 and 21.18–22. The former, as 'king of the Jews', corresponds to the charge on which he was convicted by Pilate (27.11). The other must therefore be taken to belong to the narrative in which he was convicted before the high priest, concerning Jesus' identity as 'Messiah, son of God' (26.62–4).

The events immediately preceding Jesus' arrest and trial, however, do not come until 26.1. The intervening material comprises (1) an episode in the Temple, embodying Jesus' claim to be accredited by John the Baptist; (2) a series of parables on Israel's disobedience; (3) announcement of Israel's punishment and the end of the world. The alternative entrances were combined by being placed side by side, as though, having entered Jerusalem, Jesus went outside again and returned (21.17). To facilitate this device, there had to be some action taking place after the first entrance. This was procured by bringing forward from the second entrance the earlier part (21.12–16) of the original episode in the Temple (21.12–16 + 21.33–7). This deprived the challenge 'by what authority?' (21.33) of its subject-matter.

21.1 'Approach', ἐγγίζειν εἰς, is not found elsewhere in the book. Bethphage occurs here only. The awkward apposition of a familiar place to an unknown one suggests that it may have been intended to replace B. by the Mountain of Olives. That is to be the scene of the eschatological discourse (24.3), and it recurs at 26.30. Its only occurrence in the Old Testament, besides 2 Sam. 15.30, is (significantly) Zech. 14.4.

21.2 The incident provided the model for the preparations for the Passover below (26.17–19). Both have the same verb συνέταξε 'instructed' (21.6), so used here only in the New Testament and besides in the Old Testament at Zech. 11.13 LXX (quoted at 27.10).

21.5 The Old Testament citation is the first of the sort since 12.17 and 13.35, and otherwise since 4.14. The commencement of the citation of Zech. 9.9, 'Rejoice exceedingly, daughter of Zion; declare it, daughter of Jerusalem', has been replaced by 'Say to the daughter of Zion' from Isa. 62.11. The description of the animals does not conform precisely with Zechariah, either M ('on a he-ass, on a male ass the foal of she-asses') or LXX ('upon a beast of burden and a young foal'). 'Beast of burden' (ὑποζύγιον) and 'foal' (πῶλος) are not specific to asses.

The expression in Zechariah was intensive, 'an ass, nay, the foal of an ass'; but it is taken literally by the fulfilment narrative to imply two animals. The older is made feminine, no doubt in order to identify it as the mother and so account for two animals being procured, as the she-ass would not leave its foal. Luke (19.30) boldly substituted a single animal, a πῶλος ('colt'), and scrapped the citation: there is nothing to indicate that he intended the 'colt' to be the 'colt of an ass'. Mark (11.2) followed him.

21.6 It is implied, as below at 26.19, that the anticipated objection eventualized and was answered in accordance with Jesus' instructions. 'He sat upon them' (cf. 28.2 ἐκάθητο ἐπάνω) leaves the problem of two beasts, one rider, unsolved; but the reference to the disciples putting 'the clothes' on the animals as a makeshift saddle is too awkward. 'The clothes' belong with the crowd in the next sentence. The model is 2 Kgs. 9.13: 'I have anointed you king over Israel. And hearing they made haste and took each his own cloak and put it under him on the top of the steps.'

21.8, 9 'Hosanna', ωσαννα, only in this passage (= Mark 11.9, 10; John 12.13) in the gospels; Luke pointedly omitted the line (19.38). Ps. 118.25 הושיעה נא 'save, pray' (LXX σῶσον δή), an imperative from the same root as 'Jesus', is the only occurrence in the Old Testament. The dative '*to* the son of David' is peculiar, unless it is to be construed as 'give victory to the son of David'. Equally difficult is ἐν ὑψίστοις: ὕψιστος here only in this book but common—of God—in Luke (θεὸς ὑ.), whence Mark 5.7 (= Luke 8.28), and in the Old Testament. The expression ἐν ὑψίστοις, meaning apparently 'in heaven', is found in the Old Testament only at Ps. 148.1, 'Praise the Lord from heaven, praise him in the highest', αἰνεῖτε τὸν κύριον ἐκ τῶν οὐρανῶν, αἰνεῖτε αὐτὸν ἐν τοῖς ὑψίστοις, במרומים. '*Most* of the crowd' appears deliberate, as if implying that not all hailed Jesus as Davidic king. 'Blessed is he' etc., a simple formula of welcome, which immediately follows Ps. 118.25 (above) ברוך הבא בשם יהוה.

21.10 A sequence of events has been created which would enable, indeed oblige, 'the high priests' etc. to arrest Jesus and hand him over to the Roman governor (27.2). (1) The 'whole city' is thrown into uproar (ἐσείσθη); (2) Jesus enters the Temple and violently interrupts procedures essential to the sacrificial routine; (3) he acknowledges and accepts the crowd's acclamation of him as 'son of David'; (4) the high priests, who are angered (ἠγανάκτησαν) by all this, receive no reply to their challenge: 'by what authority (ἐξουσία) do you do these things?' (21.23).

In the course of combining this narrative with an original, which led up to the Jewish trial for blasphemy, major alterations have been introduced, some of a palliatory character.

'Was shaken', ἐσείσθη, is absolute, equivalent to ἐταράχθη at 2.3, a perhaps not unintended echo. If 'the crowds' knew that Jesus was 'the son of David', how came 'the whole city' to be asking 'Who is this?' or the crowds which had hailed him 'son of David' to be answering the question with so derogatory an understatement as 'the prophet from Nazareth in Galilee'? Those who regarded Jesus as no more than a prophet (13.57, 16.14, 21.46) can hardly identify him as 'the son of David'.

21.12 The violent action attributed to Jesus has no preparation and no sequel, attracts no reaction, and is not referred to again. It would have been tantamount to causing a cessation of the Temple routine. As this required arrangements for worshippers to acquire money for the Temple dues and animals for sacrifice, the practices could not in themselves be open to objection. Had extortionate prices justified Jesus' measures, that essential point would not have been left unmentioned.

Why should those who were *buying* be selected for expulsion? The object of creating an antithesis to 'prayer', προσευχή, gave rise to an illogicality. Luke (19.45) reduced the victims to 'the sellers', while John 2.14ff. elaborated by explaining that the beasts sold were bulls and sheep and arming Jesus with a whip. Mark (11.16) inserted 'and did not allow a σκεῦος to be carried through the Temple', which, whatever the point, is inappropriate since, unlike the expulsions, it would involve ongoing surveillance—unless it meant 'stopped someone who happened to be carrying a pot through the Temple'.

The money-changers were dependent upon their 'tables'. The corresponding requisite of the dove-sellers was not their 'seats'—they could sell doves without sitting on chairs—but the 'cages' in which they kept the doves, παγίδας, not καθέδρας, were indispensable.

21.13 The proof-text, Isa. 56.7, 'my house shall be called a house of prayer *for all the gentiles*', has been mutilated by excising the crucial conclusion, 'for all the gentiles', and by adding a spurious charge of simony, backed by Jer. 7.11, as a motive for the action attributed to Jesus.

21.15, 16 The high priests etc. were angered by 'seeing the things which Jesus did', i.e. his actions in the Temple; but the allusion is diverted by the introduction of healings (21.14) and the unique description of them as τὰ θαυμάσια, 'miracles'. Spurious likewise is τοὺς παῖδας τοὺς κράζοντας ἐν τῷ ἱερῷ: it was not 'children', let alone 'in the Temple', who had been shouting (21.4) 'Hosanna'. Giving 'children' its encoded meaning, 'gentiles' (νήπιοι), the second proof-text becomes as pro-gentile as the first: it is the gentiles who will acclaim Jesus as saviour. By asking Jesus if he 'heard' them, the high priests are inviting him to disavow the style. The proof-text from Ps. 8.3 fits the context all the better with 'praise', αἶνον (LXX), preferred to עז 'strength' (M).

21.17 'Left them', as at 16.4, is the conclusion to a snub or confrontation. 'Lodged', αὐλίζομαι, here only (= Luke 21.37) in the New Testament. Like Bethphage (21.1), Bethany is treated as known, which it is not outside the New Testament.

21.18 The incident, which Luke omits, is preposterous—to use the power of faith and prayer to shrivel a disappointing fig-tree. The apostrophe to the tree is not only irritable but absurd—fig-trees don't last 'for eternity'—εἰς τὸν αἰῶνα, an expression which occurs here only in the book (like παραχρῆμα 'instantly' and μηκέτι, 'nevermore') but is a favourite of John. Absurd too is the promise to the disciples: if you have faith, you too can go around shrivelling fig-trees and shifting mountains.

'By the road', ἐπὶ τῆς ὁδοῦ, shows that aor. ἐπαναγαγών, 'having made his way', should be pres. ἐπανάγων, 'while making his way'.

21.19 ἐπείνασεν 'grew hungry' is a false lead. The grotesqueness of
the incident only disappears when it is understood as an allegory
of the fate awaiting a sterile Jerusalem that refused to allow the
gentiles to share in the salvation offered to it and to them. The
21.20, 21 curse on the fig-tree symbolizing the city which 'bears no fruit'
(cf. Jer. 8.13, 'there are no figs on the fig-trees; even the leaves
are withered') has been converted into a pointless and vindictive
miracle by being rounded out with a dialogue with the disciples
(see on 17.14–21).

21.22 The gloss has trivialized the allegory: it stimulated Mark's rewriting (11.23, 24).

21.23 The expostulation 'By what authority do you do these things [i.e. the intervention in the Temple]. Who gave you this authority?' belongs directly after 21.16, from where it has been severed by Jesus' absence (21.17). Jesus' appeal to John is more than cheap repartee ('tell me A, and I will tell you B'). It is a substantive claim to authentication by the Baptist: the son of God has, as such, sufficient authority. The high priests are hard put to it to find reasons for their indispensable silence; no doubt they were grateful to take the hint at 14.5. It was not to the 'teaching' of Jesus that they objected as unauthorized but to his *actions*: διδάσκοντι (21.23) marks an attempt to suggest a meaning for ταῦτα ποιεῖς.

21.24 'A thing', λόγον ἕνα, a Hebraism: דבר = λόγος = 'thing'.

21.25 John's 'baptism', βάπτισμα (rather than e.g. κήρυγμα 'announcement'), is a conscious cross-reference to 3.13–17. Jesus is doing what John foretold.

21.27 The requisite reply, 'we do not know', is embarrassingly lame.

21.28 In the two parables, omitted by Luke and Mark, which follow without introduction, work in the vineyard is used to signify converting the gentiles. The first is akin to 20.1–15 (where ὕπαγε and ἀπελθεῖν occur in a similar context), with the moral that it is better to say No and then obey than to say Yes and disobey. The question posed (in the singular) is precisely stated, but remains unanswered, namely, who are represented by respectively the first brother, who initially agreed to obey but then disobeyed, and the second brother, who was defiant at first but afterwards became obedient? They are reminiscent of Acts, where Peter (11.2ff.) accepted the command to admit gentiles but then let the matter lapse, whereas Paul (13.46ff.) persecuted the church but then repented (μεταμεληθείς) and became 'the apostle of the gentiles'. It is because the second (repentant) son obeyed that the tax-gatherers etc. will be in the kingdom and the Jews will not (21.31).

.31, 32 'The tax-gatherers and whores' represent the gentiles (see on 9.10). 'Be before you in the kingdom' is euphemism for being in the kingdom *instead of* you, the high priests and elders of the people. For 'kingdom of God' see on 3.2.

21.33 The 'vineyard' in the second parable has the same allegorical meaning as in the first: God has left Israel in charge of it, but when the due time (καιρός) comes for the 'fruits' (of gentile conversion) to be produced,* Israel violently resists two successive requests and finally, seeking to monopolize the property, slays God's own son. At this point the figure of the absent owner

* The distant owner's unrealistic demand to receive ripe fruit illustrates how allegory (καρπός 'fruit') can conflict with the story of a parable.

is replaced by that of an avenging potentate, who destroys Israel and turns the inheritance over to tenants who will obey his demands. The pedestrian interpretation at 21.43 hardly needed to be interpolated. Great care has been taken to contrive not just one but two rebuffed approaches to the tenants, prior to that of the owner's son, in which the owner's servants are physically maltreated. This would appear to correspond with the persecution of 'the prophets before you' (5.12) and with being 'partners in the blood of the prophets in the days of your fathers' (23.30). Evidently the gentile church was careful to claim two phases of persecuted predecessors in the same cause previous to the death of Jesus.

21.33 For the interpolated 'owner' in apposition to 'man' see on 20.1. The citation, which Luke virtually eliminated (20.9), is a direct quotation of Isa. 5.2. The Hebrew has 'fenced it and stoned it and planted a choice type of vine (שרק) and built a tower in the middle and dug a wine-vat in it'. LXX translates this exactly apart from substituting for 'stoned' (סקל) 'provided it with (vine-) poles' (ἐχαράκωσα). The citation here includes neither 'stoned' nor 'poled', omits the special term שרק, and brings 'planted' up to the beginning because in the original a vineyard has already been mentioned before the point at which the quotation starts. The particular citation is chosen to recall the curse, with which the passage in Isaiah terminates, calling down destruction upon the vineyard because (like the fig-tree) it produced no 'fruit'. The parable represents a progression, introducing, as a collateral reason for the punishment, the killing of God's son.

21.34, 35 The first servants to be sent were maltreated short of homicide. 'And another they killed' is an interpolation: it is tautologous if 'stoning' implies killing; if not, it destroys the intended climax. The second, 'more numerous' despatch of servants, merely to be treated 'the same', adds nothing to the story. This evident determination to arrange previous 'rounds' before the climax, at whatever cost in probability, suggests a connection with 23.37, which—anachronistically, of course—implies the presence and repeated persecution of some element in Jerusalem before its fall. The flogging administered to the first lot of messengers recalls 10.27.

21.37 After what had happened, the owner had little reason to expect his son to be 'respected' (ἐντρέπεσθαι here only in Matthew), a puzzle which Luke (20.13) did not much alleviate by inserting ἴσως 'perhaps' (unique in the New Testament). There is an important similarity with 22.6, where there was less occasion for unwilling guests to proceed to extreme measures against the messengers. Plainly 22.6 is not original, being out of harmony with 22.5. The fact that in the next parable the reference to an incredibly violent reaction of the offended host is a later insertion raises the probability that 21.40, 41 are a similar insertion.

21.39 The heir being 'thrown out of the vineyard' suggests an extramural place of execution.

In the elicited answer—the classical idiom κακοὺς κακῶς here only in the New Testament—owners whose rent-collectors have been rebuffed or even murdered do not 'destroy' the tenants, though they may seek to have them punished. The underlying meaning has broken through the allegory. The letting of the vineyard to other tenants does not imply that the new 'nation'—ἔθνος (sing. here and 24.7 only) is taken to represent the gentiles—will take over Jerusalem but that they will inherit the kingdom.

21.42 The vacuous and superfluous interpretation of the parable interpolated at 21.43 interrupts the item, 21.42 + 21.44, which is also out of place. The citation of Ps. 118.22, 23 and the allusion to Dan. 2.34, 35, 44, 45, which appears to have been attached to it, are wildly inapposite to the parable of the vineyard. The formula used for introduction ('Did you never read . . . ?') should preface rebuttal of an attack or reproof, as it does above at 21.16.

'The scriptures', αἱ γραφαί—obscure at 22.29 and 26.54, 56 (the only other occurrences in Matthew)—is here applied to a Psalm (118.22, 23). It corresponds to כתובים, the parts of the Hebrew scriptures which are neither the Law nor the Prophets. The crucial expression in the citation is κεφαλὴ γωνίας, ראש פנה. It must in the context denote a stone which is structurally essential, upon which the stability of a building depends—in fact, the equivalent of 'cornerstone' or 'keystone'.

21.44 The next sentence but one would then be a not very successful attempt, with the assistance of Dan. 2.34, 35, 44, 45, to provide a relevance, perceived to be missing, for the citation. The verbs θλᾶν 'smash', and λικμᾶν 'crush' (lit. 'winnow'), unique here (= Luke 20.18) in the New Testament, are common in LXX, recurring twelve and eighteen times respectively (including Dan. 2.44, 6.25). The sentence is absent from one manuscript tradition.

.45, 46 The horrified expostulation of the high priests (21.15 and 21.23) ought to be directly followed by Jesus' arrest and arraignment before Pilate. Why that did not yet happen it was essential to explain, by alleging fear of 'the crowds' (cf. 21.26). It was not because of his parables—the high priests would hardly have failed to get the drift of them—but for his subversive actions that they wished to arrest Jesus. They listen impassively enough to the parables which follow. Luke (19.47, 48), followed by Mark (11.18), tried to make amends by placing the passage after 21.13, so that the incident in the Temple should provide the motivation.

In the next parable God, having destroyed Jerusalem ('their city', 22.7), calls in the gentiles to fill the table at his son's (Messianic) bridal feast.

22.2 The parable is designated a 'kingdom parable'. For 'is likened' see on 13.24. εἶπεν ἐν παραβολαῖς αὐτοῖς λέγων is equivalent to 13.3 ἐλάλησεν αὐτοῖς πολλὰ ἐν παραβολαῖς, although only one parable follows. The groom's father is glossed as 'a king' because of what happens below.

22.3 The summons, preliminary to the final one at 22.4, provides the requisite double 'round' of warning (see on 21.34, 35). This gave rise to the awkward repetition in two senses of καλεῖν ('invite' or 'call') in καλεῖν τοὺς κεκλημένους. The 'bulls', οἱ ταῦροί μου, are suspicious alongside τὰ σιτιστά, implying an absurd antithesis between 'bulls' (thin bulls?) and 'fatlings'; and this in turn brings into question τὸ ἄριστόν μου ἡτοίμακα, 'I have my breakfast ready', a flat paraphrase superfluous to the graphic details and πάντα ἕτοιμα which follow. Being a morning meal, ἄριστον is less appropriate to a wedding than δεῖπνον (contrasted with it in Luke 14.12), which would carry the revelry on into the evening and night. Luke (14.16) substituted δεῖπνον and eliminated the wedding. He also, in true midrashic fashion, elaborated the excuses (14.18–20).

22.7 'Those' in '*those* murderers', like '*those* tenants' at 21.40, adds a dramatic touch of pathos.

22.8, 9 'Wedding', γάμος (γάμοι below), is used in lieu of 'wedding-feast'. 'Worthy' recalls its specialized sense in 10.11 (q.v.) but the antithesis is not satisfactory, as would be e.g. ἦλθαν instead of ἄξιοι ἦσαν, and the sentence is superfluous. The host did not need to describe to his servants a situation which was perfectly obvious to them. 'The highways', τὰς διεξόδους [τῶν ὁδῶν]: 'thoroughfare' is the meaning of δ., to which τῶν ὁδῶν ('thoroughfares of the roads') can scarcely be appended: it probably represents a gloss, τὰς ὁδούς, turned into the genitive on being taken into the text. (Weirdly, ὁδῶν causes similar difficulty in Herodotus 1.199.2 in the vicinity of διέξοδος.) It is not clear what the choice of the unusual word was intended to add. The same gloss may account for the interpolated εἰς τὰς ὁδούς in the next sentence, which is impossible after διεξόδους.

22.10 In '*those* servants' the demonstrative pronoun marks, as in 21.40 and 22.7, the approach of a climax. 'Bad and good' has a colloquial rather than a moral flavour, viz. all sorts and conditions; it does not imply that the original invitees were 'good'. νυμφών, here only in the New Testament apart from the mysterious 9.15 (q.v.), must mean the room in which the celebration including the feast took place, and not, as in Tobit 6.17 (the only occurrence in LXX) the bridal bedchamber. ἀνακειμένων ('the room was filled with guests sitting at table') is uncalled for.

22.11–13 The unreasonable behaviour of 'the king' in this passage, contradicting the drift of the parable as a whole, marks it as a riposte to counter the parable's pro-gentile tendency: it is, it indicates, all very well for the gentiles to be 'called', but too bad if they do not observe the legal requirements (circumcision?).

22.13 The word διάκονος, elsewhere in this book only at 20.26 (= 23.11), means specifically a servant who waits at table (cf. on 8.15 διακονεῖν).

22.14 The 'moral' applies not to the main parable, where the uninvited guests are at least as numerous as those invited, but to the polemical tailpiece: it is all very well to 'call' large numbers of gentiles, but only those properly dressed, i.e. the relatively few Law-observers, will be 'chosen'. 'Called', κλητοί, and 'chosen', ἐκλεκτοί, words equated at Rev. 17.14, are contrasted. The stock formula about 'outer darkness' (8.12; 13.42, 50; 24.51; 25.30) was a missile used by both parties to the controversy.

22.15 After the interposed parable 22.1–14, the 'high priests and the Pharisees' (21.45), here reduced to 'the Pharisees', still anxious to arrest Jesus, lay a trap to enable them to accuse him of denouncing the payment of 'tax to Caesar'. They conceal their hand by sending 'their disciples' in the company of 'the Herodians'.

'Herodians' is mysterious. A word of Latin form, derivative from 'Herod', not known apart from this passage (= Mark 12.13) and Mark 3.6, where it is inserted into the similarly worded sentence corresponding with 12.14 above, it should signify 'agents of Herod'; but though 'tax to Caesar' was levied in Judaea from AD 6, no Herod was responsible for raising it except Herod Agrippa between AD 40 and 44. παγιδεύω (here only in the New Testament) means at Eccles. 9.12 (LXX) 'catch in a trap or net' and at 1 Sam. 28.9 (LXX) (exactly as here with ἐν τῷ λόγῳ τούτῳ following) 'inveigle someone into incriminating himself'. Mark relieved the awkwardness by simply 'sending some of the Pharisees and of the Herodians' (12.13), while Luke removed all problems by substituting (20.20) 'agents pretending to be righteous'. ἀληθής and ἀλήθεια, here only in Matthew, 'truthfulness', of a person. 'You care (μέλει here only in this book) for no one' is equivalent to 'you are no respecter of persons', οὐ βλέπεις [εἰς] πρόσωπον ἀνθρώπων. βλέπειν πρόσωπον (cf. 18.11) is fixed by the context as meaning the opposite to obeying God. Luke substituted λαμβάνειν 'accept' for βλέπειν and omitted ἀνθρώπων. πρόσωπον λαμβάνειν is the implied basis of the words προσωποληπτεῖν,—λήπτης, -ληψία, which occur only in Acts and the Epistles and have the different sense of discriminating between man and man, suggesting the possibility that these may have been Christian locutions derived from this very passage in Luke (cf. Gal. 2.6 πρόσωπον ὁ Θεὸς ἀνθρώπου οὐ λαμβάνει). Jude 16 has π. θαυμάζειν. The meaning here has to be 'you do not put man before God', but the whole redundant wording καὶ οὐ μέλει σοι περὶ οὐδενός. οὐ γὰρ βλέπεις εἰς πρόσωπον ἀνθρώπων can be seen as an early gloss to explain ἀληθής.

22.17 For 'tax', κῆνσος, see on 17.25.

22.18, 19 'Badness', πονηρία (here only in Matthew), the noun from πονηρός, for which, as a standing epithet of 'the Pharisees', see on 9.4. They are 'hypocrites' because they themselves have devised means to 'pay tribute to Caesar', as their possession of the 'tribute money' reveals.

22.21 The inscription was in the possessive. The equally elliptical answer therefore signifies: 'it bears Caesar's likeness and the inscription says that it belongs to him'.

The addition of the words 'God what is God's' wrecks the force of the retort by answering a different question: the issue was whether anything should be given to *Caesar*.

22.23 'On that day', merely a formal transition: see on 13.1. The next attempt to render Jesus arrestable is entrusted to 'the Sadducees', who deny 'the resurrection'. This is perilous, if accepted. If there is no resurrection, the kingdom promised by Jesus to his followers, the ζωὴ αἰώνιος of 19.16, must be terrestrial, i.e. the supersession of the Roman empire—his kingdom must be 'of this world' (cf. John 18.36). Jesus declines to concur but relies instead upon the promise, referred to at 8.11, that 'many will come from the east and the west and feast with Abraham and Isaac and Jacob in the kingdom of heaven'.

λέγοντες μὴ εἶναι ἀνάστασιν (22.23), which means no more than 'denying (on this occasion) that there is a resurrection', was misunderstood as a general description by Mark (12.18), a conclusion avoided by Luke (20.27).

With the simple trap of denying 'the resurrection' has been combined, καὶ ἐπηρώτησαν (22.23), a conundrum derived from the Mosaic prescription (cf. 19.7) of remarriage of childless widows, which implies an embarrassment at 'the resurrection', which Jesus dismisses as absurd.

22.34 Getting no joy from the effort of 'the Sadducees'—'silenced', ἐφίμωσεν, is no doubt selected under the influence of 22.12—'the Pharisees' put their heads together—the wording evokes Ps. 2.2 (LXX), 'the rulers of the earth *take counsel together* (συνήχθησαν ἐπὶ τὸ αὐτό) against the Lord and against his anointed'—and make a last attempt to impale (πειράζειν, cf. 22.19) Jesus upon the wording of the *shema*ʿ, which the interrogator must have assumed would be Jesus' response to the question. Literally taken, the שמע overrides any loyalty or obedience except to God. The bleak quotation of Deut. 6.5 is therefore self-sufficient; but Jesus evades the trap by answering a different question, viz. there is also 'a second commandment' (see on 5.43–8).

22.35 'Lawyer', νομικός, a word occurring only here in the book, and not at all in Mark (= 12.28 εἷς τῶν γραμματέων) or John, but frequently in Luke (not only 10.25, derived from this passage, but generally as equivalent to γραμματεῖς in combination with Φαρισαῖοι). The word seems to be chosen with a view to the content of the dialogue and may be interpolated.

22.36 'Teacher', διδάσκαλε, is the form of address carefully attributed to all three interlocutors (also 22.16 and 22.24), as conceding to Jesus no more than the status of a rabbi.

For μεγάλη, 'greatest', cf. 20.24–8. 'Which' is here ποῖος, an interrogative found only in the latter half of this book (19.18; 21.23–7; 24.42, 43).

22.37 The LXX of Deut. 6.5 has 'strength' (δύναμις) instead of 'thought' (διάνοια), which, though abundant in LXX, is found in the gospels only in this rendering (= Mark 12.30, Luke 10.27) and in Luke's psalm 1.51. The Hebrew has מאדך, a word unique in the Old Testament indicating 'muchness'. The sense required no addition to 'heart and soul'.

22.39 The reply to the question was complete with the first sentence (Deut. 6.5). To add, as if by afterthought, the citation of Lev. 19.18 was to conform with a familiar association of the two commandments (see 19.19).

'As thyself', כמוך, is necessarily translated into Greek with the accusative reflexive, 'as (thou lovest) thyself', but means no more than 'as thou', i.e. '(because he is) as thou', the point spelt out in Lev. 19.34 'thou shalt love him (the stranger) as thou, because you also were strangers in the land of Egypt'.

The parallelism of ἀγαπήσεις τὸν θεόν and ἀγαπήσεις τὸν πλησίον, and consequently the association of the two passages, is nowhere previously found, though implicit in the 'excess' righteousness expounded at 5.21ff. The expression 'each his neighbour' is the Hebrew reciprocal ('one another', ἀλλήλους) איש את רעהו. There is no distinctive force in 'neighbour' such as can naturally be given to the Greek literal translation, ὁ πλησίος or ὁ πλησίον (as Luke 10.29 understands it).

22.40 The 'prophets' are a gratuitous irrelevance, and 'hang' (κρέμαται) gives the wrong sense (unexampled if it means 'depend'): it was inserted as a result of overlooking the understood verb 'to be'.

22.41 The connection—συνηγμένων refers back to συνήχθησαν (22.34)—is artificial: Jesus took the opportunity of 'the Pharisees' being all together to turn the tables upon them by purporting to prove, again from 'the scriptures' (Ps. 110.1), that the Messiah (for claiming to be which he will be convicted in the high priest's court) cannot be the 'son of David' (for claiming to be which he will be convicted by Pilate). The argument is pointedly denoted (22.46) as conclusive.

The citation does not prove the point: even assuming it relates to the Messiah and is spoken by David 'under inspiration' (for ἐν πνεύματι cf. 4.1), David could still acknowledge his descendant as his 'lord'.

22.44 LXX and M have 'footstool', ὑποπόδιον, הדם, instead of ὑποκάτω, 'beneath', here, which suits 'put' (θῶ) better. The identification of 'my lord' in Psalm 110 with the Messiah is arbitrary. The repetition of 'lord', κύριος, is due to the substitution of אדני for יהוה in the Hebrew, 'the utterance of Yahweh to my lord'.

23.1 A polemic follows against the rabbinical schools which arose in the wake of the sack of Jerusalem. From these the church is sharply differentiated: the Law remains mandatory; the rabbinical elaboration of it is not.

The change of focus is emphasized by the description of the hearers as 'the crowds and his disciples', a combination the awkwardness of which Luke acknowledged ('said to the disciples *in the hearing of* all the people', 20.45). At first 'the scribes and the Pharisees' are accused of devising burdensome obligations to impose upon others, which they do not themselves discharge. This invective is cognate with 11.28, 29 (where also φορτίον), but it adds the fresh accusation of insincerity. The desire to be 'observed by men' (23.5) echoes 6.1ff. in content and in wording (θεαθῆναι in both places) and leads into a contrast with the behaviour prescribed for 'you' of eschewing being called 'rabbi' or 'father' or 'founder', which is related to 18.4 (ταπεινῶσαι ἑαυτόν in common) and to 20.26–8 (διάκονος, διακονεῖν in common).

23.4 It is not that burdens are first bound up and then put on men's shoulders; 'and put them' is interpolated due to failure to construe δεσμεύουσιν with ἐπί: the burden is strapped to the shoulders. The reference to 'finger' is contrary to the sense. Naturally, if the burdens were heavy, they could not be 'moved' with a finger, but κινεῖν cannot mean 'touch' or the like: no wonder Luke (11.46) replaced it with προσψαύετε, 'put out a hand to'.

23.5 The passage implies acquaintance on the reader's part with Jewish practices: φυλακτήρια, prayer-bands on the forehead, so called because of the similarity to amulets ('preservatives'). Jesus himself at 9.20 has a 'fringe', κράσπεδον.

23.6 The terms πρωτοκλισία and πρωτοκαθεδρίαι, places of honour at table and front seats in the synagogues, appear not to be found elsewhere.

23.8 The first and third prohibitions are synonymous, possibly representing expansions of a gloss or glosses on *rabbi*: 'be not called "rabbi"'; 'be not called instructor' (the parallel would be even more exact with καθηγητά, sing., rather than καθηγηταί). καθηγητής, unique in the New Testament and LXX, is found from the first century BC in the sense of 'professor, founder of a school', the exact equivalent of רבי 'my master' in post-biblical Hebrew.

23.13–36 There follows abruptly a passage which comprises an initial series of four reproaches, where the common formula οὐαὶ ὑμῖν, γραμματεῖς καὶ Φαρισαῖοι ὑποκριταί, ὅτι has been expanded with elaborations on the theme of 'blind leaders' (ὁδηγοί τυφλοί, cf. 15.14)—23.16, 24, 26. The fifth 'woe' (23.27, 28), retaining the common formula, appears to be merely a restatement of the fourth. The sixth goes off into a full-scale denunciation of a second generation which will not escape the punishment for its 'fathers' having murdered unspecified 'prophets' and 'righteous', a persecution they are doomed to repeat in the present.

The section ends (23.36) with the asseveration that 'all this will come (i.e. be visited) upon this (present) generation' and an apostrophe to Jerusalem. An explicit prophecy *ex eventu* of the destruction of Jerusalem (or of the Temple) follows (24.2), introduced embarrassingly by Jesus' disciples 'showing him' the buildings (24.1).

'Woe betide', οὐαί, first found (repeatedly) in LXX with nominative or (as here) with dative, represents various Hebrew exclamations: אוי, אוֹ, הוי, הוֹ; cf. 11.21. For ὑποκριταί, here only in apposition, see on 6.2.

23.13 The present tenses εἰσέρχεσθε and εἰσερχομένους in the second sentence have to be understood as future: 'you will not enter', 'those who (would otherwise) enter'. The Judaizers bar the kingdom of heaven to 'men' (the gentile world) by telling them they must observe the Law, instead of relying upon faith in Jesus' identity and action. They thus will not get in themselves and will prevent others who could.

One manuscript tradition inserts, before or after the first 'woe', the following: 'Woe to you, sanctimonious scribes and Pharisees, because you devour the houses of widows, though praying at length on any excuse; therefore you shall receive additional condemnation.' It is a garbled copy of the sentence which Luke (20.47 = Mark 12.40) substituted here for the 'woes', which he removed to 11.39–52.

23.15 The next 'woe' is a bitterly polemical reflection upon Jewish converts: they are absurdly few in number ('one convert') and will be 'doubly' damned as a result of the pernicious doctrine they imbibe. Logically, one can be a 'son of Gehenna' once but not twice or three times over. The exaggerated adverb expresses the ironical bitterness of the denunciation. διπλότερον here only in the New Testament.

'Son of Gehenna' is a Hebraism for 'one doomed to G.' For G. as the opposite fate to entry into the kingdom, cf. 10.28, 18.9. 'Convert', προσήλυτος (here only in the New Testament except Acts 2.11, 6.5, 13.43), has a different meaning in LXX, where it is frequent as 'stranger' or 'sojourner', viz. non-Jew living in Israel. 'Land', ἡ ξηρά ('the dry'), here only in the New Testament.

23.16–22 The repetitive 'woes' formula is interrupted in order to insert a mockery of halakhic doctrines on a binding oath. At the end of it the knife is twisted by applying the principle that an oath 'by X' is an oath by whatever is on X, so as to argue that an oath 'by heaven' is an oath by God's throne and therefore by God himself (cf. 5.34).

23.24 The ironical 'camel' of 19.24 reappears.

The accusation is that discharge of minuscule obligations in the law of tithes (Deut. 14.22) covers up the evasion of more important requirements of the Law. The mocking comment 'sieve out the gnat' etc. renders superfluous the luckless attempt of one glossator to specify these more important requirements and of another to make the moral clear.

23.25 The next 'woe' brings up the theme of purity, external or ritual and internal or moral, which was explored in ch. 15. Those attacked are careful of the cleanliness of the exterior (τὸ ἔξωθεν) but careless of the defilement of the interior (ἔσωθεν). The contrast has been ruined by an interpolation which supplied a physical identification of the exterior (the 'cup' and the 'bowl'), and an absurd deduction based upon it which enjoins cleaning the inside first 'so that the outside too may become clean'. The result is a cup and bowl full of 'robbery and incontinence'. The impurities alleged, of ἁρπαγή (cf. 7.15, where 'false prophets' are ἅρπαγες) and incontinence, are abusive and treated as notorious.

Luke (11.39) saw the difficulties but was not happy in his conjectures, 'cup *and plate*' (πίναξ), and made the contrast between those who cleanse '*their* exterior' while 'their interior' is full of 'robbery and wickedness (πονηρία)'. The illogical comment 'cleanse first the inside so that the outside may be clean too' he completely romanced away: 'did not he who made the outside make the inside? Howbeit give the contents away in alms and everything will be clean for you.' 'Incontinence' (ἀκρασία) is unsatisfactory. 'Uncleanliness' (ἀκαθαρσία), as at 23.27 below, would at least have provided an intelligible antithesis. Luke (11.39) replaced the word with πονηρία, 'wickedness'.

23.27 The following 'woe' makes the identical point, using in part the same terminology (ἔξωθεν, ἔσωθεν, γέμειν), which raises the possibility that it may have been composed as an alternative to 23.25, 26, perceived to be difficult and unintelligible.

'Resemble', παρομοιάζειν, is unique not only in LXX but apparently in Greek. Luke (11.44) altered the subject to 'concealed' (ἄδηλα) tombs, the presence of which is not suspected, perhaps reading or understanding κεκονιμένοις 'covered with dust', i.e. hidden so as to be walked upon unknowingly.

23.29 The concluding 'woe' is on a different pattern. Those attacked are described as building the tombs of 'the prophets' and adorning the graves of 'the righteous' while declaring that, if they had been around in their fathers' time, they would not have taken part with them in 'the blood of the prophets'. (κοινωνοί 'partners' here only in the gospels apart from Luke 5.10, where the meaning is partners in an enterprise.) On this the comment is made that thereby they admit being the sons of those who 'murdered the prophets'. They are not themselves accused of having done the dark deeds perpetrated a generation ago. Luke (11.47, 48) attempted to produce a paradox by accusing them of approval of the murders: 'so you are witnesses to, *and approve of*, your fathers' deeds'. The real paradox, however (without which the obvious fact of their being sons of their fathers would be irrelevant), is that despite their disclaimer, they have inherited the retribution which will overtake them: being 'the offspring of vipers', they cannot escape 'judgement'; as predicted below at 23.36, 'all these things' (i.e. the punishment for the murders) 'will be visited upon this generation'. They are heirs to a curse similar to that created by 'all the people' at 27.25 when they cried out: 'His blood be upon us and upon our children.'

23.32 There were evidently two distinct 'classes of person', both described as προφῆται, whose victimization has created an inescapable curse: (1) those in the previous generation, 'the days of our fathers', προφῆται and δίκαιοι; and (2) in the more recent past, those 'sent' with a view to 'filling up the measure', namely προφῆται καὶ σοφοὶ καὶ γραμματεῖς.* The two classes no doubt correspond to the two groups sent in the parable by the owner of the vineyard (21.34 and 36) before he sends his own son.

The later class is associated with the Judaizing church by the material shared with 10.17–35 and particularly by the formula 10.16 ἰδοὺ ἐγὼ ἀποστέλλω ὑμᾶς. That would leave the earlier class available to be identified with the followers of John the Baptist (to whom the epithet δίκαιοι, 'righteous', would be apt). The respective dates of the two persecutions have to be (1) a generation before the fall of Jerusalem and (2) the period immediately pre-

* Luke (11.49), nonplussed, substituted the empty term ἀπόστολοι, the noun corresponding to the verb ἀποστέλλω.

ceding it. The most exhaustive search* has failed to find evidence of penitential tomb-building in the first century AD; but the latter period is fixed by the curious detail supplied at 23.35.

πληρώσατε, imperative, would have to be understood as ironical advice: πληρώσετε, future, matches the context (ἀποκτενεῖτε etc. 23.34) better than ἐπληρώσατε, aorist.

23.33 'Serpents' is a gloss on 'offspring of vipers', which it assumes to be a Hebraism, whereas the context here implies that the phrase is meant literally: the fathers are the 'vipers' and their sons the 'offspring'. 'Of Gehenna' is also a gloss, on 'judgement'—the same equation as at 5.22.

23.35 The fall of Jerusalem is made the retribution for the shedding of 'righteous blood' throughout the whole of the past. However startling might seem the introduction of Abel at the beginning of the series, it was not unintelligible: he was murdered because his offering to God was accepted, making him a forerunner and type of those who would offer Jesus as an acceptable and sufficient propitiation. The same thought is spelt out in Heb. 11.4. The terminal deed in the series did not need to be specified; indeed, the words which follow 'Abel the righteous' are dispensable, and the symbolism of Abel is clearer without them. In any case, the list could not stop in the reign of Joash (ninth century BC), when according to 2 Chr. 24.21 a Zacharias was stoned to death 'in the Temple court'. By an audacious anachronism an event during the siege of Jerusalem itself was made the terminal point. Josephus (*BJ* 4.343) relates how in AD 68–9 zealots murdered 'in the middle of the Temple' a worthy citizen called Zacharias.† The careful description, not derived from Josephus, of the exact spot of the murder (which proves that the reference is not to 2 Chr. 24.21) suggests that the event was notorious and remembered long after the siege.

23.37 Several successive attempts to gather Jerusalem's 'children' together have failed. Jerusalem is apostrophized, then referred to as 'it', then as 'thou' ('thine'), and finally called 'you' (plural). Who are these 'children' of Jerusalem, whom God made repeated attempts to gather together there but was prevented because those under attack 'did not want it'? The gentile churches were in

* See a monograph on the subject by J. Jeremias: *Heiligengräber in Jesu Umwelt* (Göttingen, 1958).

† In the MSS of Josephus the father of this Zacharias is variously 'Baris', 'Baruch', and 'Barischaeus'. Zacharias son of Barachiah was the prophet who gave his name to the (first part of) the canonical Old Testament book.

a filial relation with Jerusalem and sought to be acknowledged by it as chicks by their hen; but they were rejected, and as a result God quit the Temple.

The key to the allusion of the lyrical outburst is in the word ἐπισυνάγειν 'gather together in a place'. The speaker is not saying, 'I frequently tried to protect you, as a hen covers its chicks'—'under its wings' is possibly interpolated—but 'I frequently tried to bring your children to you here'. The owner of the vineyard and the bridegroom's father had sent a series of messages (ποσάκις) but were always rebuffed. The 'children' are the gentile churches which repeatedly sought to be accepted as a fowl acknowledges her chickens: ὄρνις, here (= Luke 13.34) only in the New Testament, probably means specifically 'hen'. The punishment for the refusal is that the Temple becomes an empty shell: Jesus has attempted to bring the gentiles to Jerusalem but they were rejected. Very well, then: 'your house is left deserted—sacked, destroyed'. The original source (Jer. 22.5) runs, 'this house shall be laid desolate'. It is not so much Jesus who will disappear as God who is leaving the Temple. Josephus (*BJ* 6.299) reports a voice heard in the Temple during the siege, 'We are departing hence', immediately preceding his account of Jesus son of Ananias who four years before the rebellion could not be prevented from crying 'Woe to Jerusalem'. God will not return until greeted with the words which in Ps. 118.27 follow 'Blessed is he' etc., viz. 'God is lord (κύριος), and has manifested himself to us (ἐπέφανεν ἡμῖν)', i.e. not until the divine identity of Jesus is recognized. As above (see on 21.13), the key words of the proof-text were left to memory to supply—or have been deleted.

24.1 As at 13.1 and 15.21, 'went out' is a pure formula of transition. The words do not, as the interpolator supposed, imply that Jesus went out of the Temple, as though everything since 21.23 had been spoken there. Similarly, ἐπορεύετο 'he was going his way', as at 19.15, is a link formula. Here, however, the aorist (ἐπορεύθη) has been replaced by the imperfect (ἐπορεύετο), a form found nowhere else in the book, in order to facilitate insertion of the prophecy following. The contrived occasion which is created for that prophecy is exceptionally insipid. There was no reason for the disciples to 'show' Jesus the Temple: 'buildings' (οἰκοδομάς, plural) (= Mark 13.1, 2) is apparently unique. The sense requires 'Do you see?', not 'Do you *not* see?'; nor is 'all these things' (ταῦτα πάντα) natural after οἰκοδομάς. The underlying prophecy was 'Not a stone shall be left (standing)'; but failure to understand ἀφεθῇ as absolute gave rise to the two alternative glosses, one of which, ἐπὶ λίθον, is ungrammatical for ἐπὶ λίθῳ.

24.3 The long discourse 24.5–25.46, pronounced as it were *ex cathedra* (cf. 5.1, 15.29, 28.16) 'on the mountain' (see on 21.1), following Jesus' prediction of Jerusalem's downfall in retribution for past wrongs, is delivered in response to the enquiry 'Tell us when this will happen.' That simple question has been expanded to embrace the contents of both parts (see below) of the discourse. The term παρουσία, here first occurring, has been obtained from below; it appears in the New Testament elsewhere only in the Epistles, 1 Cor. 15.23, 1 and 2 Thessalonians, James, 2 Peter, and 1 John.

24.5 The discourse which begins at 24.5 comprises two separate parts. The first runs to 24.25, where its conclusion is signalled by 'Lo, I have told you in advance', words which belong at the end, not in the middle, of a prophetic discourse. It concludes by repeating (24.23, 24) the caution against being misled by 'false Messiahs' with which it had commenced at 24.5. With the exception of 24.14 ('and then shall come the end'), it is a description, in apocalyptic language, of the period spanning the Jewish revolt and the siege and fall of Jerusalem. The 'end', to be described in the second part, does not occur within that period, which is marked throughout by a θλῖψις or persecution, described in terms closely related to those used of the Judaizing church in 10.17ff. (q.v.). When the besieging army (cryptically indicated by allusion to Daniel) arrives at 24.15, 'those in Judaea'—evidently one section of those at whom the discourse is directed—are advised to lose no time in taking to the hills, advice which would be absurd (especially in its limitation to Judaea) in the face of the apocalyptic events to be described in the second part. At this time the oppression (θλῖψις) will intensify. But this is palliated by the assurance that it will be of short duration: its length 'was shortened (ἐκολοβώθη) for the sake of the elect', a term procured from the description of the 'end' in 24.31 and meaning (as there) those destined for salvation.

'In my name', ἐπὶ τῷ ὀνόματί μου, unlike τῷ σῷ ὀνόματι at 7.22, has in this context to mean not 'invoking my name', but 'assuming my name', i.e. 'the Christ', Messiah, which Jesus thereby implicitly acknowledges. They are called ψευδόχριστοι, 'false Messiahs', at 24.24 below.

24.6 The highly unusual (and illogical) future of μέλλω, 'you will be going to', seems intended to render the prediction still more tentative. ἀκούειν πολέμους should mean 'hear wars', not 'hear *of* wars'; nor is there any difference between 'hearing of wars' and 'hearing reports of wars', unless the implication is that the reports will be unfounded, in which case nothing will have actually happened. Luke (21.9), on a wild surmise, wrote πολέμους καὶ ἀκαταστασίας, 'wars and anarchies'. More likely, 'wars' was merely a variant to 'reports of wars'. 'Pangs', ὠδῖνες, here only (= Mark 13.8) in the gospels but frequent in LXX, means literally birthpangs. The allusion is to the civil disturbances throughout the Empire in the 'year of the four emperors', AD 69, most of which took place in the west.

24.12 The strangely overwrought expression, τὸ πληθυνθῆναι (here only in Evv.) τὴν ἀνομίαν—'the fact that unlawfulness has been multiplied'—does no more than repeat portentously what has been said just before. ('The many', τῶν πολλῶν, represent the 'many', πολλοί, who have defected (24.10). ψύχειν 'chill', here only in the New Testament, and ἀγάπη 'love', here only in this book.) Otherwise the passage reads like a summary of 10.17–21, the second sentence and the conclusion being in the identical terms of 10.22.

24.14 The sentence καὶ κηρυχθήσεται κτλ. is out of place here: it belongs with the second part of the discourse, which is concerned with describing τὸ τέλος. 'As a witness to all the gentiles' echoes 10.18. 'The gospel of the kingdom', τὸ εὐαγγέλιον τῆς βασιλείας, is always found with κηρύσσω (4.23, 9.35, and, with τοῦτο as here, 26.13): the superfluous τοῦτο here and at 26.13 is meaningful, implying that there is more than one 'gospel of the kingdom'.

'The world', ἡ οἰκουμένη, here only in this book.

24.15 'The abomination of desolation', τὸ βδέλυγμα τῆς ἐρημώσεως, is not of itself intelligible. ἐρήμωσις means the sack of a city etc. Apart from this passage (= Mark 13.14), βδέλυγμα occurs only in Revelation and in Luke (16.15), where it has its natural meaning ('what is lofty among men is an abomination in the sight of God'). Luke (21.20) could make nothing of the phrase and substituted a statement of the obvious, 'when you see Jerusalem surrounded by camps, then know that its sack is imminent'. However, as the annotation observes ('Let the reader note'), the phrase is from Daniel, where the expression occurs in three places: 9.27 'at the end of seven (days) the sacrifice and drink-offering shall be taken away and upon the Temple shall be βδέλυγμα τῶν ἐρημώσεων (plural)'; 11.31 'and hands shall be lifted by him and shall remove the sacrifice and make βδέλυγμα τῆς ἐρημώσεως'; 12.11 'from when the sacrifice is done away altogether and τὸ βδέλυγμα τῆς ἐρημώσεως is prepared to be given'. In all these places βδ. ἐρ. is linked with the suspension of the Temple sacrifices. In 1 Macc. 1.54 'in the 145th year he built a βδ. ἐρ. on the sacrificial altar', the expression is particularized—not just (as in Dan. 9.27) 'upon the Temple', but as 'built on the altar'.

The most probable origin of the inherently meaningless expression is that Ζεὺς Ὀλύμπιος, whose statue was erected by Antiochus Epiphanes on the Temple altar in 167 BC (2 Macc. 6.2), was translated Baʿal Shamayim (Lord of Heaven) and this in turn mockingly altered by replacing Baʿal with 'abomination' (the substitution of באש, shame, for Baʿal was normal), and שמים 'heavens' (plural) with (מ)שומם 'devastated'—whence the plural ἐρημώσεων in Dan. 9.27, elsewhere changed (for the sake of sense) to the singular ἐρημώσεως as here. 'Standing' or 'set up', ἑστός, in this passage suggests that the expression was taken as referring to an image.

In the context here, however, in view of 'see' and the reference to 'those in Judaea', it is likely that Luke's guess was right and that the expression alludes not to the desecration itself but to those who brought it about—the besiegers. The bold (and unique) annotation, 'let the reader note' was evidently thought necessary to underline this allusive meaning.

24.17 The 'person on the rooftop' presupposes a flat roof with direct access from the ground. So far from participating in the armed resistance, those addressed are advised to take flight—advice exculpatory from the Roman point of view.

24.19, 20 A joke has been indulged in at the expense of the Judaizers by way of a snide allusion to strict observance of the Sabbath (cf. on 12.1)—always a problem in wartime or emergency, with which the Maccabees had frequently to cope.

24.21 There has evidently been use of Dan. 12.1 'that is the day of oppression (θλῖψις) such as was not since days began until that day', and Joel 2.2 'its like has not been from of old, and after it shall not be repeated for generations'.

24.22 The lapse into the aorist ἐκολοβώθησαν betrays consciousness that the event already lay in the past. κολοβῶ 'dock', here (= Mark 13.20) only in the New Testament, is apparently nowhere else applied to time.

24.23 The first part of the discourse, originally a prophecy *ex eventu* of the Jewish revolt and its sequel, ends, as it began, with a warning against the spate of false Messiahs which accompanied those events. It is known* that at the subsequent Judaean revolt of AD 131—which may have been precipitated by Hadrian's proposed erection of a temple to Jupiter on the Temple site—Bar Kochba, the leader, was hailed as the Messiah and performed miracles and that Christians who rejected him were persecuted. There may have been similar events accompanying the earlier revolt.

24.24 The words 'if it were possible' cause difficulty. They can neither mean '*with the object*, if possible', of leading even the elect 'astray', which Mark (13.22) attempted by replacing ὥστε with πρὸς τό; nor can they mean 'so that, if it *had been* possible, even the elect *would have been* led astray'. Without 'if possible', the passage is a positive statement that 'even the elect *will* be led astray', so that the term οἱ ἐκλεκτοί denoted not those irrevocably predestined to salvation but a self-styled and vulnerable élite. Only in this discourse is πλανῶ used in the book in the sense of leading believers astray. There is a recollection of Deut. 13.2, where also δοῦναι 'give' (נתן) with σημεῖον and τέρας. The same situation, with Satan instead of the 'false prophets', is outlined at 2 Thess. 2.8–12.

24.26 The purpose of the first part of the discourse was to inculcate that the sack of Jerusalem is not the end of the world, nor the coming of the kingdom. These events cannot happen before the gospel has been preached throughout the inhabited world (24.14), and in any case—see the second part of the discourse, which the introduction (24.3) has been framed to foreshadow—they will be supernatural and unheralded in their instantaneity.

The second part of the discourse, which describes the παρουσία and consists (unlike the first part) of events which are supernatural, starts at 24.27. It is attached to what preceded by a sentence which insipidly duplicates 24.23, 24: the writer was even reduced to copying 'do not believe it', words which apply as much to the cry 'in the desert' as to the cry 'in the closet' (a term borrowed from 6.6—and reborrowed from here by Luke 12.3). The purpose of the duplicate was to provide something to which to attach 24.27, the knock-down argument 'if they had been genuine, the παρουσία would already have happened by then'.

24.28 Comparison with the uncanny speed with which carrion-

* See E. Schürer, *History of the Jewish People*, trans. Vermes and Millar (Edinburgh, 1973), 543–5.

eating birds arrive on the scene of a death adds nothing to the simile of lightning: it is symptomatic of the desire for rhetorical padding which characterizes the prophecy. 'Like lightning' is all that was necessary. Luke found the comparison superfluous and disposed of it (17.37) by attaching it, prefaced by the question 'where?', to 24.41 below. Job 39.30 was in mind. 'Eagle' (ἀετός, here only in the gospels) is used generically for birds of prey.

24.29 The words 'after the tribulation of those days', referring back to 24.21, 22, produce an intolerable contradiction: if the παρουσία is immediately after an event which will happen in this generation, it has ceased to be dateless and unforeseeable. Without the words, which are dispensable, εὐθέως 'immediately' would read straight on after 24.27, emphasizing the suddenness of what follows.

The παρουσία is described in apocalyptic terms, which mark it as the evident demise of the existing physical world. The quotation appears to be from Isa. 13.10: 'the stars of heaven and the constellations thereof shall not give their light; the sun shall be darkened in its going forth, and the moon shall not cause her light to shine'; but the two halves have been inverted and the first half paraphrased: 'the powers of heaven' represents כסיליהם 'its (heaven's) constellations', and the verb 'will not give light' has been replaced by 'fall from heaven' and 'be shaken'. The quote is thus more a pastiche or paraphrase. As with the other Old Testament allusions in this discourse, there is no express appeal to the texts as authority.

24.30 The nature of the 'sign' remains unspecified. The following clause appears to be Zech. 12.12 'and the earth shall mourn tribe by tribe' (καὶ κόψεται ἡ γῆ κατὰ φυλὰς φυλάς), and the next Dan. 7.13 'and lo, upon the clouds of heaven as it were a son of man came'. The remainder reflects Isa. 27.13 'and in that day they shall sound with the great trumpet, and there shall come those that perished in the land of Assyria and those that perished in Egypt and shall worship the Lord on the holy mountain in Jerusalem'. Despite Zech. 12.12 κόψονται and ὄψονται are alternative readings both of which have entered the text.

24.31 The παρουσία, instantaneous and unmistakable, reaches its consummation with the gathering of the 'elect' (i.e. into the kingdom); and the distinction between it and the events of AD 66–70 has been firmly drawn. A new theme is now taken up: the παρουσία is not only sudden but unpredictable in date (24.36–44), from which follows logically the duty always to be 'ready'. This is argued and explained in 24.36 (περὶ δὲ τῆς ἡμέρας ἐκείνης)–25.30. Just because there will be no forewarniang of the παρουσία, that is no reason not to push ahead in haste with the work of conversion, so as to have the results to show when the time comes. The moral is inculcated by three parables: the bad and good steward during the master's absence (24.45–51), the wise and foolish maidens (25.1–13), and the servants who do or do not invest in anticipation of the master's return (25.14–30). The above logical sequence is preceded by a passage (24.32–5) which not only flatly contradicts it but presents severe internal difficulty. To recognize new leaves as a sign that summer is approaching, it is fatuous to take the fig-tree (whether that at 21.19 or any other) as a 'parable' (whatever that may mean); and refusal to name a date for an event is blankly inconsistent with stating, even with the support of an asseveration repeated from 5.18, that it will occur before 'this generation' is past (cf. 17.28).

24.36 The construction 'know about', instead of the accusative as at 25.13, is unique. For 'the son', thus unqualified, see on 11.27. For 'angels of heaven', cf. 'angels in heaven' at 18.11, 22.30 (q.v.), which Mark (13.32) substituted here.

24.37 The similarity of Noah's flood to the παρουσία is the unpredictability and comprehensiveness of the catastrophe. That one is taken and one left is part of the nature of the event: there is nothing that the one left can do to escape. 'Being awake' will not help. As in the parables, those at risk must produce results to show, and without delay—the results being, in line with the denunciation of unfruitfulness, the conversion of the gentiles.

24.38 The vocabulary is distinctive: ἄχρι 'until', here only in this book; τρώγω 'eat', here only in the New Testament, outside John; ἦρεν 'carried away', which Luke (17.27) replaced by 'destroyed', ἀπώλεσεν. Luke also took the opportunity to insert a parallel and more elaborate piece on Lot as a counterpart to Noah.

24.41 μύλος 'mill' (cf. on 18.6) is given the meaning of 'place of grinding' (μυλών), which Luke (17.35) found strange, replacing it with the colourless ἐπὶ τὸ αὐτό, 'at the same place'. The expression implies a two-handed quern.

24.43, 44 'Wakefulness' (24.42) was a false trail which the author of the simile of the householder and the burglar followed up: the 'precise hour of night' (ποίᾳ φυλακῇ) assumed that the householder already knows in which *night* the burglar will come. The analogy of the 'thief in the night' is shared with 1 Thess. 5.6.

4.45–51 What follows the proverb-like simile of the householder and the burglar is not in form a parable, though it might have been so shaped. It has been severely dislocated. The steward was not 'faithful and wise' until proved so by his behaviour, nor is there anything for 'that bad servant' (24.48), which Luke (12.45) deleted, to refer back to. There is only room in the story for one steward; the basic story should be simply: 'A certain householder, on going away—ἀποδημῶν (cf. 21.33), an indispensable detail, lost perhaps between ὅν and κατέστησεν—appointed one of his servants etc. Happy is that servant if, when his master comes, he finds him doing as he was told . . . But if he (the same servant) says to himself. . . his master will come and cut him in two.' The dislocation could have been caused by interpolation attaching 'good servant' and 'bad servant' labels to what thereby became two servants instead of one. Alternatively, there could have been polemical identification with two actual individuals heading opposing factions. The rhetorical question, editorially propounded ('Who then . . . ?', τίς ἄρα), is unhappy. It would fit, if at all, only the conclusion, not the commencement of a narrative.

The inappropriateness and ferocity of the householder's punishment recall those of the owner of the vineyard at 21.41 and belong to the same allegorical meaning. God has left Israel in his absence with the equivalent of a stewardship. Returning—in the person of his son (cf. 21.37)—he finds that Israel has withheld from his servants their (eucharistic?) nourishment, even beaten them (cf. 10.17), and wasted his estate. The triumphant coda about 'weeping and wailing' etc. occurs only after polemical encounters (8.12; 13.42, 50; 22.13).

24.45 οἰκετεία 'household', unique in LXX and the New Testament, is precise, meaning 'household slaves' (σύνδουλοι below). ἐν καιρῷ 'at the right time' is superfluous, but perhaps an echo of Ps. 145.15 δίδως τὴν τροφὴν αὐτῶν ἐν εὐκαιρίᾳ. The pleonastic 'and an hour he does not know' may have been designed to replace rather than duplicate 'a day he does not expect'.

24.51 The violent punishment διχοτομήσει (δ. apparently so here only) is inappropriate in apposition to the periphrastic expression 'give him his portion' etc. μέρος 'destiny' is curiously classical, cf. μερίς in Ps. 49.18 (of which there may be an echo) μετὰ μοίχων τὴν μερίδα σου ἐτίθεις. The use of ὑποκριταί equated with the condemned reprobate seems deliberately ironic. Luke was fain to substitute ἄπιστοι 'unbelievers' (12.46). Noticeably, 'that bad servant', though he 'eats and drinks' with the 'drunkards', is not accused of getting drunk himself. There is a code here, to which we do not possess the key.

25.1 Attempts to match the parable of the wise and foolish maidens with real marriage customs are foredoomed to failure. The parable is an allegory of the coming of the son of man to take possession of the kingdom. In order to enter it with him—there will be no subsequent admissions—the 'elect' are summoned (if necessary from the sleep of death, to which all ten maidens had succumbed, ἐκάθευδον) by trumpet (24.31 = 'shout' 25.6) to 'meet' him. The scene of the 'meeting' (ἀπάντησις, the same word as here) is described at 1 Thess. 4.17. For the maidens, however, there is an indispensable ticket of admission: they must bring lights, lighted lamps or torches (the latter being the normal meaning of λαμπάς). The maidens who are 'foolish' and not, like the 'faithful servant' (24.45), φρόνιμοι are shut out because they have with them no 'lights': no converts, no new churches.

In conformity with the context, the fault of those whose lamps are out is that they have not made converts while there was still time. The lamps are churches or congregations sustained by a continuing flow of converts. The oil is the supply of converts to keep the churches shining in the world (cf. 5.16); and the moral is: no converts, no entry into the kingdom.

The dramatic details and the dialogue, which give the story its liveliness, need not have had specific analogues. There is not even a 'bride', though one family of manuscripts supplied her after 'bridegroom' in 25.1. Her place is in a sense occupied by the maidens and their lighted lamps. Luke (12.35) found it all so unintelligible that he rewrote the parable to apply to servants who stay up late with lamps lit to let their master in when he comes home from a wedding. The last sentence, 25.13, which draws the wrong conclusion—even the 'wise' maidens did not keep awake!—repeats 24.42.

'Then' (25.1) gives an impression of sequential prophetic narrative. So also does the future ὁμοιωθήσεται (meaning 'will be like', not 'will be compared with'), instead of ὡμοιώθη as at 18.23 (q.v.) etc.

25.4 As in Num. 4.9, ἀγγεῖα with reserve oil were a normal appurtenance of lamps.

25.7 The curious verb κοσμεῖν (lit. 'adorn') has to be given the meaning 'trimmed', i.e. did what would need to be done to lamps which had been burning while they were asleep. The required sense, however, is rather 'lit' or 'picked up': ἐκόμισαν?

25.9 μήποτε, elsewhere (e.g. 5.25) 'lest . . .', is here 'perhaps'.

25.14 The initial words ὥσπερ γάρ, 'For just as', are left hanging in the air, as if someone had intended to frame a sentence on the pattern of 24.38, concluding with 'even so will be the παρουσία of the son of man', and then either abandoned the intention, or else words to that effect were deleted. A sign, which has survived intact, of hasty draftsmanship?

No simple emendation of the words ὥσπερ γάρ solves the problem. Mark (13.34) tried to read 25.14 as running on from 25.13, but found himself obliged by this to invent a new injunction to a 'doorkeeper' to 'keep awake'. The cruder device of simply repeating ἀποδημῶν as ἀπεδήμησεν found its way into the text, separating εὐθέως from the καί which should immediately precede it (as at 8.3; 13.5; 14.22; 20.34; 26.49, 74; 27.48).

The parable continues the same theme of the disastrous consequences of failing to reap a 'harvest' from the propagation of God's endowment, like the 'good seed' at 13.8, 23. This is confirmed by the condign punishment of the 'unprofitable servant' who produces no accretion and by the repetition of the stereotyped coda of damnation (25.30 = 24.51, q.v.). The reward of those whose churches expand and multiply will be increased authority, while those who opposed them will lose even their own claim to salvation. There may be intended significance in the fact that it is the holder of the largest sum who annexes what the discredited servant has forfeited.

Luke (19.12–27) found the sums in 'talents' (see on 18.21–35) too enormous to be credible or to be contrasted as 'little' with 'much' at 25.21. He therefore altered τάλαντα to μναῖ (unique in the New Testament) and amended πολλῶν 'many' conjecturally to πόλεων 'cities', having rationalized the story by giving ten servants (like the ten maidens?) one *mina* each and rewarding their graduated profits with graduated preferment in a province their master had acquired.

25.15 'To each according as he willed', κατὰ τὴν ἰδίαν δύναμιν, cannot mean 'in accordance with their respective capabilities': ἰδίαν must refer to the subject, as immediately above τοὺς ἰδίους δούλους, 'his (own) servants'. The expression, which has to mean 'in accordance with his (arbitrary) will', is chosen to fit the allegory: the commissioning by Jesus of the mission to the gentiles is attributable to his 'power'.

25.16 For 'gain', κερδαίνω, in the sense of 'win over, convert', cf. 18.15.

25.21, 23 Each of the first two servants receives the identical, unexplained reply. 'Your master's joy' cannot mean his 'favour'; nor can there well be a reference forward to 25.34.

25.24–6 The servant was 'afraid', φοβηθείς, (to take risks with the money) because his master was 'strict' or 'harsh', σκληρός. Yet to 'reap where one has not sown' is not a mark of σκληρότης, and the reference to it by the master makes the servant illogically convict himself (cf. Luke 19.22). Allegory has overpowered parable: the Judaizers had been given plenty of prior warning that the gentile world was to be evangelized. They sinned, therefore, against the light and deserved their punishment.

25.26 The master's ὀκνηρέ 'timid' picks up 'afraid', φοβηθείς; but in its code meaning (see on 9.4) πονηρός 'bad' is in place. 'Reap where I have not sown' is pure tautology in this context for 'gather where I have not scattered' (see on 12.30), suggesting that the former glossed the latter. Jesus expects to find believers in regions he never trod himself: the gentilizing polemic is overt.

25.28 The master's switch from addressing the servant to ordering others to deal with him is curiously abrupt. For the irony cf. 13.12.

25.30 The parable was complete already without the sentence from 22.13, which brings it into line with 24.51.

25.31 The scene at the παρουσία is suddenly resumed from 24.31 in order to append a judgement scene at the end of the discourse. The 'elect' have already been picked up to 'meet' the son of man. He now assumes a judgement seat, and 'all the nations are brought together in front of him'—a general resurrection still not being distinctly mentioned. They it is whom he proceeds to judge. The 'elect', whether resurrected or still alive, are already 'with him for ever' (cf. 1 Thess. 4.17): it is not upon them that judgement is passed—they have already been saved through Jesus. Those now assembled are judged, and consigned either to the kingdom or to destruction, upon one criterion, and one only—the way they have behaved, not in general but specifically towards the son of man's 'brethren' ('these', οἱ ἐκλεκτοί). The nature of that astonishing sole criterion—good behaviour to Christians—explains why the discourse was extended to include this appendix.

The gentile churches had a problem over their relationship with Rome. It would be fatal if their 'kingdom of heaven' were to be confused with that intended by those who raised the nationalist rebellion with its catastrophic ending in AD 70. The flight to the mountains recommended at 24.16 to 'those in Judaea' has acquitted the church of involvement in that. A future 'kingdom of heaven', however, albeit remote, such as the extended discourse foreshadowed, presented, by involving the power of judgement over the whole world, an explicit challenge to the Roman domination. Now this difficulty was to be met by populating the 'kingdom' with Christians, οἱ ἐκλεκτοί, *plus* those pagans now living at peace and on good-neighbourly, benevolent terms with them. There would therefore be no antagonism or incompatibility between the empire and those who were living in expectation of Christ's kingdom and in preparation for it. Such an offer could be extended only on behalf of churches already in existence in broadly 'all the nations' (cf. 24.14).

25.32 αὐτούς, 'divide *them*', refers, despite the masculine gender, to 'all the nations', πάντα τὰ ἔθνη. Goats and sheep were often pastured together, but the two were folded separately. πρόβατα means 'sheep' generically; and in this, the only passage in the gospels where the goat is mentioned at all, ἔριφοι (lit. 'kids') is used for 'goats' in generic antithesis to sheep, possibly because αἶγες (not in the New Testament) means 'she-goats' and τράγοι 'he-goats'. In Ezek. 34.17 LXX God says, 'I will distinguish (διακρινῶ) between sheep and sheep, rams and he-goats' (προβάτου καὶ προβάτου, κριῶν καὶ τράγων), and in 34.20, 22 'I will distinguish (διακρινῶ) between a strong sheep and a weak sheep' and again 'between a ram and a ram'.

25.33 Jesus will not put on one side of him or the other actual sheep and goats—the inserted equivalents are interpolations—but those equated with them in the simile, which has influenced the gender, τὰ μέν . . . τὰ δέ instead of τοὺς μέν . . . τοὺς δέ.

25.34 The subject, 'the king', ὁ βασιλεύς, would not be missed if it were absent, and is specially significant after he has just been denoted 'the son of man'. It recurs in 25.40 but is not repeated before the subsequent dialogue with the damned, of whom presumably he will not be 'the king'. The use of the term firmly identifies his παρουσία with the commencement of the kingdom. 'Of my father' is attached to 'blessed', as if equivalent to 'blessed *by*'.

The verb 'inherit', κληρονομήσατε, requires 'the kingdom' as the object to be 'eternal life' (cf. 19.29) rather than 'kingship' or 'rule' (cf. 21.38). Strong and no doubt significant emphasis is laid on the pre-existence of 'the kingdom', which is ready waiting at the παρουσία for the outcome of the judgement: it has existed 'from the creation of the world'. This is incompatible, presumably designedly, with an earthly 'kingdom' in this world, and obliges the universe after the παρουσία to be conceived in terms which exclude the continued existence of the present world.

25.41 'Accursed', κατηραμένοι (here only in this book), the antithesis of εὐλογημένοι, is unqualified. The 'eternal fire' (18.8) is also, corresponding with the 'kingdom', pre-existent and prepared for 'the Devil and his angels', with whom those 'on the left' are equated. The expression does not necessarily imply familiarity with the 'war in heaven' (Rev. 12.7, where also οἱ ἄγγελοι αὐτοῦ). In the only other occurrence of διάβολος in the book apart from the temptation scene 4.1–11, he is 'God's enemy' who has sown the world with 'the sons of the evil one' at 13.39. 'The Devil and his angels' is a savage description for the opponents of the son of man, who will be disposed of in a manner opposite to that which awaits his well-wishers.

25.46 The concluding sentence is not quite the same as Dan. 12.2: 'and many of those sleeping in the depths of the earth will arise, some to everlasting life and others to reproach [v.l. dispersal] and others to everlasting shame'. As the antithesis with ζωή 'life' shows, κόλασις (here only in the gospels) means, as e.g. Wisd. 3.4 and frequently in LXX apocrypha, not 'punishment' but 'destruction', it being the fate of the unrighteous to be eliminated by fire (see 3.12, 13.30).

26.1 The sentence, to τοὺς λόγους τούτους, is a conventional transition (cf. 7.28 q.v., 11.1, 13.53, 19.1), followed normally by another action of Jesus. The function of the sentences that now follow is to facilitate the insertion of two items which play no practical part in the subsequent narrative, viz. (1) the Passover, and (2) the purported 'betrayal' by Judas.

26.2 Whether οἴδατε is understood as interrogative ('do you know?') or as imperative ('be it known to you'—οἴδατε for classical Greek ἴστε), the disciples were as well aware as Jesus when the Passover fell, though no indication of its being the reason for their journey to Jerusalem has been given. Nothing about the meal as described at 26.20–30 suggests Passover: the lamb, for instance, is not only not mentioned but is ignored by the 'bread' (26.26). There was in any case no need to explain Jesus sharing a meal with his disciples. The motive for introducing the Passover may be to provide, as explained at 26.4, 5, a reason in the feast for the 'betrayal' by Judas.

26.3–5 The place where 'the high priests and the elders of the people' met was obtained from 26.57, 58. Mention of 'the high priest' (singular) in the same breath as 'the high priests' (plural) (see on 2.4) is a curiosity. αὐλή, here used for the high priest's official residence, is derived, like the high priest's name, from 26.58 and 26.69 below, where it means 'courtyard'. In the event Jesus' enemies did not proceed to arrest him δόλῳ 'by a trick'. The sentence is preparatory to Judas' approach and offer, which originally immediately followed, as if that had been what made up their minds despite fear of the people (recalled from 21.46). συμβουλεύεσθαι for 'take counsel, resolve' here only in this book—elsewhere (12.14; 22.15; 27.1, 7; 28.12) συμβούλιον λαμβάνειν is used.

26.14 But for the episode 'at Bethany' inserted here from after 8.15 (q.v.), the approach of Judas to the high priests would have followed directly upon 26.5. The words ὁ λεγόμενος belong between Ἰούδας and Ἰσκαριώτης (on which see on 10.4); their displacement suggests that ὁ λεγόμενος Ἰσκ. may have been interpolated. 'The twelve', οἱ δώδεκα, only here, 20.17, and 26.47 below; elsewhere always οἱ δώδεκα μαθηταί.

26.15 ἀργύριον as a coin here only: Mark 14.11 and Luke 22.5, who omitted the sequel (27.3–9), simply have ἀργύριον = 'money'. But there is a close resemblance to Zech. 11.12, καὶ ἔστησαν τὸν μισθόν μου τριάκοντα ἀργυροῦς 'and they weighed out for my wage thirty silver pieces' (ἀργυροῦς, unique in LXX as a noun, כסף). The verb ἱστάναι (ἔστησαν) probably here means 'weigh out' (cf. שקל, whence 'shekel') and thus 'pay cash down'; but Mark (ἐπηγγείλαντο) and Luke (συνέθεντο) understood it in the more classical sense of 'fix by agreement'. The implication of 27.3ff. is that Judas had the cash already before Jesus' arrest and was not merely promised it.

Judas undertakes to 'hand Jesus over' (παραδώσω αὐτόν), but it was the Jews who 'handed him over' (παρέδοσαν) to Pilate in the crucifixion narrative (27.2). To be 'handed over' is the prediction repeatedly made by Jesus himself—17.22 'into men's hands', 20.18, 19 'to the gentiles', 26.2. The Jews on their own showing, even if they denied Jesus to be the son of God, were guilty of the ultimate crime of 'handing over' a Jew to the gentiles. It is as if Judas, the archetypal Jew, was used to personify that crime.

26.16 For 'from that time', ἀπὸ τότε, cf. 16.21; and for 'sought an opportunity', ἐζήτει εὐκαιρίαν, cf. 21.46 ζητοῦντες κρατῆσαι,

26.59 ἐζήτουν ψευδομαρτυρίαν. The alleged 'betrayal' by Judas, comprised in four separate pieces of text (26.14–16, 20–5, 47–50; 27.3–10), is not essential to the narrative.

1. Judas is nowhere stated to have done or disclosed anything which enabled Jesus to be arrested: there is no quid pro quo in his bargain with the high priests, and the conclusion 'he sought an opportunity to hand him over' is self-consciously vacuous.

2. Though Judas accompanies the high priest's emissaries at 26.47, it is not suggested that he had told them where to find Jesus (even if he knew), and the 'signal' of the kiss, though it aggravates the 'betrayal', was no more necessary than any other way of identifying Jesus (if any was needed).

3. Judas' presence at the supper is contrived by the repetition (26.21 and 26) of ἐσθιόντων αὐτῶν, 'as they ate'; there is no sequel, and nothing is done to prevent his implied departure, though he is identified by Jesus as the betrayer in a formula, σὺ εἶπας, obtained from the trial scene at 26.64—inappropriately, because strictly it is Judas' denial (μήτι ἐγώ εἰμι;) which it affirms. The use of the formula has grotesquely involved the disciples in all saying 'Surely it is not I?' (26.22).

The figure of Judas, whether or not created for the purpose ('Ιούδας = 'Ιουδαῖος?), represents betrayal in the abstract. In a narrative already complete without him, there was nothing for him actually to do. Significantly, he insists, unlike the other disciples, on addressing Jesus as 'rabbi'. The problems posed by Matthew's narrative were perceived by the other gospel authors, who attempted to meet them. Mark (14.21) and Luke (22.21) omitted the overt detection of the betrayer at the supper, and Luke altered the kiss from a mark of identification into a gesture repudiated by Jesus. John's measures were more elaborate: he arranged (13.26–30) for Judas to quit the supper early without detection, and to 'know' (18.2–5) to what spot Jesus would repair, where Jesus then identifies himself.

26.17–19 The function of the passage is to establish Jesus as eating the Passover with his disciples, i.e. that they were eating together the flesh of the Paschal lamb sacrificed in the Temple. The disciples' question had to be asked not later than—and, consistently with 26.2, actually on—the morning of 14 Nissan, the day when the Passover was sacrificed. The seven days during which leaven was prohibited (Exod. 12.15 etc.) were from 15 Nissan (i.e. from the evening of the day of 14 Nissan) to 21 Nissan; but the expression 'on the first of the days of unleavened bread' must have been intended to include 14 Nissan itself, as being the first day of the Passover period. The disciples' question is a response to the intimation of Jesus at 26.2, but also the preface to a special direction for identifying the venue of the meal. That direction and the sequel are modelled on 21.2–7. The ambiguous 'the lord (the owner) needs' (21.3) could not, however, be repeated and is replaced by the irrelevant 'My time is near'. What was necessary was for the disciples to have some 'sign', corresponding to the tethered she-ass and colt, to find the predetermined place. Luke (22.9–13), whom Mark (14.12–16) followed, realized this and supplied the incident of the man with the water-jar to introduce the element of predetermination. Had that incident been original, it would scarcely have been subsequently rejected.

26.18 ὁ δεῖνα occurs nowhere else in the New Testament or LXX but was used by Aquila to translate פלני in Ruth 4.1 and מקים פלני in 1 Sam. 21.3 (also Symmachus) and 2 Kgs. 6.8. In the latter passages LXX transliterated the Hebrew; but in Ruth, where the sense is clearly 'Hey you, come over here and sit down', it translated the Hebrew with κρύφιε 'secret, hidden one'. The sense demanded here is 'the first person you meet'; but in classical Greek the meaning was So-and-So, and Luke (see above) saw and attempted to remove the absurdity and irrelevance of Jesus giving the disciples a specific name and address to go to. For πρός σε 'at your house' cf. 13.56 πρὸς ἡμᾶς.

26.21 It was deemed necessary to show Jesus to have been aware of the 'betrayal', so that the voluntary and predetermined nature of his immolation remained intact. Hence the embarrassing scene in which Jesus announces the betrayal and discloses knowledge of the betrayer but no action is taken to inhibit it.

26.22 'Exceedingly grieved', λυπούμενοι σφόδρα, as at 17.23 ἐλυπήθησαν σφόδρα, in similar circumstances. It is quite unnatural for each disciple to ask Jesus if he is himself the 'betrayer', and Jesus' response to the disciples is tautologous, intelligible only if it were proverbial or a quotation: it seems related to Ps. 41.9 'which did eat of my bread'. If the betrayer is one who dips in the communal dish, that does not distinguish him from the rest.

26.23 It is not 'the hand' but the (understood) sop that is dipped by each diner in the common sauceboat: τὴν χεῖρα is an unlucky interpolation.

26.24 No specific prediction of the son of man being 'betrayed' has been identified in any known 'writings', γραφαί (cf. 22.29, q.v.).

The choice of the word ὑπάγει (in the indicative here only in this book), 'goes his way', as perhaps a euphemism for 'is betrayed', is curious. The thought of the next sentence is the same as at 18.8ff. (where also (18.7) δι' οὗ 'through whom' and καλόν = 'preferable').

26.26 Divested of the connection with the Passover and with Judas' alleged betrayal, the meal of Jesus with his disciples (the 'Last Supper') establishes on his authority the meaning of the sacramental bread. An insertion enjoins the additional practice of all participants drinking from a sacramental cup, a practice then still the subject of controversy.

The ritual of the bread and the cup is not 'instituted': the narrative establishes its significance, but does not enjoin its repetition, which is presupposed. A living person, even one about to die, cannot without absurdity point to bread and say, 'That is my body'; nor indeed could those words be used by one who was physically resurrected. They are only capable of attribution to such a person if no longer on earth but still normative, which is what in defiance of dramatic propriety the narrative achieves.

σῶμα 'body' is used (like σάρξ 'flesh' in 16.17) as the antithesis of αἷμα 'blood', representing בשר ודם.

26.27 A striking feature is the asymmetry between the treatment of the two commands. The brevity of the command to eat the broken bread, which 'is my body', contrasts with the command that 'all' drink from the cup, which is supported by two lengthy and divergent reasons: (1) it is 'my blood of the covenant, shed for remission of the sins' of 'many'; (2) it is the last drink with Jesus before the kingdom comes, when new wine will be drunk. The second reason, superfluous and almost trivial, downgrading the circulation of the cup to the level of a farewell ceremony, throws the whole weight of attention on to the first reason, which it suggests an intention to supplant and suppress.

Unlike the first command, to partake of the bread, which is noted almost as a matter of course, the second is treated as controversial and requiring justification. That justification is remarkable: instead of the parallel assertion 'this is my blood', it affirms a new concept, 'my blood of the covenant'—albeit the phrase already stood in Zech. 9.11—and explains it by the affirmation of 'taking away sins'. This can hardly have been intended to withhold that effect from the bread but rather to endow the cup with irresistible significance: the 'covenant' is the promise secured by Jesus whereby sins are forgiven as the counterpart of his death. The implication is that ritual circulation of the cup was still a subject of controversy, which those who claimed it felt the need to justify and explain. To emphasize that drinking from the cup must apply to 'all' present, and not be, for example, restricted to the officiant, would also be part of the polemic purpose of the words attributed to Jesus.

The pompously pleonastic gloss 'product of the vine' (cf. Isa. 32.12) and 'it' are perverse because ἐκ τούτου is manifestly 'from this cup'. καινόν by itself means 'new wine': in the kingdom everything, including the wine, will be new, nothing being carried over from the previous age.

26.28 ἐκχυννόμενον (see on 23.35) is ambiguous in point of tense between past and present. Unique in this book is ἄφεσις ἁμαρτιῶν 'remission of sins' for an (unspecified) 'many'—the same 'many' as at 20.28, where Jesus' 'life' is given as λύτρον ἀντὶ πολλῶν—though the implicit active verb ἀφιέναι has occurred in 6.14 and 9.4–6.

26.30 This anticipates and duplicates the actual departure at 26.36 (τότε ἔρχεται). The dialogue which follows the singing of a hymn, understood to be customary, is a part of the description of the meal, not conversation on, or on the way to, the Mountain of Olives.

26.31 Jesus' grim prediction that 'all' his disciples 'will fall away' from him 'on this night' forms the necessary prelude for Peter's boastful assertion and its verbal and practical rebuke (26.34, 58, 69–75).

26.32 The special significance of 'Galilee' as the scene of the ascension (see on 28.17) explains the mention of it here, though unintelligible to, and ignored by, the disciples.

For σκανδαλίζεσθαι ἐν see on 11.6: the meaning 'defect' is unalloyed by any suggestion of being forced or induced to do so. 'Deny' (ἀπαρνᾶσθαι) (26.34, see on 10.32) is the overt mark of defection. Both terms were part of a specialized vocabulary.

Once again, the citation is from Zechariah (13.7), where the textual situation is obscure. M has 'O sword . . . smite the shepherd and scatter the sheep, and I will turn my hand against the lambs (הצערים)'. LXX has 'smite (πατάξατε, v.l. πάταξον, whence perhaps πατάξω here) the shepherds, and snatch (ἐκσπάσατε) the sheep, and I will turn my hand against the shepherds (v.l. μικρούς, little ones)'; but LXX(A) has, instead of the intolerable ἐκσπάσατε ('snatch'), 'shall be scattered', διασκορπισθήσονται, the special word for sheep (see John 10.12).

Possibly it was the expression 'the little ones' in M which secured the application of the text to the disciples (see on 18.6).

26.36–46 The humiliation of Peter is counterbalanced (cf. 17.1) by an incident which exhibits all three—Peter and the sons of Zebedee—in an equally embarrassing light. In order to contrive this, Jesus, whose 'unease' is a necessary part of the composition, leaves behind not only the disciples generally but (illogically) the chosen three, and goes aside to pray. Despite the lack of witnesses, a prayer is provided which, in defiance of the narrative at large, consists of a last-minute plea to avoid the impending doom. Having been used once, it cannot be repeated on the next two occasions but is perfunctorily summarized. The artificiality of the incident is confirmed when it turns out, in the vacuous and inappropriate sentence 'Awake, let us be going' (26.46), that there was nothing for the three disciples to do when they did wake up. The ironical 'sleep and take your rest' was as powerless to counteract this difficulty as was the proverbially buttressed sentence (26.41) about avoiding 'temptation'. The 'agony in the garden' is transparent fiction.

Luke (22.40–6), who saw the problems, telescoped the three prayer sessions into one and inserted an insipid supernatural answer to the prayer ('there was seen by him an angel from heaven strengthening him').

26.36 The place of Jesus' arrest, like that of his execution, had for authenticity to have a name, otherwise unknown. Γεθ- represents either גת '(wine)press' or גן 'garden' and -σημανει Aramaic שמני 'olive oil'. John 18.1 substituted a 'garden (κῆπος) across the brook Kedron'. χωρίον 'spot', here only in this book.

αὐτοῦ 'where you are', here only in this book. Lack of a point of reference for ἐκεῖ 'there, thither' is a symptom of artificiality.

26.37 ἀδημονεῖν 'be distressed' is found here (= Mark 14.33) only in the gospels and not in LXX (although once in Aquila and several times in Symmachus). 'Exceedingly grieved' points to Ps. 43.5, 'wherefore art thou exceedingly grieved, O my soul?', but 'even to death' is out of place here.

26.46 ἐγείρεσθε, 'awake', is natural; but what is to be made of ἄγωμεν? It is used in similar circumstances by Mark 1.38, ἄγωμεν ἀλλαχοῦ 'let us go off somewhere else'.

The drama of the arrest has been ruined by superfluous touches. Jesus cannot both say ἰδοὺ ἤγγικεν ἡ ὥρα and then immediately ἰδοὺ ἤγγικεν ὁ παραδιδούς με. The sentence 26.46 is dispensable.

26.47 After the preceding descriptions of Judas and his betrayal, 'one of the twelve' is inconceivable even as an interpolation: it implies a stage when Judas only appeared here at the arrest and when the rest of the Judas insertions had not yet found their place in the text. καὶ εὐθέως relates directly to Ἰούδας ἦλθεν, and 26.48 is superfluous: the kiss was not a preconcerted signal, but an act of infamy: the cue for Jesus to be seized is his own answer to Judas, 'Do your business' (ἐφ' ὃ πάρει).

26.48 ἔδωκεν has to be taken as meaning ἐδέδωκεν 'had agreed a preconcerted sign'. Indeed, Mark 14.44 so amended it, also changing σημεῖον into σύσσημον.

It was not necessary for Judas to kiss Jesus in order to designate him. All he needed to do was to point, 'There he is; don't let him get away.' To provide matter for actual betrayal, it would be necessary to suppose (what is neither stated nor implied) that Judas had anticipated and made known to the authorities where Jesus would go after the meal. John (18.3), who also thoughtfully provided torches to illuminate the scene, met the requirement by observing that Judas 'knew the place, because Jesus often forgathered there with his disciples'.

26.50 ἐφ' ὃ πάρει was a colloquial expression for 'good luck to you', lit. '(may you get) what you have come for'. It was a common inscription round the lip of drinking-cups.

.51, 52 The disciple involved in so significant an incident could hardly have been left anonymous as 'one of those with Jesus'. Probably this masks a Petrine incident which has been depersonalized (cf. on 26.6, and 27.32). But why should the reader be supposed to assume that 'the high priest's servant' was there? A sort of tipstaff? The crowd had come simply 'from the high priests and elders of the people'.

The words ἀπέσπασεν τὴν μάχαιραν αὐτοῦ, 'snatched away his sword', are a displaced gloss on ἀφεῖλεν αὐτοῦ τὸ ὠτίον, which last word ('little ear') has ousted the term for a weapon. There is reason to think that it was ξιφίδιον 'dagger, side-arm', because ξιφίδιον and ὠτίον both have the same secondary meaning of a sort of shellfish. The verb ἀπέσπασεν does not mean 'drew', nor ἀφεῖλεν 'cut off'; for ἀποστρέφειν 'put back' cf. στρέφειν at 27.3 below (cf. Gen. 43.21, 44.8 LXX).

The words 'your sword to its place', with the awkward 'its

place' to mean the scabbard, were interpolated after the corruption had occurred. That the original text involved no violent act is proved by the absence of any such sequel as would have imperatively been necessary if blood had been shed—a sequel which Luke (22.51) supplied in the shape of a miraculous healing.

26.52 The command to refrain from physical resistance is justified on the general ground that violence provokes violence—a pointed allusion to the Jewish rebellion of AD 66–70 and its disastrous outcome.

26.53 ἤ, 'or', frequently introduces a new argument in the form of an ironical question (7.4, 9; 12.5, 29; 16.26; 20.15). The neuter plural πλείω 'in excess (of)', referring to fem. λεγιῶνας, is paralleled by Xenophon, *Historia Graeca*, 2.2.16 τρεῖς μῆνας καὶ πλείω. The ironical disclaimer of willingness to invoke divine protection, underlined by the grotesque exaggeration 'more than twelve legions', is explained by the necessity for αἱ γραφαί, 'the scriptures', to be fulfilled. No such 'scriptures' are cited; nor have any been discovered.

26.55 There has been a disturbance of the original order: 26.55 ought to follow directly upon 26.50.

Whether καθ' ἡμέραν means 'in the daylight' or 'daily', it is not the opposite to 'with swords and staves'. The interpolator has answered incorrectly the rhetorical question 'Do you take me for a bandit, that you came out armed to arrest me?' Jesus' words belong with the foregoing call for non-resistance. διδάσκων ἐν τῷ ἱερῷ was obtained from 21.23.

26.56 For τοῦτο ὅλον γέγονεν cf. 1.22. αἱ γραφαὶ <u>τῶν προφητῶν</u> is an illicit combination: the prophets and αἱ γραφαί are separate categories of Scripture. The sentence is tautologous after 26.54.

26.57 Compared with 26.3, and 26.47, the 'high priests' have been replaced by 'scribes'.

26.58 ἰδεῖν τὸ τέλος can scarcely mean 'to see how the thing would end'. In any case Peter is not stated to have witnessed 'the end'. Perhaps a marginal note ('see conclusion below') directed attention to a marginal sign against 26.69?

The narrative of Peter's shame is split into two parts (26.58 and 26.69–75) and inserted on either side of the trial, with which it has no integral connection but which its second part gives the appearance of rounding off.

26.59 Jesus is condemed to death by the high priest's court (for συνέδριον see on 10.17) for the blasphemy of claiming to be 'the Messiah, the son of God'. Since that identification had hitherto not been made openly (16.20), he could be convicted only out of his own mouth; there could not be true witness available—only 'false witness'. At 26.62, when the high priest says 'Do you hear what these men are witnessing against you?', Jesus remains silent. The high priest then obtains the conviction by putting Jesus himself on oath to declare himself. This logical course of events, where the unsatisfactory nature of the available 'false evidence' enables, and obliges, the high priest to act as he does, has been wrecked by the insertion of ὕστερον δὲ . . . οἰκοδομῆσαι, a specific allegation, known by the reader to be false despite the allusion to 24.2. The accuser cannot then proceed to ask the prisoner, 'What is this accusation?' The same reaction to general accusations is copied at the trial before Pilate (27.13). Mark (14.58) took the interpolated accusation seriously and used the opportunity to invent the allegory of a 'temple not made with hands', ναὸς ἀχειροποίητος, i.e. Jesus' body.

26.63 It is curious that 'the living God', ὁ θεὸς ὁ ζῶν, occurs in the gospels only here and 16.16 (q.v.) in the same context. (Has τοῦ ζῶντος here been transferred after the first τοῦ θεοῦ from after the second, which would be its more natural position?) ἐξορκίζω, 'make a person (e.g. a witness) answer upon oath', here only in the New Testament and here only (apparently) with κατά + gen. instead of acc. for the person or thing sworn by. The high priest could not force Jesus to swear 'by God'; but Jesus was unwilling before God to deny his sonship. (Mark 14.61 and Luke 22.70 suppressed the conjuration.)

26.64 The admission implicit in the reply 'You have said it' neither required nor admitted of anything further—least of all an announcement that something would presently happen which signally failed to occur. The attribution of further words to Jesus represents the endeavour to supply a sufficient reason for the forthcoming condemnation. The materials from which it was composed are to be found at 16.27 and 24.30. The second half is identical with 24.30; the first, though reminiscent of Ps. 110.1, has no exact Old Testament original—'the power' is substituted in it euphemistically for 'God'. The court will not in fact 'see' Jesus in glory; and the author of Stephen's defence (Acts 7.55, 56) was fain to attribute the vision to the accused.

26.66 Having passed sentence of death, the court must proceed to carry it out by stoning Jesus to death (cf. 21.35, 23.37) in pursuance of Lev. 24.16. Nothing has suggested—see especially 26.59 ὅπως θανατώσωσιν—any incapacity on its part to do so without further proceedings. The execution has been deleted after 26.68 or 26.75, in order to add a trial and execution by the Romans. The members of the court content themselves instead with spitting upon Jesus and buffeting him. The spitting and striking are impliedly acts of aversion, apotropaic, following upon the condemnation for blasphemy; but the game of blind man's buff is absurd. Even if προφητεύω could mean 'guess', blindfolding, which is not mentioned, would have been an essential preliminary. Luke (22.63), who brought Jesus outside at this point to witness Peter's discomfiture, supplied it with περικαλύψαντες αὐτόν, 'having covered him up'. Jesus would have had to be assumed to know the members of the court individually by name.

26.69 'Outside in the court' contradicts 26.58 (ἔσω, i.e. τῆς αὐλῆς); but without the resumptive words 'And as Peter . . . courtyard' the text runs straight on after 26.58 without problems, suggesting that the passage about Peter's denial was embodied piecemeal into a pre-existing text. 'With the servants' (26.58) is preparatory to the 'approach' of the 'servant girl' (26.69).

26.74 καταθεματίζειν, non-existent and incorrect, is amended by Mark 14.71 to ἀναθεματίζειν, 'make asseveration by a curse' (ἀνάθεμα), e.g. 'God blind me if . . .'.

The climax reached through three successive stages, which would be expected, is flawed. There is an appropriate gradation from 'denied' to 'denied with an oath' to 'began to curse and swear'. Not so the three answers, 'I don't know what you mean', 'I don't know the man', and again 'I don't know the man', which last is not the appropriate rebuttal of 'You are one of them'. The third challenge is introduced by μετὰ μικρόν, here (= Mark 14.70) only in the New Testament, a pointless note of time. Did they only gradually recognize Peter's patois? And was Peter chatting, or did his brief reply to the previous challenges suffice to betray his accent? The second serving girl simply duplicates with minor variation the challenge of the first; and οἱ ἑστῶτες 'those standing' is curious after τοῖς ἐκεῖ 'those there' and ἔμπροσθεν πάντων, 'in front of them all'. It is as if there had originally been only two denials—one inside and one outside the high priest's courtyard. δῆλον ποιεῖν 'betray' (like 12.16 φανερὸν ποιεῖν), here only in the gospels.

26.75 The conclusion, especially with the adverb 'bitterly', comes as a lame anticlimax, which strengthens the suspicion that 27.32 (q.v.) was the original sequel.

27.2 Nothing has so far hinted that 'the high priests and elders' were not competent to try Jesus and, if they found him guilty on a capital charge, to put him to death. Judas himself, the conclusion of whose story is inserted here, had no doubt about the sentence of the Sanhedrin being final (27.3 κατεκρίθη)—a fact which dates his introduction into the narrative to a stage when it still contained only the Jewish trial and execution. Suddenly Jesus' enemies, having in terms identical with those at 26.59 made a plan to put him to death, arraign him before 'Pilate the governor' (who appears as a known figure) on what subsequently turns out to be the charge that he claimed to be 'king of the Jews'. Reluctantly Pilate, tricked and threatened, after having declared Jesus innocent and disclaimed the blood-guilt, sentences him to be scourged and crucified.

The trial before Pilate is demonstrably constructed from the trial before the high priest—demonstrably, because features of the latter are reused without regard to their original significance. The Roman trial ends, instead of beginning, with accusations and begins, instead of ending, with the accused's self-incrimination in the formula 'you say it', σὺ λέγεις, a variation upon that 'you have said it', σὺ εἶπας, which placed the words 'Christ, the son of God' on the lips of the high priest. No such devastating irony results from Pilate's question 'Are you the king of the Jews?' In both trials the prisoner remains silent in the face of unspecified charges. In the Roman trial too the charges are unspecific, 'all that they are accusing you of', and the silence which provoked the detonation of the high priest's challenge serves only to cause Pilate to 'marvel greatly'. In short, literary material has been appropriated from where it was purposefully and exquisitely used and re-employed crudely to create an alternative.

If the crucifixion is secondary and not primary, the consequence has to be faced that the trial and execution of Jesus by the Romans as putative king of the Jews has been combined with what it was designed to supplant—his trial and execution by the Jewish establishment as putative son of God; and a death by stoning for blasphemy has been dropped in order to admit an execution by crucifixion for insurrection.

The theological conflict between two identifications of Jesus, between the gentile churches and the Judaizers, has reached crisis-point. A price, however, for accepting so daring a combination was exacted. Pilate and the Romans must be exonerated and the blood-guilt accepted by the Jewish people. The fulfilment of this condition in literary terms by a detachable graft (27.15–25) had the incidental effect of reducing Pontius Pilate to an incredible and un-Roman figure; it also enabled the gentile churches to escape alienation from the rest of the Roman world.

27.1 πρωΐα 'morning' here (= John 21.4) only in the New Testament (πρωΐ at 21.18, John 18.28). There is nothing to prevent 27.1 following immediately upon 26.56: proceedings in the morning were the sequel to the night-time arrest. The narrative which begins with 27.1 was designed as an alternative to the whole text which originally followed 26.56.

27.3 The high priests—it was they alone who in 26.14–16 gave Judas the money—and the elders would not accept the money back, but Judas put them in a fix by throwing it down and leaving it with them. (He could not have thrown it 'into the holy of holies', ναός). ἀθῷος 'innocent', here only (and in Pilate's mouth at 27.24) in the New Testament but common in LXX, viz. ἐκχέειν ἀ. αἷμα, e.g. 1 Macc. 1.37, 2 Macc. 1.8.

27.6 The story has reached its natural, and dramatic, close with 'hanged himself'. How the high priests disposed of the pieces of silver did not need to be related. The only effect of the prolongation 27.6–8 is to adduce an allegedly contemporary placename as if it were evidence of the event.

27.7 The high priests decided to use Judas' money for burial (εἰς ταφήν) of the miscreant. Failure to see that the 'burial' is the burial of Judas resulted in an interpolation supplying τοῖς ξένοις. It creates the puzzle why the high priests should wish to provide a (new?) burial-ground for visitors—the only other use of ξένος in the book is in 25.35–44—and if so why the ground should be called Bloodfield.

The passage breaks new ground in the book by appearing to appeal to the reader's knowledge, or ability to verify the existence, of a named site in or near Jerusalem, and by referring to 'the present day' (ἡ σήμερον sc. ἡμέρα). The phenomenon is repeated at 28.15, which reports the persistence μέχρι τῆς σήμερον 'among the Jews' of a rationalist explanation of the resurrection. The phenomenon, of which 'Golgotha' at 27.33 could be another instance, is sufficiently striking to raise a query whether the passage was aimed at visitors (pilgrims) to Jerusalem. Members of the gentile churches visiting Jerusalem would naturally be eager to see on site traces of the gospel narrative. The end of the Judas story was omitted by Luke and Mark, although they had included its commencement (Mark 14.10, 11; Luke 22.4–6) and its consummation (Mark 14.43–5; Luke 22.47, 48). They might have found the local reference irrelevant for their readership. (Luke has no passage corresponding to 28.15.)

The previous name of the plot, 'the potter's field', is taken for granted as known because an explanation is to follow immediately. The Old Testament precedent of the 'price' of the 'shepherd' in Zech. 11.12, 13 has already been adopted for the 'thirty pieces' above (26.15). To that passage it was natural to have recourse for the eventual destination of the money. In M it runs: 'And I said to them, "If you think good, give me my price; and if not, forbear!" So they weighed out for my price thirty pieces of silver. And the Lord said to me, "Cast it unto the potter"—a goodly price that I was prized at by them—and I took the thirty pieces of silver and cast them to the potter in the house of the Lord.' There is nothing in Zechariah about a potter's field, and purchase is not implied by 'giving to the potter'. The idea of purchase was obtained by reference to Jeremiah (32.9), where God commanded the purchase of a field (for seventeen shekels). 'Potter' itself is not secure in Zechariah. Instead of it LXX has τὸ χωνευτήριον, 'the smelter's' or 'the assayer's', suggesting that יוצר 'potter' has been substituted by error for יוצק 'smelter', which appears to fit the context better.

27.14 In 'answered him not a word (ῥῆμα) to anything', the analogy of 15.23 shows that ῥῆμα (like λόγον there) is the object of ἀπεκρίθη. πρὸς οὐδὲ ἕν, if genuine, means 'in reply to anything', though the emphatic οὐδὲ ἕν for οὐδέν is unexplained.

27.15 Jesus' self-incrimation left Pilate no option but to convict and sentence him. He does so at 27.26: παραδιδόναι is the technical term for judicial sentence. Before that, however, there intervenes an ingeniously constructed passage in which Pilate strives to avoid that outcome. It is possible to reconstruct how the passage was put together. To enable Pilate to make the attempt to release Jesus, there was attributed to him a gubernatorial custom of free pardon 'at the time of a feast', of which no other evidence exists. The problem still remained, however, why Pilate failed to carry out his intention. To explain this, the power to choose the prisoner had to be given to 'the crowd', which Pilate was then obliged to try to circumvent by offering only a choice between two prisoners—whence 'the notorious' (ἐπίσημος) Barabbas. In the end, despite the supernatural warning conveyed by Pilate's wife—an insertion which disjoins Pilate's question (27.17) from the answer to it (27.20)—the high priests etc. secured the crucifixion of Jesus in defiance of Pilate. κατὰ ἑορτήν, 'at the time of a feast' (not τὴν ἑορτήν, '*the* feast'), may be intended to generalize the alleged custom. Apart from the repetitive καθ' ἡμέραν (e.g. 26.55) 'daily', κατ' ἔτος, etc., there seems to be no parallel in the New Testament.

27.16 'He had', εἶχε, sing.—i.e. Pilate was holding in prison—is required instead of εἶχον 'they had', plural, which would attribute possession of the prisoner to the populace.

27.23 περισσῶς (= Mark 15.14) is used, surprisingly, in the sense of 'all the more' instead of μεῖζον as at 20.31, which is being echoed. Its correct meaning, 'extra', 'out of the ordinary', is as in 5.47 τί περισσὸν ποιεῖτε; If Pilate's original expostulation had been τί περισσὸν ἐποίησεν;, that would be an appropriate reaction to the
27.24 call for crucifixion—viz. 'what has he done to deserve *that*?'—and κακόν would be a lame gloss on περισσόν. Pilate's words of disclaimer, including ἀθῷος and ὄψεσθε, are shared, as ὄψεσθε here betrays, with the Judas story (27.4).

27.25 The 'populace' when it accepts the blood-guilt, is described no longer as a 'crowd' (ὄχλος) but as λαός, 'the people' (of Israel).

27.26 The scourging (φραγελλώσας, Lat. *flagellare* Graecized, here only = Mark 15.15) is curious, partly because of the merely participial reference and partly because Pilate is no more the actual executant of the scourging than of the crucifixion. A suspicion arises that the scourging was originally part of the offer in 27.17, 21. Luke (23.16) in fact transferred it thither, replacing the barbarous φραγελλώσας with the urbane euphemism παιδεύσας.

σταυροῦν (from σταυρός 'stake'), the word conventionally rendered 'crucify', was a form of execution adopted by the Seleucids and applied in Judaea by Antiochus IV, as also by Alexander Jannaeus *c.*88 BC (Jos. *Ant.* 13.380; *BJ* 1.97). It appears to be referred to in the Qumran commentary on Nahum 2.13 as 'hanging men alive on the tree' (Schürer, *History of the Jewish People*, i. 225n.).

Polybius (1.86), writing about 130 BC, had applied the verb to the Carthaginians and their rebellious mercenaries in 241 BC: τοὺς . . . αἰχμαλώτους ἐσταύρωσαν ἐπιφανῶς . . . πρὸς τὸν σταυρὸν ἀγαγόντες ἐκεῖνον μὲν καθεῖλον, τοῦτον δὲ ἀνέθεσαν ζῶντα. In the fifth century BC the synonyms ἀνασκολοπίζειν (from σκόλοψ) and ἀνασταυροῦν had been used by Herodotus interchangeably of impaling inflicted by the Persians, and by Euripides of other barbarians: *Iphigenia in Tauris*, 1430 σκόλοπι πήξωμεν δέμας; cf. *Electra*, 898. Also Plato, *Republic*, 362a ὁ δίκαιος . . . πάντα κακὰ παθὼν ἀνασχινδυλευθήσεται, a word otherwise known only (with κ-, ἀνασκινδυλεύειν) in the lexicographers, suggesting substitution for ἀνασταυρωθήσεται, in order to deaden the Christian echo; cf. *Gorgias*, 473c ἀνασταυρωθῇ ἢ καταπιττωθῇ.

27.26 The Roman execution would be no less indebted to the Jewish execution than the Roman trial to the Jewish trial, though the suppression of the Jewish execution has made the dependency less traceable. Mockery before execution by the Roman soldiery is the counterpart of the Jewish mockery (26.67, 68). Both related to the charge on which the accused was respectively convicted.

The Roman mockery is authenticated by a flurry of self-conscious Latinisms.

27.27 πραιτώριον, a Latin word not exemplified in Greek literature outside the New Testament, is no more Greek than *legio* at 26.53 or *flagellare* above. The unnecessary precision of *cohort* (σπεῖρα here and Acts 10.1) is part of the same phenomenon. παραλαβόντες, 'taking charge of Jesus', is absolute, leaving εἰς τὸ πραιτώριον governed (like ἐπ' αὐτόν) by συνήγαγον. Everything from the trial onwards took place in the governor's house (which is what *praetorium* means).

27.28 χλαμύς, a military cloak (here only in the New Testament), also used in Latin, *chlamys*, is another Roman touch, though 'red' cloaks seem to have been restricted to generals and emperors. στέφανον πλέκειν means 'plait a wreath' (as of laurel etc.) and ἄκανθος, as opposed to ἄκανθα, 'a thorn', means an acanthus plant, as seen ornamenting Corinthian capitals. Such an adornment would be at least as mock-regal as a 'crown of thorns' and more convenient to make.

27.30 The unexpected action of striking Jesus on the head with the reed (or sceptre, ῥάβδος) replicates ἐρράπισαν at 26.67.

The insertion—it is clearly such, because the next sentence, commencing 'when they had mocked him', must originally have followed directly upon the crowning, enthronement, and homage (i.e. 27.29)—makes the correspondence of the two mockeries closer and increases the dependence of the Roman on the Jewish.

27.31 The return of Jesus' own clothes—not, incidentally, implying that he retained the crown!—an apparently superfluous detail, is preparatory to the casting of lots for them at 27.35 and proves that the mockery and the crucifixion were composed as one piece.

27.32 The isolated sentence begins with the seemingly pointless participle, 'as they were going out'. In so doing the soldiers 'found'—not a natural word for stopping a passer-by—someone by the name of Simon. There was, however, another person of that name who would be 'found' outside the high priest's palace by those 'going out' to execute the sentence of that court. The words hark back to 26.75, where Simon Peter 'went out' and 'wept bitterly'. His humiliation was not complete until he was forced to assist in the execution of the master whom he had denied. As elsewhere (see on 26.6), the identity of Peter has been obliterated by the unique naming of a minor figure on the scene. Mark (15.21) knew the names of his two sons. 'By name', ὀνόματι, common in Luke, is unique in this book.

The word ἄρῃ (αἴρειν) does not mean 'carry, transport': that is φέρειν. αἴρειν means 'pick or lift up, raise', as in αἴρειν ἱστίον 'raise a sail'. Simon was not to *carry* the cross instead of Jesus doing so. That would in any case demand explanation why Jesus was not able to. Why Jesus could not *raise* the cross himself, the reason was clear: he would already be on it. Once the victim was affixed to whatever the σταυρός was, there had to follow the laborious task of hauling it into a vertical position like a maypole to drop into the prepared hole or socket. This sweaty job, which might well require tackle and a team of men or animals, was work for which the Roman soldiers preferred to find forced labour. Mark (15.21), though he knows the names of Simon's sons, has the identical words ἵνα ἄρῃ τὸν σταυρὸν αὐτοῦ. Luke (23.26) expands the misinterpretation and makes it specific: 'they put the cross upon him (Simon), to carry (φέρειν) behind Jesus'.

It would have to follow that the misunderstanding formed the basis for 16.24 (where cross-carrying is associated with 'behind me' and with 'denial'), and that this is reflected in 10.38. John (19.17) expressly, even defiantly, made Jesus 'carry' (βαστάζειν) the cross himself (ἑαυτῷ): Jesus could hardly expect others to αἴρειν their crosses if he had not done so with his own.

27.33 The Aramaic for 'skull' is *Gulgalta*, Hebrew *Gulgoleth*, גלגלת — for whatever reason, the second 'l' has been omitted. There was no need for the exact location of the crucifixion to be specified. Attempts at explanation of the name are merely fanciful. The context called for no more than 'when they came to the place of execution' or 'where he was to be crucified'.

The narrative of the crucifixion is an assemblage. The framework consists of four citations from Psalm 22, where the psalmist complains of abandonment by God: (1) 'they divided my raiment'; (2) 'they wagged their heads'; (3) 'he trusted in God, let him deliver him'; and (4) 'My God, my God, etc.' To these have been added: (1) a citation—in two halves—from Psalm 69; (2) the superscription of the 'Roman' charge; (3) a mocking; and (4) a humorous misunderstanding of the last citation from Psalm 22.

27.34 The allusion is to Ps. 69.22: 'they put bile in my meat and in my thirst they gave me vinegar to drink', where the word translated in LXX by χολή ('bile'), as here, represents Hebrew ראש. This latter is usually in the Old Testament used in parallel with לענה, LXX πικρία ('bitterness'), translated 'wormwood'. Both words appear to be nowhere used literally but to be metaphors for bitterness: the assumption that ראש and hence χολή (also used in Greek metaphorically for 'bitterness') denoted a herb is superfluous. Misunderstood as literal instead of metaphorical, 'bile' had to be rendered manageable. This was done by writing 'they gave him *wine* to drink *mixed with* bile', and stating that the resultant mixture was refused. A purely literary cause has created an alleged incident. The second part of Ps. 69.22 was accommodated below at 27.48 (ἐπότιζεν) in an evident insertion, suggesting that the citations of Ps. 69.22 are an afterthought.

27.35 The allusion is to Psalm 22, of which the soldiers themselves were presumably unconscious.

27.37 The affixing of the so-called *titulus* comes too late. It was needed before the soldiers settled down to keep watch. 'Attached' (ἐπέθηκαν) is awkward in the sense of attaching to the cross, nor is the statement Jesus' 'offence' (αἰτία). His 'offence' was to have *claimed* that he was king of the Jews. The difficulty was felt by all the other gospels, and most comprehensively removed by John 19.19. All, however, omit αἰτία. The alleged wording was curiously prolix for an inscription: later artists were to abbreviate it to four (Latin) letters, *I.N.R.I.*

27.38, 44 The two sentences about the pair of crucified 'robbers' (see on 20.22–3) are detachable: Luke (23.39–43) perceived their dramatic possibilities and exploited them, having introduced the two characters at a more natural earlier point; but here (and in Mark) they remain functionless. Isa. 53.12, 'he was numbered with the transgressors', is insufficient to account for them.

27.40 The mockery has been lifted whole from another scene: the two references to 'the cross' ('come down from the cross') are in insertions designed to adapt the passage to a crucifixion. καὶ κατάβηθι ἀπὸ τοῦ σταυροῦ (27.40) is an anticlimax after σῶσον σεαυτόν; and as regards 27.42, the failure of one claiming to be son of God to 'come down from the cross' is a taunt logical and appropriate to the Jewish but not to the Roman conviction—a king of Israel is as helpless on a cross as anyone else. When the references to the 'cross' are removed, all allusions are to the Jewish trial and Jesus' claim to be the son of God, which the two companions crucified with him now reject (τὸ αὐτὸ ὠνείδιζον αὐτῷ). The choice of the word βλασφημεῖν (27.39) for 'insulting' someone being executed for βλασφημία would be (presumably intentionally) ironical.

27.42 'Others he saved' (ἄλλους ἔσωσεν) appears to concede too much; ἔσωζεν, 'he purported to save', would be more appropriate.

27.45 It is not without significance that the universal darkness—it had begun at high noon—came to an end with Jesus' death. It was his death that lifted the metaphorical darkness in which the gentile world lay. The darkness is allegory: search for solar eclipses is powerless to discover it. The darkness, not described as due to an eclipse of the sun, may allude to Isa. 60.2, 'darkness shall cover the earth, and cloud the peoples'.

27.46 The death of Jesus is signalled by the citation of Ps. 22.1 uniquely in Aramaic, so as to make possible the mishearing of a call to Elijah. (The reaction to this, 'This fellow is calling for Elijah: let us see if Elijah will come to save him'—cf. 27.43—has been split in two to receive the remaining half of Ps. 69.21: see on 27.34.) It is hardly credible that the jocularity of an absurd mishearing was intended at this point in the narrative. This being so, and given the identification of John the Baptist with Elijah (cf. 11.14), the conclusion is difficult to avoid that John is in fact being invoked as a witness to Jesus' death. (The Greek translation of the Aramaic would, on this hypothesis, not be original.) Mark 15.36 improved matters slightly by attributing the second half of the remark to the man with the sponge. Presumably κάλαμος (lit. 'reed', cf. 27.29, 30) means no more than a stick on which the sponge was held up to Jesus' mouth: if it had been to act as a pipe, the man would have had to stand at a higher level to secure gravity feed.

27.50 The second cry, of which no content is specified, is an anticlimax after the first and serves no dramatic purpose. Luke (23.46) furnished words from Ps. 31.5. It is possible that originally there was no more than 'at the ninth hour Jesus uttered a loud cry and gave up the ghost'.

πνεῦμα ἀφιέναι, 'give up the ghost', is precedented (Euripides, *Hecuba*, 571; cf. *Orestes*, 1171); but πνεῦμα is open to interpretation as more than 'the breath of life'. At the beginning of the book the incarnation of God, begotten by the 'holy spirit' (1.20), was certified by supernatural means. Supernatural means are now applied to the disincarnation, in two phases. The second relates to the body, and is placed after the burial (28.2). The first relates to the spirit and occurs at the immediate point of its being 'given up' (ἀφῆκεν τὸ πνεῦμα).

27.51 The death is accompanied by supernatural events, hailed by gentiles as evidence that Jesus was 'truly the son of God'. There follows a narrative, to which the women are introduced as witnesses, leading to the assertion, 'prevalent among the Jews to this day' (28.15), that the disciples removed the body: (1) in the evening, the body is buried; (2) the next day, a guard is provided by Pilate; (3) the day after, the guard alleges that while it was asleep the disciples had stolen the body. The allegation is refuted by Jesus' appearance in Galilee: there is no specific mention of the tomb being found empty.

By the rending of the Temple veil, the ἅγιον πνεῦμα has, allegorically, rejoined the Father in his habitation, in a manner which visibly excluded human agency but is not unexampled as a metaphor for Jesus' action (Heb. 10.19, 20).

27.52 The salvation which Jesus effected by his death is symbolized by the opening of the graves of dead believers (ἁγίων) and their resurrection. The insertion of 'after his resurrection' removed an apparent contradiction, making the resurrection of Jesus rather than his death the critical event. (ἔγερσις here only in the New Testament.)

'The' tombs are by implication those hewn in 'the' rock; cf. 27.60. 'Those asleep' (τῶν κεκοιμημένων) is qualified by 'saints' (ἁγίων) to restrict the privilege of resurrection. κεκοιμημένοι here only in this book for 'the dead' (cf. on 25.5); and similarly ἅγιοι 'saints'. This and 4.5 are the only places where Jerusalem is periphrasized as 'the holy city'.

27.54 The (hitherto unmentioned) centurion and his men might 'see' the earthquake but were in no position to observe the other 'happenings' (τὰ γινόμενα). Having witnessed the execution of Jesus for claiming to be king of the Jews, the Roman soldiers would hardly exclaim, 'Truly this was the son of God.' No steps have been taken to relieve the anomaly. Luke (23.47) attempted unsuccessfully to deal with the difficulty by substituting 'righteous' for 'son of God' and making it the manner of Jesus meeting his death by which the centurion was so impressed.

27.55 The 'many' women are described as watching, like Peter at 26.58, ἀπὸ μακρόθεν, 'at a distance', and thereby deliberately precluded from being witnesses of the actions and words at the crucifixion, a difficulty which John (19.25) took steps to remove. The 'disciples' having 'all' fled (26.56), the remainder of the narrative, viz. burial and resurrection, required friendly witnesses. They are produced here at the outset—with that narrative in view, as is proved by the expression καὶ ἡ ἄλλη Μαρία 'and the other Mary' at 27.61 and 28.1, intelligible only in the light of 27.56. The 'mother of the sons of Zebedee' (see on 20.20) is mentioned, though last and perhaps as an addition; but she is pointedly dropped out of the action (27.61, 28.1) and as a result does not witness the angelic announcement nor become one of the messengers of the resurrection.

'Mary of Magdala' is unknown to a reader of the book—'Magdala' has been no more than a variant to 'Magadan', where Jesus is recorded as having gone after one of the miraculous feedings (15.39); and to discover that 'the other Mary' was the mother of Jesus, the same reader would have to find 'James and Joseph' among the four brothers of Jesus listed at 13.55.

27.57 The narrative had to continue after Jesus' expiry with the removal and burial of the body. There is no further reference to the cross. Jesus' disciples were not available. An appropriate agent appears in the person of Joseph, who performs it, having on hand a suitable rock tomb. 'Had become' a disciple, ἐμαθητεύθη (cf. 13.52), is curious instead of simply 'was a disciple'. Like Simon's (27.32), his place of origin is given. (Strictly 'from A.' ought to be construed with 'came' rather than as 'an Arimathaean'.) Arimathaea appears to be הרמתים (i.e. Rāmāthaım with definite article); 'Αρμαθαιμ, used only in 1 Sam. 1.1 for the home of Samuel, is doubtfully identified with Ram, 5 miles north of Jerusalem.

27.59 Unnatural stress is laid on the cloth being 'clean'—one would not otherwise have supposed it to be dirty!—and on the tomb being 'new'. The same expression 'hew oneself a tomb' is in Isa. 22.16. Curious also is the use of the Aristophanic verb ἐντυλίσσω for 'wrap up', otherwise not occurring in the New Testament or in Greek versions of the Old Testament. It was natural enough not to put the body in a tomb already containing one or more bodies; but the stress on a 'clean' winding-sheet—Luke (23.53) and John (19.40) omitted the description, but Mark (15.46) described Joseph as having 'bought' the sheet—is striking and presumably therefore intended to be significant. If the significance was liturgical, the reference could be to the 'fair linen cloth' spread on a stone altar. The allegorical requirement for the tomb to be 'new' and also to be of stone made it necessary to explain how a new but empty rock tomb came to be available instantly: Joseph had (just) made it for himself. The man has been fitted to the moment. Hence the embarrassments in the narration: the reader ought not to have been assumed to be aware ('put it in *his* new tomb, which' etc.) that Joseph had made himself a rock tomb; and the aorist tense ἐλατόμησεν instead of the pluperfect is surprising if, as must be implied, Joseph had already 'hewn' the tomb.

27.61 To make possible their forthcoming act of witness, the two Marys are enabled to pinpoint the location of the tomb.

27.62 Jesus' body has been buried. If he was king of the Jews, his execution put an end to his existence. If he was the son of God, neither the spirit nor the body which it had begotten could be earthbound: the son of God would be immortal. Those who denied that Jesus was the son of God must necessarily deny the resurrection. The remainder of the narrative reflects the debate, still unresolved, between these opposites. Those who denied the resurrection devised a plan, which they superimposed upon the account of it. They did not dispute that the tomb was found empty, but they offered a natural explanation: the body was taken away by the disciples—as had been that of John the Baptist by his (14.12). To make this explanation 'stick', they required witnesses: they would produce a guard, a Roman guard, to furnish it and use seals in evidence of a physical intrusion in the tomb.

If the high priests feared the disciples stealing the body, the delay of a whole night in securing the tomb was inexcusable: their explanation, 'we have remembered', is too feeble—they needed to take their measures without delay after the interment, if they were to forestall the mischief which they feared. 'The morrow', ἡ ἐπαύριον, here only in this book. There was no need to identify 'the morrow', i.e. of the entombment just described: 'which is after' has to be strained to mean 'the day next after

. . .'; but that would be the Sabbath, and the tense ('is') is wrong. παρασκευή (lit. 'preparation'), translated 'Friday', is used to denote the Sabbath eve in the passion narrative, Mark 15.42, Luke 23.54, John 19.14, and in an imperial decree cited by Jos. *Ant.* 16.163. This is the only appearance of the 'Pharisees' after 22.41.

27.63 The terms of the request to Pilate give the show away. He would have been puzzled to learn that the person whom he convicted and executed for claiming to be the king of the Jews had expected to 'arise after three days'. The term πλάνος, 'impostor', is specific for a pseudo-Messiah (cf. 24.5). It is as such that Jesus' enemies were concerned to avoid a sham resurrection.

The term κύριε, 'lord', 'sir', used to Pilate, is highly obsequious. Jesus is nowhere reported saying publicly that he would rise on the third day—16.21, 17.23, and 20.19, whatever their status, were private communications. The attribution of a public prediction provided the necessary motivation to take the precautions.

27.65 The pure Latin term* κουστωδία, though taken below (μετὰ τῆς κ.) and at 28.11 as meaning 'a guard', means 'power of custody'. Pilate does not say 'take some soldiers', for which ἔχετε would be inappropriate, but 'You are in charge', an impatient, offhand response.

28.1 The indications of day and hour are confusing. ὀψὲ σαββάτων 'late on the Sabbath' could mean shortly before its termination, i.e. early in the morning on Sunday. On the analogy of μιᾷ τοῦ μηνός (Gen. 8.13 LXX) 'on the first day of the month', μία σαββάτων could mean 'the first day of the week' if σαββάτων means 'week'; but even if that meaning were valid, σαββάτων would scarcely be used at so short an interval in different senses. κατὰ μίαν σαββάτου in 1 Cor. 16.2 appears to mean 'each Sunday' and δὶς τοῦ σαββάτου in Luke 18.12 'twice a week'; but the other occurrences in the New Testament (Mark 16.2, 9, Luke 24.1, and John 20.1) are derived from here and no non-Christian examples appear to be cited.

τῇ ἐπιφωσκούσῃ εἰς has to mean, as the other gospels interpreted it, 'in the early light of'. The verb is found neither previously nor subsequently; ἐπιφαύσκω, possibly meaning the same, occurs only in LXX of Job (three passages) and Eph.

* Another (see on 27.27) conscious Latinism; in *Oxyrhynchus Papyri* 294.22 of AD 22 it means 'prison'.

5.14. By way of cleaning up the chronology, Luke wrote of the time of the interment (23.54) 'It was Friday—παρασκευή (from 27.62)—and Sabbath was coming on' ἐπέφωσκεν (from here). The sentence here he altered (24.1) into 'on the first day of the week in early dawn'.

The stated object of the women's visit—'to watch the tomb'—is vacuous. They were necessary there to be witnesses. Luke (24.1), feeling the embarrassment, supplied a practical purpose derived from 26.12, and was followed by Mark (16.1).

28.2–11 The 'big earthquake' serves no purpose. If *it* had been what rolled away the stone, all would have been straightforward: 'a great earthquake occurred and rolled the stone away; and an angel of the Lord descended from heaven and came and sat upon it'. The angel's business is with delivering a message: in itself an empty tomb is no evidence that the person buried there has 'risen from the dead'.

'I know why you have come' is peculiar in the angel's mouth. A question—'Are you looking for (ζητοῦντες) Jesus who was crucified?'—would be more natural. The women conspicuously ignore the invitation to look inside the tomb, as though the invitation made its own point.

The physical appearance of Jesus himself to the women is not only incompatible with the command to the disciples to go to Galilee, but adds nothing to the narrative: Jesus simply repeats what the angel of the Lord has said. It is therefore probably an insertion, and thus not one of 'all the happenings' which the guards reported to the high priests. Πορευομένων αὐτῶν (28.11) followed naturally upon ἔδραμον (28.8).

28.2 The 'angel of the Lord' has not made his appearance since 1.20, 24; 2.13, 19, where, however, he was only a dream figure. There was little point in his sitting on the stone after 'rolling it away' (ἀποκυλίνδω, a word which remained in the narrative of Luke 24.2, cf. Mark 16.3, whence the angelic descent has been expunged).

28.3 The writer had the transfiguration (17.2, 6, 7) in mind. εἰδέα, a form of ἰδέα, here only in the New Testament, must mean 'face' (17.2 πρόσωπον) as opposed to garments, as it does in 2 Macc. 3.16. Luke 9.29 and John 5.37 have εἶδος.

28.4 οἱ τηροῦντες masc. (27.54) is intended to refer to the soldiers of the *custodia*; hence the angel's conventional (see on 1.20) 'do not fear' is addressed only to the women (ὑμεῖς). 'Lo, I have told you' appears to be purely peremptory (cf. 24.25).

28.9 'Met', ὑπήντησεν, only here and 8.34 (ὑπάντησις) in this book. χαίρετε 'greetings', elsewhere only 26.49. 'Prostrating themselves', προσκυνεῖν, as did the mother of the sons of Zebedee at 20.20, is bathos after the clasping of the feet, which can itself be part of προσκύνησις but betokens dread and supplication, whence followed here naturally by μὴ φοβεῖσθε, the formal address of an apparition (see on 1.20). 'My brethren', οἱ ἀδελφοί μου: Jesus does not elsewhere, except by implication at 12.49, call his disciples his 'brothers'.

28.12–15 The rationalistic explanation for the empty tomb which the guards were induced to give (28.13) is not only incompatible with the announcement made by the 'angel of the Lord' but inherently unsound: if asleep at the time, the guards would have no means of knowing who it was that 'stole' the body. The guarantee of immunity given to the soldiers is also unrealistic: how could the high priests or the guards be so sure of the success of an attempt to pervert Roman discipline?

πείθω, 'persuade' (act.) (cf. Acts 12.20), is found here only in the gospels; and the particle τε in συμβούλιόν τε λαβόντες, which occurs in only two other passages in the book (22.10, 27.48), both in the passion narrative, is nowhere else in it used as here to mark one action following another. ἱκανά 'considerable (money)' is again unique in this book, where the only other occurrences of the adjective are 3.11 and 8.8. 'Heard in front of the governor' is a convoluted expression, while ἀμέριμνος has a technical legal flavour: its only other occurrence in the New Testament is 1 Cor. 7.32, in a different sense. For διαφημίζειν 'noise abroad' cf. 9.31.

28.15–20 The still continuing prevalence among 'the Jews' of a rational explanation for the empty tomb is noted without further comment. That does not prepare the reader for what he is about to encounter. The 'eleven' make their way, as instructed, to Galilee and there see and adore Jesus; 'but some of them had doubts', οἱ δὲ ἐδίστασαν, though οἱ δέ does not naturally mean, without a preceding οἱ μέν, 'but some of them'.

The startling statement is then completely ignored. What cannot have been intended was to conclude the book on a note of doubt and disagreement, leaving Jesus, so to speak, still 'on stage'. Doubt, if mentioned at all, had to be mentioned only so that it could be resolved incontestably—for example, by an ascension into heaven. Luke (24.51) resorted to conjectural emendation to solve both problems: 'he separated himself (διέστη) from them and was carried up into heaven'.

28.15 The term Ἰουδαῖοι ('Jews') is unique in the book except in the title 'king of the Jews' (2.2; 27.11, 37).

28.16 Those who were 'the disciples' in the angel's announcement and 'my brethren' in Jesus' words are now, for the first time, referred to as 'the *eleven* disciples', i.e. minus Judas. In his instructions (26.32, 28.16) (ἐτάξατο thus here only in the New Testament) Jesus did not refer to a 'mountain' in Galilee. The disciples simply made their way 'to Galilee, *where* Jesus had told them (i.e. to go)'. εἰς τὸ ὄρος is an officious interpolation.

28.17–20 The unique locutions and the formal reference to the Trinity increase the impression that the last column of the book (like the original end of Mark) was lost, and its loss has been made good perfunctorily by the farewell speech attributed to Jesus. The lost text will have contained what Luke (24.51) saw to be lacking—an ascension, to round off the book and provide proof of Jesus' resurrection.

28.19 'Make disciples', μαθητεύειν, elsewhere in the book only in the passive (13.52, 27.57 q.v.), is apparently used here in the sense of 'convert' rather than 'make disciples of': so in Acts 14.21 correlatively with εὐαγγελίζεσθαι as here with βαπτίζειν. Nowhere else is Jesus reported as either baptizing or enjoining baptism. Baptism 'in the name of' the three persons, thus linked here only in this book, implies knowledge of the admission ritual in established churches. ('The holy spirit' is connected with baptism—in a different context—in 3.11, attributed to John.)

28.20 'And lo . . .', a no doubt intended echo of Gen. 28.15 (in Jacob's dream). For the συντέλεια 'end' of the age see on 13.41–3. 'All the days', πάσας τὰς ἡμέρας, here only in the New Testament.

INDEX

The index covers the Introduction and Commentary only.